MW00365023

FIGURES, CHARACTERS, AND AVATARS, SECOND EDITION

THE OFFICIAL GUIDE TO USING DAZ STUDIO™ TO CREATE BEAUTIFUL ART

Les Pardew

Course Technology PTR
A part of Cengage Learning

COURSE TECHNOLOGY
CENGAGE Learning®

Australia, Brazil, Japan, Korea, Mexico, Singapore, Spain, United Kingdom, United States

Figures, Characters, and Avatars, Second Edition: The Official Guide to Using DAZ Studio™ to Create Beautiful Art

Les Pardew

Publisher and General Manager, Course Technology PTR:
Stacy L. Hiquet

Associate Director of Marketing:
Sarah Panella

Manager of Editorial Services:
Heather Talbot

Senior Marketing Manager:
Mark Hughes

Senior Acquisitions Editor:
Emi Smith

Project Editor:
Jenny Davidson

Technical Reviewer:
Cris Palomino

Interior Layout Tech:
William Hartman

Cover Designer:
Luke Fletcher

Indexer:
Larry Sweazy

Proofreader:
Mike Beady

UNIVERSITY OF COLORADO
COLORADO SPRINGS
WITHDRAWN
OCT 15 2012
KRAEMER FAMILY LIBRARY

© 2013 Course Technology, a part of Cengage Learning.

ALL RIGHTS RESERVED. No part of this work covered by the copyright herein may be reproduced, transmitted, stored, or used in any form or by any means graphic, electronic, or mechanical, including but not limited to photocopying, recording, scanning, digitizing, taping, Web distribution, information networks, or information storage and retrieval systems, except as permitted under Section 107 or 108 of the 1976 United States Copyright Act, without the prior written permission of the publisher.

For product information and technology assistance, contact us at **Cengage Learning Customer & Sales Support, 1-800-354-9706.**

For permission to use material from this text or product, submit all requests online at **cengage.com/permissions**. Further permissions questions can be emailed to **permissionrequest@cengage.com**.

DAZ Studio is a trademark of DAZ Productions in the United States and other countries.

All other trademarks are the property of their respective owners.

All images © Cengage Learning unless otherwise noted.

Library of Congress Control Number: 2012930786

ISBN-13: 978-1-4354-6120-8

ISBN-10: 1-4354-6120-7

Course Technology, a part of Cengage Learning
20 Channel Center Street
Boston, MA 02210
USA

Cengage Learning is a leading provider of customized learning solutions with office locations around the globe, including Singapore, the United Kingdom, Australia, Mexico, Brazil, and Japan. Locate your local office at: **international.cengage.com/region**.

Cengage Learning products are represented in Canada by Nelson Education, Ltd.

For your lifelong learning solutions, visit **courseptr.com**.

Visit our corporate website at **cengage.com**.

Printed in the United States of America
1 2 3 4 5 6 7 14 13 12

Acknowledgments

I want to acknowledge and thank all of the many people who have helped me create this book. My deepest thanks go to my family and especially to my wife, who has put up with living with an artist and all of the ups and downs that brings. I also want to thank the many mentors who have taught me about art. They may never know how much they have influenced my life. Special thanks go out to Cris Palomino for her work on the book. I also want to thank my editors Jenny Davidson, Emi Smith, and Stacy Hiquet without whose help this book would be impossible.

About the Author

Les Pardew is a recognized leader in the world of interactive entertainment. He is a video game and entertainment industry veteran with more 20 years of industry experience. His artwork credits encompass film and video production, magazine and book illustration, and more than 100 video game titles, including numerous market-leading choices. Les has also authored or co-authored 13 books on game art and game design for teens, digital art and 2D and 3D animation, drawing, and virtual models. Les started his career in video games doing animation for *Magic Johnson Fast Break Basketball* for the Commodore 64. He went on to help create several major games, including *Robin Hood Prince of Thieves, Star Wars, Wrestle Mania, NCAA Basketball, Stanley Cup Hockey, Jack Nicklaus Golf, Where in the World/USA is Carmen Sandiego?, Star Craft Brood Wars, Rainbow Six, Cyber Tiger Woods Golf,* and many others. An accomplished instructor, Les has taught numerous art and business courses, including teaching as an adjunct faculty member at Brigham Young University's Marriott School of Management. As a business leader, Les has founded two separate game development studios. He is also a favorite speaker at video game conferences and events.

Contents

Introduction vi

Chapter 1: Introduction to 3D Graphics 1

Chapter 2: The Basics 11

Chapter 3: The Scene 31

Chapter 4: The Figure 47

Chapter 5: Clothing 57

Chapter 6: The Head and Face 71

Chapter 7: Posing the Figure 83

Chapter 8: Props and Sets 103

Chapter 9: Lighting 121

Chapter 10: Animation 133

Chapter 11: Lip Sync 143

Chapter 12: DAZ Studio 4 and Traditional Media 153

BONUS chapters found on companion website (www.courseptr.com/downloads)

Chapter 13: Avatars and Game Art 163

Chapter 14: Creating Your Own 3D Models 173

Introduction

Unlocking the 3D Artist in You

In its basic sense, art has always been about depicting the artist's vision in tangible form. Whether it's the early cave drawings depicting a hunt, Michelangelo's masterwork of the creation of man on the ceiling of the Sistine Chapel, or the latest special effects for a science fiction movie, all were the result of an artist bringing his or her vision forward in a way that can be shared with others.

In the past those who wanted to be artists had to spend years, if not a lifetime, developing skills in painting, sculpture, or some other media to express their artistic vision. While these skills will always be important, they have limited the creation of great artwork to those who were able to master the craft of drawing, painting, or sculpting. A new wave of computer graphics tools like DAZ Studio is starting to break the barriers, awakening the potential artist within each of us and opening the path to amazing artwork even for those with limited painting or drawing skills.

This book will show you how to unlock the 3D artist in you using the incredible power of DAZ Studio and some of the other great tools created by DAZ 3D. In its pages you will learn how to build sets and populate them with amazing characters. You will learn how easy it is to move and pose characters. You will learn about lighting and how to make your art look real. You will learn how to create your own movies with real 3D characters including making the characters talk. You will learn how to use DAZ Studio to improve your drawing skills. Finally, if you go through all of the practice exercises and learn the program, it will make you a better artist and bring your artistic vision to life.

DAZ Studio is a very powerful art program but unlike paint programs like Photoshop or 3D programs like 3ds Max, DAZ Studio is designed to give the artist the ability to compose beautiful scenes using a vast library of existing characters, props, and sets. This enables even a beginning artist to create beautiful realistic art. The simple tools allow the artist to set up an environment and then populate it with characters or creatures that can move and act. To see what is possible we've included a gallery of art created in DAZ Studio at the end of the book. Take a look. I'm sure you'll be inspired by what you see.

Pretty amazing, isn't it? These pictures are just a sample of some of the exciting things you will be able to do with DAZ Studio. Soon you will be creating art that is similar in quality to these pictures. Can't wait to start? Turn the page and let's begin.

1

Introduction to 3D Graphics

Welcome to the world of 3D graphics and DAZ Studio. This first chapter is a basic primer for understanding 3D graphics. It will cover what 3D graphics are and what they can be used for. Along the way, you will see some amazing art. Just remember that anything you see in this book is within your power to create with DAZ Studio. You don't have to be a trained artist to create incredible art.

3D stands for three-dimensional. 3D graphics are three-dimensional objects that exist in virtual space. This means that you can rotate and look at these objects from any angle on your computer screen. You can also take a picture of the objects from any angle and print it on your computer printer. 3D objects are often referred to as 3D models.

3D Models

The term *3D model* comes from the early days of computer graphics. Back before computers were used to create graphics for motion pictures, artists would build real scale models of objects they wanted to film. As computer graphics improved, over time, the real models were replaced with computer-generated models. The versatility and realism achievable with computer-generated 3D models is so high that there is no longer any need to build physical models. For example, can you tell which of the images in Figure 1.1 is a 3D model?

Can you tell which one was created using a 3D model? Actually they all were. Each image you see is a picture of a 3D model. In fact, the images were all created in DAZ Studio.

Figure 1.1 Which of these images is computer generated?

Computer graphics have matured to the point that they are regularly used in motion pictures, TV shows, and other media interchangeably with real characters or scenes. This has given rise to a whole new generation of graphical effects in motion pictures and TV shows, allowing directors to shoot scenes that a few years ago would have been impossible. It has also given rise to a new generation of video games that seem almost lifelike.

Inside a 3D Model

A 3D model is comprised of a mesh of simple geometric planes combined to form a very complex object. It is a little like a cut diamond for a piece of jewelry. The diamond has many facets or planes that form its shape, yet as a whole the diamond can be almost any shape the jeweler desires. A 3D model uses the same concept of combining many flat planes to create a more complex shape. On a 3D model, these individual flat planes are called polygons.

The basic unit of a 3D model is the polygon. A polygon is a simple flat plane with three or more sides, as shown in Figure 1.2.

The point on the corner of a polygon is called a vertex or vertices for plural. The vertex is the mathematical point in space that a computer software program calculates.

The lines between vertices are called edges. If you started with one three-sided polygon and added another vertex, you could form another polygon, sharing a common edge with the first, as shown in Figure 1.3.

Note

This book won't cover how to plot these points. If you are interested in the concept, you can gain a better understanding from math.com at the following address: http://www.math.com/school/subject3/lessons/S3U2L1GL.html. For now, all you really need to know is that 3D software programs like DAZ Studio keep track of all the vertices in a 3D model for you.

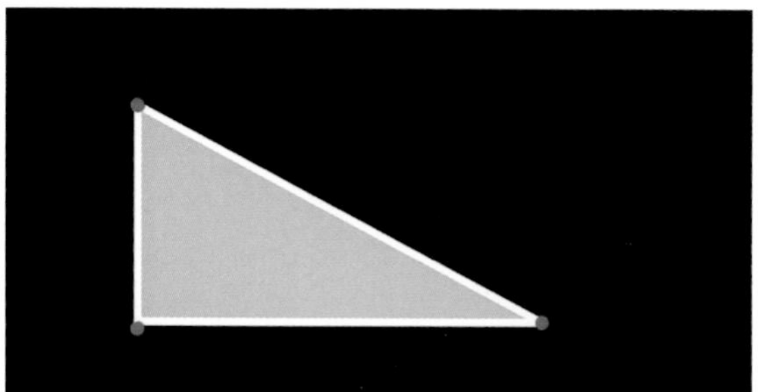

Figure 1.2 The polygon is the basic unit of a 3D model.

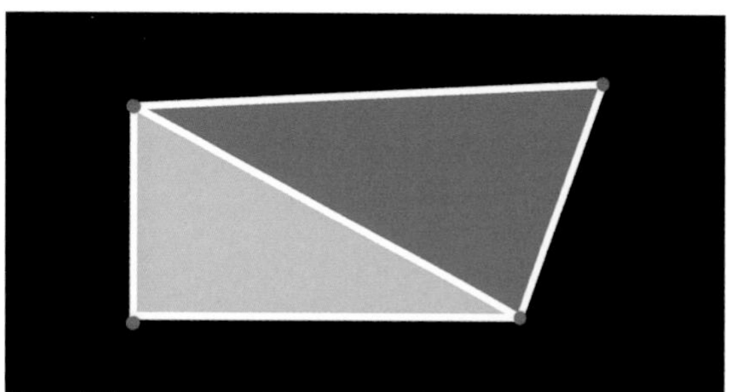

Figure 1.3 Adding a fourth vertex creates a second polygon.

Vertices and edges make up what is referred to as a wireframe mesh. Figure 1.4 shows a complex wireframe mesh of a character commonly used in DAZ Studio. As you can see, it takes a lot of individual polygons to create a realistic 3D model.

A polygon is comprised of three or more edges, usually four, connecting the vertices to form a flat plane. The flat plane of the polygon is called a face. When we look at 3D models in video games, motion pictures, or other media we are generally looking at faces and not at vertices and edges. Figure 1.5 shows the same model as Figure 1.4 with the faces showing instead of the wireframe mesh. DAZ Studio uses smoothing technology to blend the edges of the polygons to make the surface look smooth.

In Figure 1.5, all of the faces have only a single color so even though the 3D model looks good, it still lacks in detail. Polygons can also have textures mapped to them. Textures are 2D pictures that are attached to a polygon. Figure 1.6 shows the model now with textures. As you can see, the texture adds the detail that was missing in Figure 1.5.

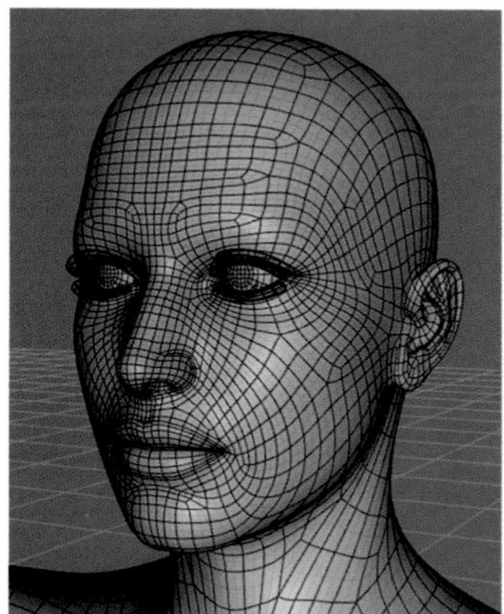

Figure 1.4 A wireframe mesh can have many individual vertices and edges.

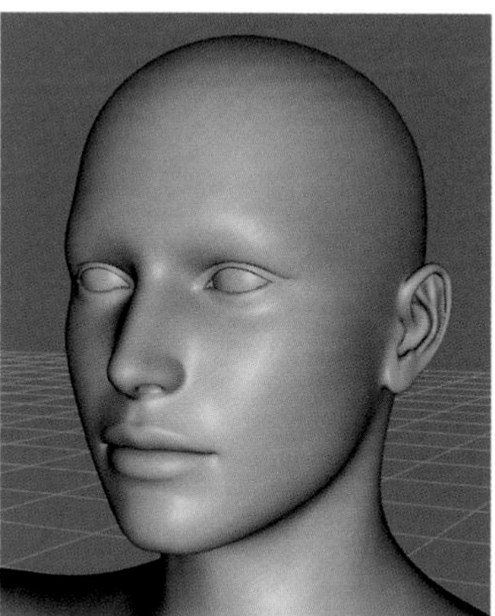

Figure 1.5 We usually see the faces of a 3D model.

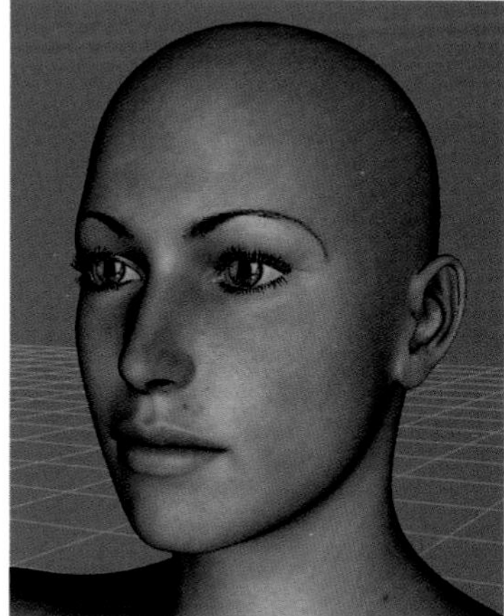

Figure 1.6 Textures on 3D models give the appearance of greater detail.

In order to understand the language of 3D models, you need to understand a few terms, which were covered above. Let's review.

- **Polygon.** A polygon is a simple flat plane with three or four sides.
- **Vertex or vertices.** A vertex is the mathematical point in virtual 3D space.
- **Edges.** Edges are lines between vertices.
- **Face.** A face is a flat surface formed by three or more vertices.
- **Wireframe mesh.** A wireframe mesh is a group of polygons forming a 3D model.

How 3D Graphics Are Used

Because of their increasing versatility and graphic quality, 3D graphics are being used in more and more industries. You can find 3D graphic artists in almost every industry from motion picture production to landscape architecture. There are 3D graphic artists creating amusement park rides, cars, video games, virtual reality simulators, Internet games, and movies. In fact there are probably fewer industries without 3D artists than there are with them. Let's take a closer look at some of the fascinating career opportunities that are available for 3D artists.

Motion Pictures/TV

Industries that are commonly thought of when people think of 3D graphics are the TV and motion picture industries. Most people are familiar with movies like *Shrek*, *Toy Story*, *Cars*, and other fully animated 3D motion pictures. What you might not be familiar with is how extensively 3D graphics are used in live-action movies. *The Lord of the Rings*, *Iron Man*, *Avatar*, and the *Transformers* movies made extensive use of 3D graphics blended with live action. Even movies like *Saving Private Ryan*, *The Bourne Ultimatum*, *Babe*, and others made use of 3D graphics in their production as well.

3D graphics for motion pictures range through almost anything you might see on the screen, but some of the basic jobs available to the movie artist are as follows:

- **Scenes and Sets.** The 3D artist may create a small part of a set like a historic building that no longer exists, or an entire set. Set artists specialize in the creation of interesting and sometimes spectacular settings for movies.
- **Characters.** Characters can be anything from a large crowd to an individual person. A character could be the main star of the show or a background character to fill out a scene. Character artists specialize in the creation of articulated actors. These actors range from the very stylized cartoon to the ultra-realistic human character.

- **Props.** Many objects in a movie are created as 3D models because the object is hard to find in real life, or maybe it is a fantasy item. Actors may actually be holding blocks of wood or some other object that is substituted for the 3D model after the scene is shot.
- **Animation.** Animators move 3D characters and objects on screen. They are the ones who are responsible for any motion that takes place in a movie. (Animation is listed separately because many times the animator and the model builder are two different individuals. Animation is the simulation of movement and is more about how a 3D model moves rather than the building of that 3D model.)
- **Special Effects.** Special effects cover a wide range of specialized visuals like rain, smoke, explosions, water, specialized lighting, and almost anything else that might be added to a film to enhance a particular scene.
- **Storyboards.** Storyboards are pre-visualization of the motion picture along with visual instructions used by motion picture and TV directors to guide the shooting of a scene. Storyboards traditionally are sketches, but more recently 3D graphics are being used in situations where very specific effects or angles are needed. 3D graphics allow a director to more fully visualize complex shots saving time and money on the set.

DAZ Studio provides many tools and features that will help a beginning artist understand and utilize many of the above-mentioned 3D models and effects. If you are interested in a career in motion pictures as a 3D artist, you will find a wealth of resources in DAZ Studio to help you get started. In Figures 1.7 and 1.8 are some examples of DAZ Studio used in motion picture production.

Illustration

Illustration is the field of commercial art that creates visual images for print material like magazines, billboards, books, advertisements, products, etc. More recently, illustrations are being used on the Internet in web pages, banner ads, and other electronic media. Illustrations are static images that enhance a message by explaining it in visual form like a picture or diagram. For example, a book illustration helps tell a story. A product illustration helps explain a product. An advertisement illustration helps sell a product or idea. In a way, illustration can be thought of as working art. It has a communication purpose.

Illustration is traditionally thought of as a two-dimensional media; however, DAZ Studio and other programs like it have given rise to a whole new way of creating stunning lifelike illustration. Through the power of 3D, artists are now able to set up scenes; populate them with characters, objects, or whatever else they need; and render them with specialized lighting. Figures 1.9 and 1.10 are examples of DAZ Studio being used for illustration.

Figure 1.7 The above DAZ character was used in a motion picture production.

Figure 1.8 DAZ Studio is used to visualize a movie scene.

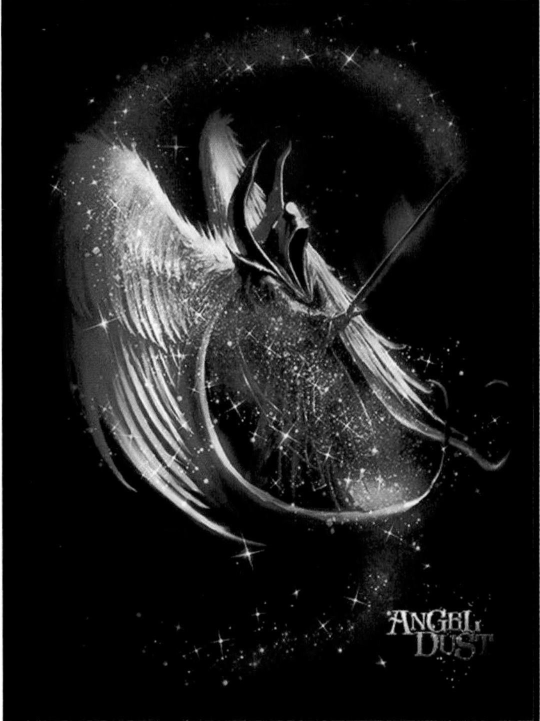

Figure 1.9 DAZ Studio helps the artist create a strong 3D environment.

Figure 1.10 DAZ Studio is used to illustrate an idea.

Video Games

Electronic games like video games have increased in popularity over the years to the point that the video game industry is one of the largest entertainment industry segments in the world. Billions of dollars are spent to buy and play video games every month. To support the demand, an army of 3D artists works to create the worlds, characters, and other game elements required by this ever-growing industry. A single video game can require the services of 20 to 30 artists working full-time for more than a year to produce.

3D graphic production for video games is similar to that of movies, requiring many of the same job functions for developing scenes, characters, animation, special effects, and storyboarding. The main difference between the two disciplines is that video game graphics have very strict technical guidelines pertaining to model complexity in order to work within the requirements of the game system. As game systems have become more and more powerful, these technical limitations have decreased, giving the game artist more and more freedom. Even with advances, however, 3D graphics still have upper limits that the artist has to maintain to allow the game to run at a decent speed.

Video game artists use DAZ Studio as a tool to help them visualize scenes and test out characters. Figure 1.11 shows a video game scene visualization.

Avatars

Related to video game art development is the development of avatars. Avatars are characters or objects that represent a person in a video game, online community, or within other applications. An avatar represents an individual; therefore, having an avatar that looks like the person or expresses the person's personality becomes important. Massive multi-player online role-playing games (or MMORPGs) like *World of Warcraft* and others make extensive use of avatars. Online communities like *Second Life* also make use of unique avatars as do social games like *FarmVille* and *CityVille*. As the need for avatars has increased so has the demand for 3D artists to create these characters.

An avatar can be something as simple as a static picture to something as complex as a completely articulated 3D character. The more complex the character, the higher the level of 3D expertise is needed to create that character.

DAZ Studio is a tremendous tool for creating avatars because it already has a huge library of pre-built characters available from humans to animals and even fantasy creatures. These characters can be imported into DAZ Studio and modified to fit the specific look that the artist wants for an avatar. Figure 1.12 shows a group of avatars that were created in DAZ Studio. While some DAZ models may have too high of a polygon count to use in some virtual worlds, DAZ has created some tools like Decimator and Texture Atlas that help in the process. There are also specific rules in the use agreements that indicate how you can legally use DAZ models for games or virtual worlds.

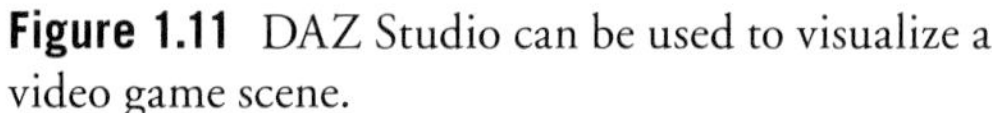

Figure 1.11 DAZ Studio can be used to visualize a video game scene.

Figure 1.12 Avatars created in DAZ Studio.

Design

The word design is a nebulous term and covers 3D graphics (3D graphics are used in the design of everything from toasters to skyscrapers). Almost everything we use, from the homes we live in to the books we read was designed by someone. Designers are the ones who decide how an automobile will look or how a toy will be put together. They are known by names like graphic designer, architect, and industrial designer. They often combine the skills of an engineer with that of an artist. Designers probably make up one of the largest groups of 3D graphic artists in the world.

With the power of 3D graphics, designers are able to design virtually before they have to go through the trouble and expense of building their design in real life using real materials. This freedom allows designers the opportunity to investigate multiple designs in a relatively short amount of time, increasing their creative output.

DAZ Studio is a great tool for designers because it allows them to visualize the product, building, or whatever they are designing in a setting with characters as if it were in a real environment. Figure 1.13 shows how an architect might use DAZ Studio to visualize a scene.

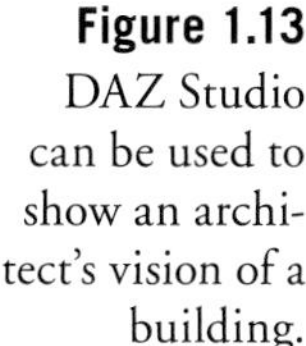

Figure 1.13 DAZ Studio can be used to show an architect's vision of a building.

Fine Art

Last but not least, 3D graphics have made their way into the world of fine art. More and more fine artists are discovering the flexibility and versatility of 3D graphics and 3D graphics software in their art. Whether artists work in traditional media like painting, drawing, or sculpture, or directly on the computer, there are many ways artists can use 3D graphics to improve and enhance their work. With a 3D program, fine artists can set up scenes and experiment with lighting, viewing angles, and frame sizes until they find exactly what they like, then use the scenes to create their art.

Many fine artists have found DAZ Studio to be an indispensible tool in their studios. With DAZ Studios, artists can develop complex compositions to use for reference in their paintings. Rather than hiring an expensive model to experiment with compositions and poses, the fine artist can work all of that out beforehand saving valuable model time. Fine artists can also use the program itself for creating amazing art. Figures 1.14 and 1.15 show two examples of fine art created in DAZ Studio.

Summary

This introductory chapter helped you visualize the creative possibilities of 3D graphics and many uses of DAZ Studio. With tools like DAZ Studio, even beginning artists can create amazing quality art. Skilled artists will find the program of immense value to sharpen skills and extend creativity.

In the next several chapters, the many fascinating features of DAZ Studio will be unlocked to give you a chance to experience for yourself some of the inspiring things you can do with this software. If you are ready to start, turn the page and let's begin.

Figure 1.14 Beautiful art created in DAZ Studio.
Image courtesy of Cris Palomino

Figure 1.15 DAZ Studio can be a great tool for the fine artist.
Image courtesy of Cris Palomino

2

The Basics

DAZ Studio is a powerful 3D application that is easy to use yet has the same features as programs that cost thousands of dollars, yet DAZ Studio is free. That is a remarkably good price for such a powerful program! This chapter provides an overview of the basic layout of DAZ Studio and its features. Before we can get into layouts and features, however, we need to go over a few basic 3D concepts.

Basic 3D Concepts

The first concept that a beginning 3D artist needs to understand is the idea of 3D virtual space. Unlike painting a picture as a 3D artist, you are not limited to one flat two-dimensional canvas to create your artwork. Instead, you have an entire virtual world to work with. This virtual world is a simulated 3D world where you can set up your environment and view it from any angle. Think of it as a virtual photography studio.

In DAZ Studio you create your art similarly to how a photographer prepares to take a picture in real life. You start by placing 3D objects and characters into a virtual scene. You place lights into the scene. Then you view the scene from different angles to find the perfect shot. When you have everything set up just as you like it, you take a picture of the scene. It is just like setting up a scene in a photography studio except that in the virtual 3D world your studio can be as large or small as you want it to be; from the smallest insect to a galactic spiral, there is really no limit to what you can do in a virtual world.

Let's cover a few terms that you will need to know to understand 3D and how to work with a virtual set.

- **Scene.** The word scene is used when referring to the virtual world as seen on the computer screen.
- **Camera.** You view the scene through a camera. There can be multiple camera views in a scene and you can move from one camera view to another to see the scene from different angles. You can also move camera views within a scene.
- **Origin.** The origin is the beginning point for your scene. It is a single point in space. Everything in your virtual world is measured from the origin point.
- **View.** A view is the direction from which you see the scene, similar to a stage with a front, back, top, bottom, left, and right. If you are looking at the scene from the front then you are in the front view. If you are looking at a scene from the top then you are in the top view.
- **Axis.** An axis is a direction. There are three cardinal axis directions—X, Y, and Z—in a 3D virtual world. That is where the term 3D comes from. These three axis directions are perpendicular to each other. Each axis begins at the origin and extends outward from there.
- **X axis.** The X axis is the horizontal axis. If you are looking at the scene from the front, the X axis measures distance to the right and left. From the origin, the numbers to the right will be positive numbers and those to the left from the origin will be negative numbers.
- **Y axis.** The Y axis is perpendicular to the X axis and is the vertical axis. It measures distance up and down from the origin point. Up is positive and down is negative.
- **Z axis.** The Z axis is perpendicular to both the X and Y axis and measures depth into and out of the scene when viewed from the front. Distance from the origin to the front is positive. Distance from the origin away from the front is negative.
- **Camera view.** There are camera views preset in the scene to help with orientation. They are placed on an axis. For example, the front view looks along the Z axis into the scene. The top view looks along the Y axis.
- **Orthographic.** There are two types of camera views, orthographic and perspective. Orthographic views are flat views similar to a drafting drawing. Items do not get smaller with distance from the camera. Orthographic views are useful in measuring distances and building scenes.
- **Perspective.** A perspective camera view simulates how we see things in real life. Items in the scene will appear smaller with distance from the camera. Perspective views are useful for seeing how a scene will look when it is rendered.
- **Render.** The process of creating an image from a 3D scene is the rendering process.

Don't worry if you don't understand all of these terms right away. As we go along in the book they will become clearer. Like everything new, you may need to work with them a little to understand them fully.

Installing the Software

DAZ Studio is a downloadable program from the DAZ 3D website. You can find it at http://www.daz3d.com/ as shown in Figure 2.1.

Once on the site you will need to open the 3D Software menu and select DAZ Studio, as shown in Figure 2.2.

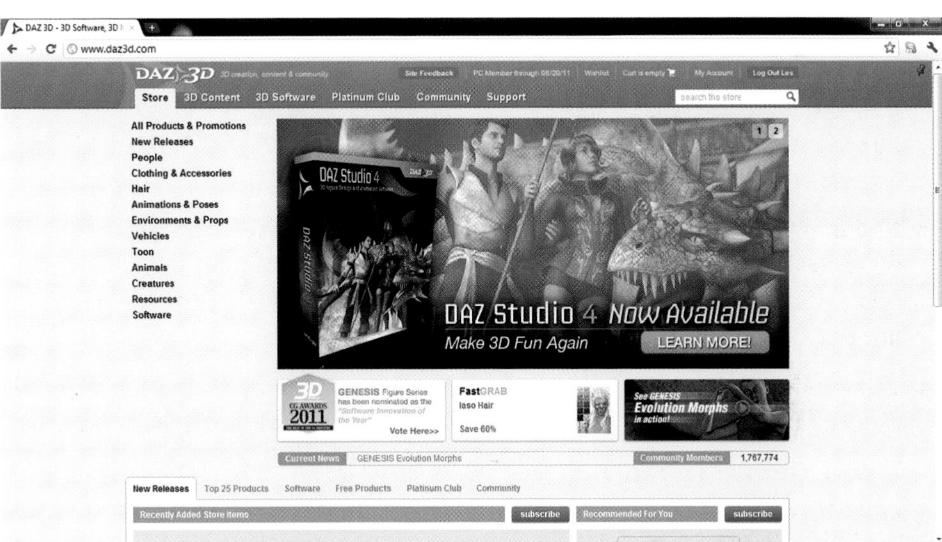

Figure 2.1 This is the DAZ 3D website at the time of this writing.

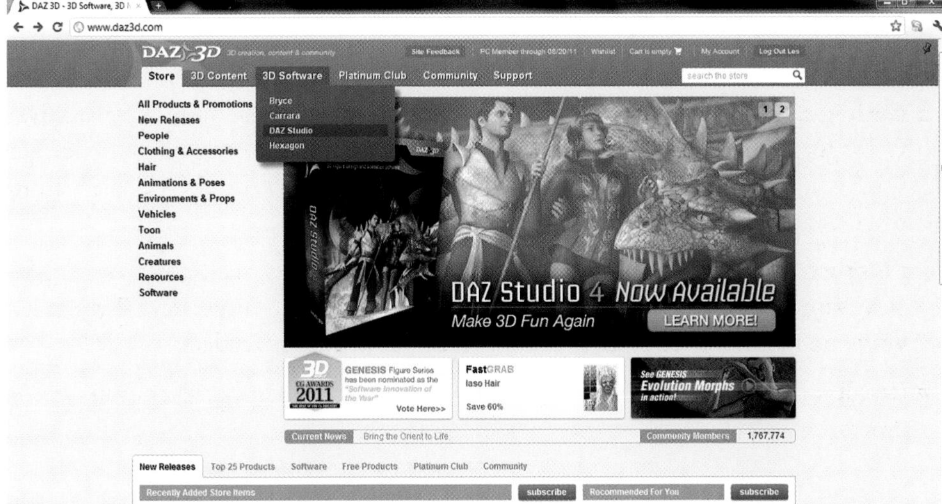

Figure 2.2 Find DAZ Studio in the 3D Software menu.

This will take you to the DAZ Studio landing page. The page will have a lot of good information about the program and even a video or two. Scroll down to the bottom of the page to find the product's purchase information. See Figure 2.3.

Currently the program is free. All you need to do is go through the purchase process, download, and install the software. Just follow the online instructions.

If you happen to have an older version of DAZ Studio on your system, the installation program will ask if you want to remove it. The older version has to be removed before you can install the new version so click Yes.

Once the program is installed, take the time to review the readme file. When you are ready to begin, start the program.

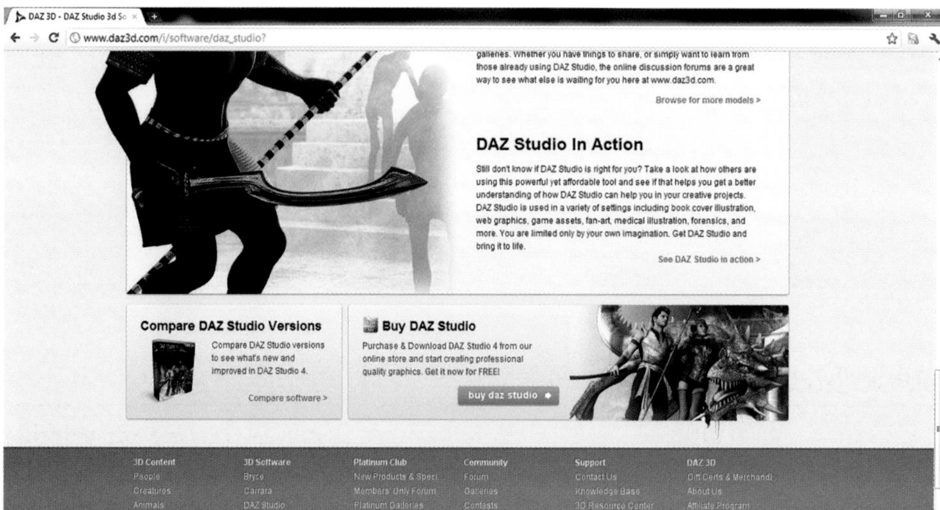

Figure 2.3
The purchase information is at the bottom of the page.

Registering DAZ Studio

When DAZ runs for the first time, you will be asked to register the program with a serial number. If your computer is connected to the Internet, you will be able to receive your serial number right away; just follow the online instructions. If you have any trouble registering DAZ Studio, you can find all your DAZ serial numbers on your account page under Available Serial Numbers.

Once DAZ Studio is registered and activated, it will load with a pop-up shown in Figure 2.4. This is a video that shows how to work with a character in DAZ Studio. It is well worth the time to view and is a good introduction to DAZ Studio.

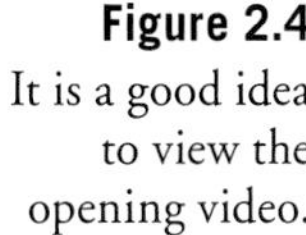

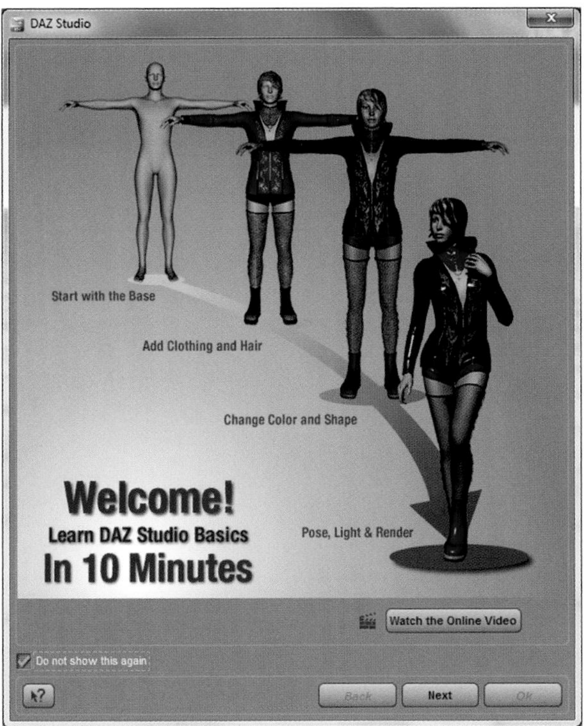

Figure 2.4
It is a good idea to view the opening video.

DAZ Studio Basics

DAZ Studio takes a different approach to creating art. Instead of drawing and painting like in Photoshop, or building 3D objects like Maya, 3ds Max, and others, DAZ Studio is more like a virtual photography studio. In DAZ Studio, the artist uses existing 3D models to create art. The program also allows the artist to modify 3D models resulting in almost limitless possibilities.

In DAZ Studio, the workflow generally goes as follows:

1. **Load a scene file.** A scene is a 3D file that contains an environment. For example, a scene might be a city park, a beach, or even a room.
2. **Load characters and props.** Characters and props are 3D models that are used to populate a scene. For example, characters can be humans, robots, animals, or any other creature. Props are objects like furniture, cars, and buildings. Props can also be objects like guns, backpacks, and cell phones.
3. **Accessorize the characters.** Once the scene elements are loaded, the artist then can modify the characters in the scene by changing or adding accessories and/or clothing. For example, the artist may want the model to wear a different outfit or add items like sunglasses or a hat.

4. **Arrange the scene.** The next step for the artist will be to arrange the scene. In this step, the artist moves the loaded elements around in the scene until everything is where it should be.
5. **Pose and shape characters.** Because characters can animate, the artist can pose and shape them in any position the artist chooses.
6. **Set up lighting.** When the scene is ready and all elements are in place and posed to the artist's satisfaction, it is time to set up the lighting. In this step, the artist adds lights to the scene.
7. **Position the camera.** The last task to complete before rendering the scene is to create the camera for the angle that the artist wants for the final rendering of the scene.
8. **Render the scene.** Rendering the scene is where you take the picture of what you created. Renders can be a single picture or multiple frames of an animation sequence.

This is a simplified list of a common workflow for using DAZ Studio. It isn't necessarily how all artists work and it can be much more complex, but it's easier for a beginner to start with a basic workflow. This book is organized so it follows this workflow, taking you through each aspect of the above steps.

Following the workflow will also help you to understand why the interface is set up the way it is. Let's move on and take a look at the DAZ Studio interface.

The DAZ Studio Screen

At first glance, the DAZ Studio screen may seem a little complex with all of the icons and menus. It really isn't that difficult to understand once you know that most of the icons and menus are just tools to help you navigate the scene and manipulate objects within the scene. They are placed in the toolbars surrounding the scene to make the program easier to use. To help you make sense of these tools, I'll go through them and explain what they are and how they are used.

General Layout

DAZ Studio's layout is designed to make it easy for the user to set up scenes. The main work area is in the center of the screen, shown in Figure 2.5. Think of this area as the stage. It is your view of the world you are creating.

In the upper-right corner of the scene view you'll see several tools that are used to help you work in the scene, as shown in Figure 2.6. They appear when you place your cursor over them. They control scene movement, zoom, display modes, camera views, and layout options.

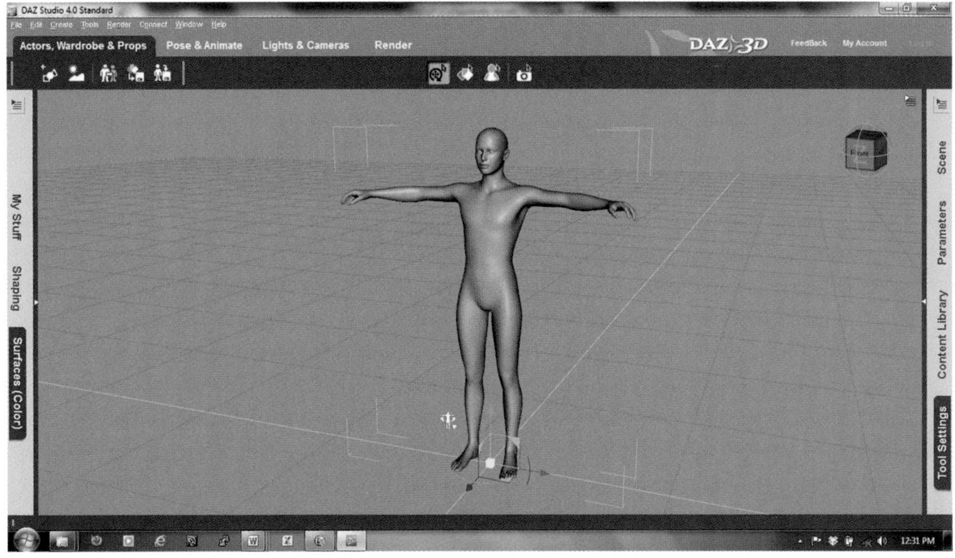

Figure 2.5 The center part of the screen shows the scene you are working on.

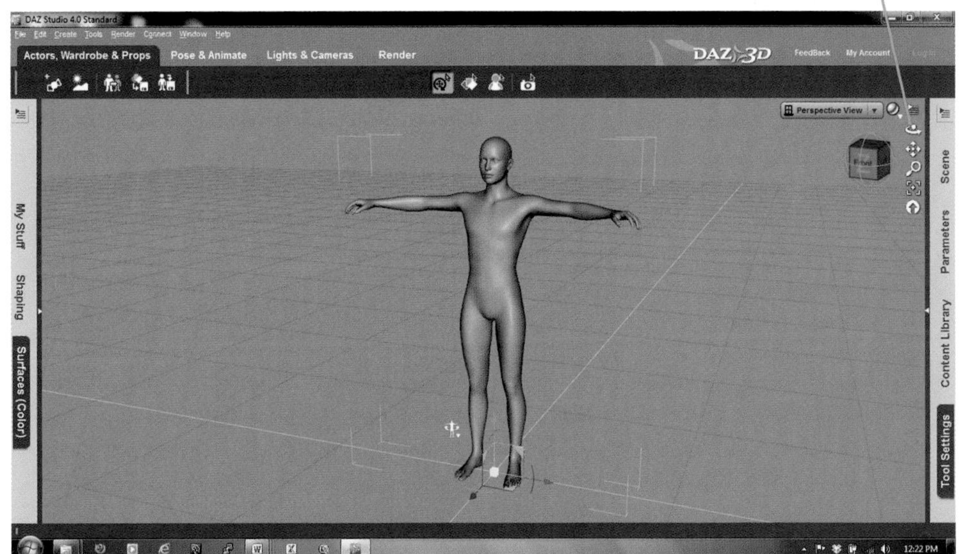

Figure 2.6 The scene tools are hidden in the upper-right corner of the scene.

Menus

Along the top of the screen, starting from left to right as shown in Figure 2.7, is a list of menu headings. When clicked, each menu heading opens a drop-down menu with several items that can be selected with a second click.

- **File.** The File menu includes options for loading, saving, importing, and exporting files into and out of DAZ Studio.

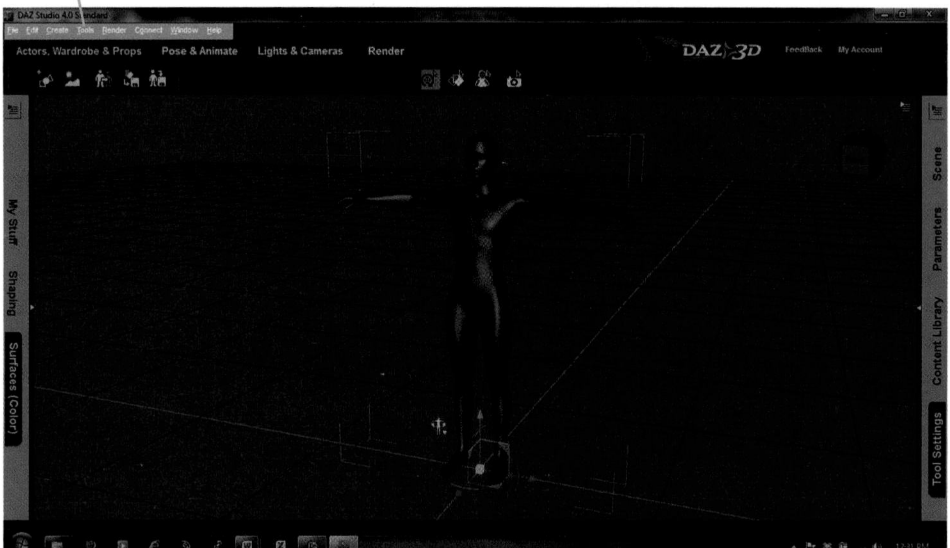

Figure 2.7
The menus are along the top of the screen.

- **Edit.** The Edit menu includes options like Copy and Paste. It also contains options for Preferences and Customize that allow you to edit how the program works.
- **Create.** The Create menu includes options that are used to create elements like cameras, lights, and objects.
- **Tools.** The Tools menu includes tools used in the program for manipulating, animating, and rendering 3D objects.
- **Render.** The Render menu includes functions directly related to rendering a scene, including those used to change rendering settings.
- **Connect.** The Connect menu provides several links to DAZ 3D to help you find new 3D models and organize your purchases. It also connects you to the DAZ art community.
- **Window.** The Window menu contains functions to change the layout of your working space. It also includes a Tabs menu that contains several floating tools used for customizing objects.
- **Help.** The Help menu provides help documents, online helps, product information, and a way for you to send feedback to DAZ 3D.

Activity Tabs

Below the menus are four activity tabs, as shown in Figure 2.8. These tabs are used to change the basic function of the program for different work purposes. If program layout included all tools for every function needed to use DAZ Studio, it would be so cluttered

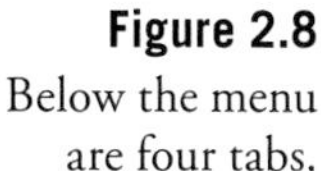

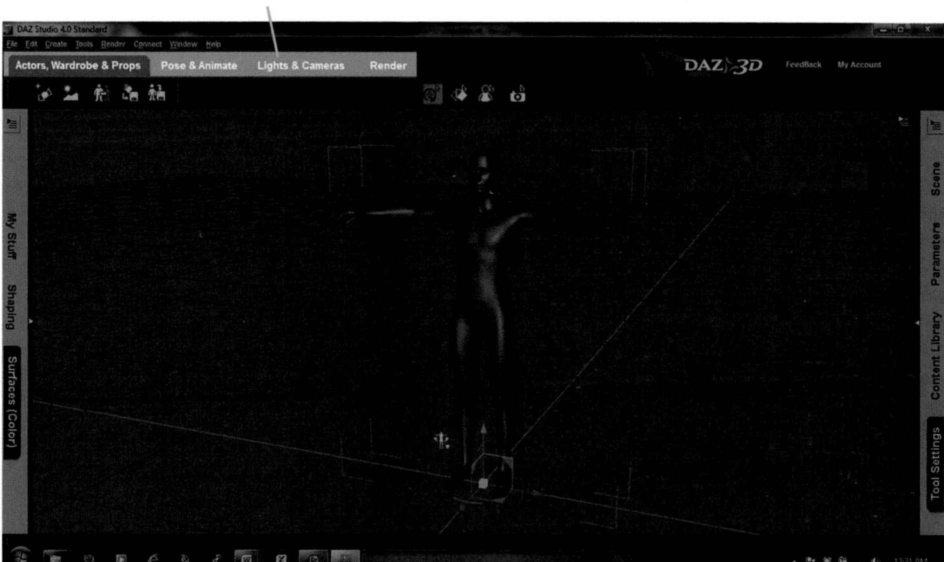

Figure 2.8
Below the menu are four tabs.

it would be almost impossible to use. To simplify the layout and just focus tools and functions to specific aspects of the art creation process, the good folks at DAZ 3D have split the functions into four separate basic functional groups.

Actors, Wardrobe & Props

The program opens with the first tab selected. The first order of business when setting up art for DAZ Studio is to populate it with the objects and characters you want to be part of your picture, movie, or 3D world. The Actors, Wardrobe & Props layout is designed to make the process of finding and loading 3D assets easier.

Pose & Animate

Once all of the 3D assets are loaded into the scene, they need to be posed or animated so you can create your artwork. Posing and animating requires specialized tools, which are present in the Pose & Animate layout.

Lights & Camera

When everything in the scene is posed and animating as it should be, you are then ready to move on to placing lights and cameras into your scene. There are many options for placing lights, including animating them, which requires special tools. Cameras are no less comprehensive. The Lights & Camera layout simplifies the process by making the tools specific to those functions more evident.

Render

The last step when making your art is to render it. This process requires putting everything together so you can get just the look you are after. Depending on the complexity of your arrangement, the rendering process can take some time to complete. There are also many options for rendering that can change the look of your art. These options are all arranged for easy use in the Render layout.

Panels

On the left, right, and bottom of the screen you'll find pull-out panels, as shown in Figure 2.9. Panels are used to make tools available as you need them along your production path. Each panel has a series of panel tabs located on the inner edge of the panel. These tabs help you navigate to tools and functions that are useful to you in your art creation. Depending on the activity tabs selected, the tabs on the panel on the left will change. The panel on the bottom only appears when you are in the Pose & Animate tab. The tabs on the right remain constant and do not change.

In order to explain how to use the panels, we need to cover them in conjunction with the tabs because many of the functions will change depending on which activity tab is chosen. To start, click on the Actors, Wardrobe & Props tab. You will find three panel tabs on the left: My Stuff, Shaping, and Surfaces (Color), as shown in Figure 2.10.

Click on the small arrow on the panel to open it. The panel should open with video options for learning how to use each panel tab.

Figure 2.9
Panels around the scene make tools and functions available as you need them.

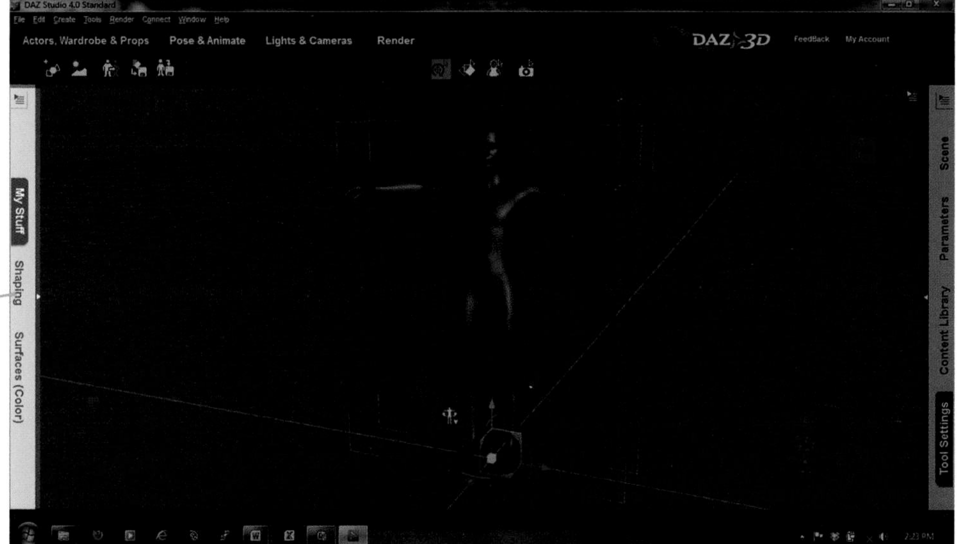

Figure 2.10
The left-hand panel contains three panel tabs.

> **Note**
>
> The fine people at DAZ have embedded several tutorial videos to help explain how to use many of the functions in the panels in DAZ Studio. These videos will appear the first time you open a panel. You can view these videos to gain more in-depth instructions on specific functions. You will need to be connected to the Internet to view the videos.

My Stuff

The My Stuff tab contains 3D assets in two views, Files and Products. The File view shows 3D assets as files. The Product view groups files into products. The advantage of the Product view is that it groups items that were created to work together, whereas the File view just list files by category. Basically, it is just two ways of sorting the files to make them easier to find. If you click on All in the Files view, you will see a long list of images that you can scroll through. See Figure 2.11.

If you want to load one of the files, double-click a file icon, as shown in Figure 2.12.

Shaping

The Shaping tab contains shape morphs that are used to change the shape of a character. Only models with morphs will have shaping options. Some models, like the Genesis model, have a number of morphs. To see the morphs for a model, double-click the model in the scene. Figure 2.13 shows the morphs for the Genesis model.

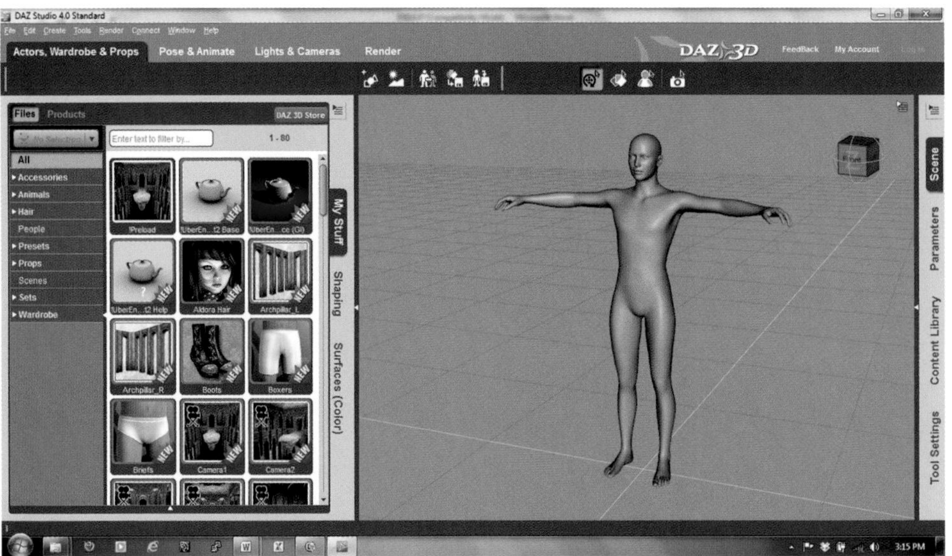

Figure 2.11
A long list of files.

Figure 2.12
The scene with a file loaded.

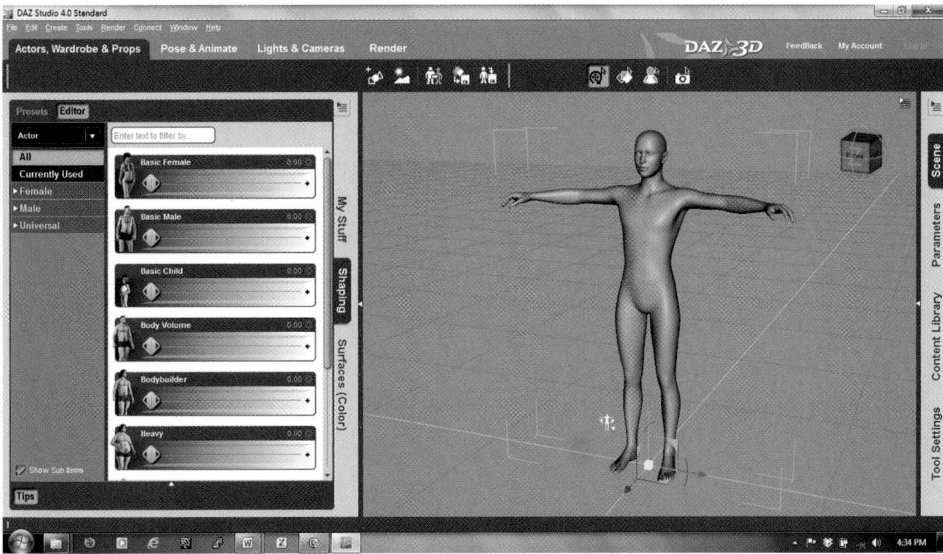

Figure 2.13 There are many morphs for the Genesis model.

Surfaces (Color)

The Surfaces tab contains choices for making surface changes to your model. Some models have more available surfaces than others but even those with limited surfaces will still let you change the color and many other attributes. See Figure 2.14.

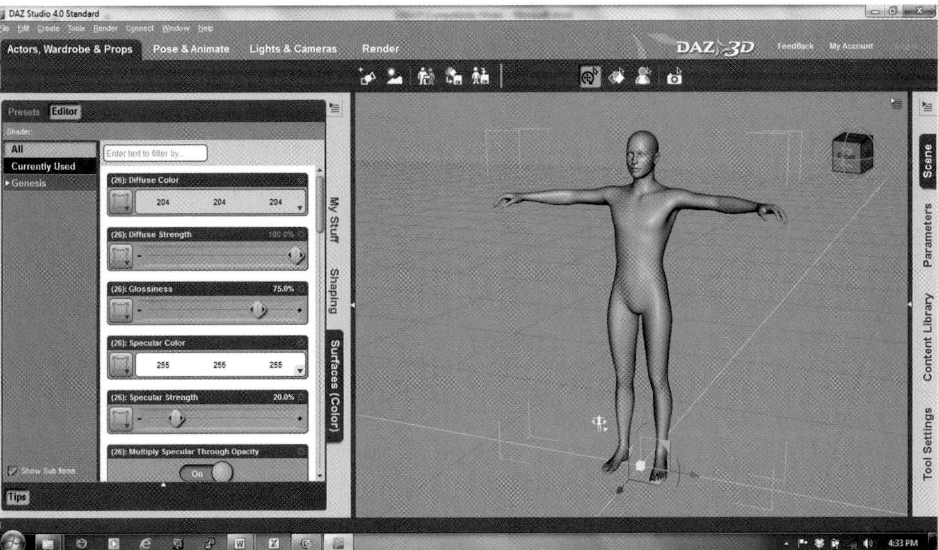

Figure 2.14 DAZ Studio gives you great control of surface attributes.

Right Panel

The tabs on the right panel do not change when you change the activity tabs. They are always there because they can be used no matter where you are in the process of creating your art.

Scene

The function of the Scene panel tab is to help you organize your scene and find any 3D object and its parts. In Figure 2.15, you can see the Genesis model and some of its sub-parts.

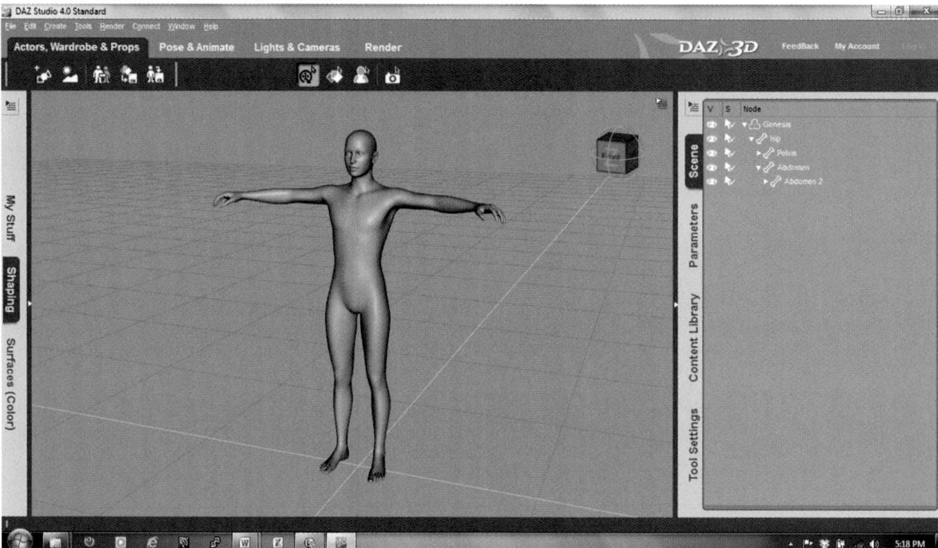

Figure 2.15
The Scene panel tab helps to keep you organized.

Parameters

The Parameters panel tab stores about anything you can modify in a model, ranging from where it is in the scene to how big any part of it is. The only things it does not contain are those found in the Surface panel tab. You can see the Parameters panel tab in Figure 2.16.

Content Library

The Content Library panel tab is where you will find all models and files that can be loaded into DAZ Studio. It is basically a hierarchal system for finding and sorting your content. Unlike the My Stuff panel tab, Content Library contains all files including those not included with the metadata needed to work in My Stuff. This includes older models and those created for use in programs that are compatible with DAZ Studio. You can see in Figure 2.17 some items colored blue. These are categories that contain content that is compatible with DAZ Studio.

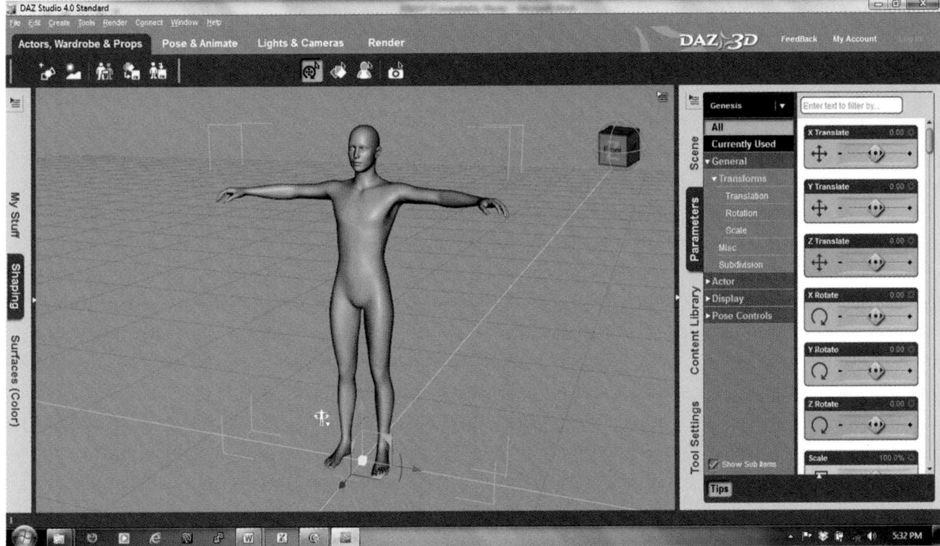

Figure 2.16
The Parameters panel tab holds functions to adjust your model.

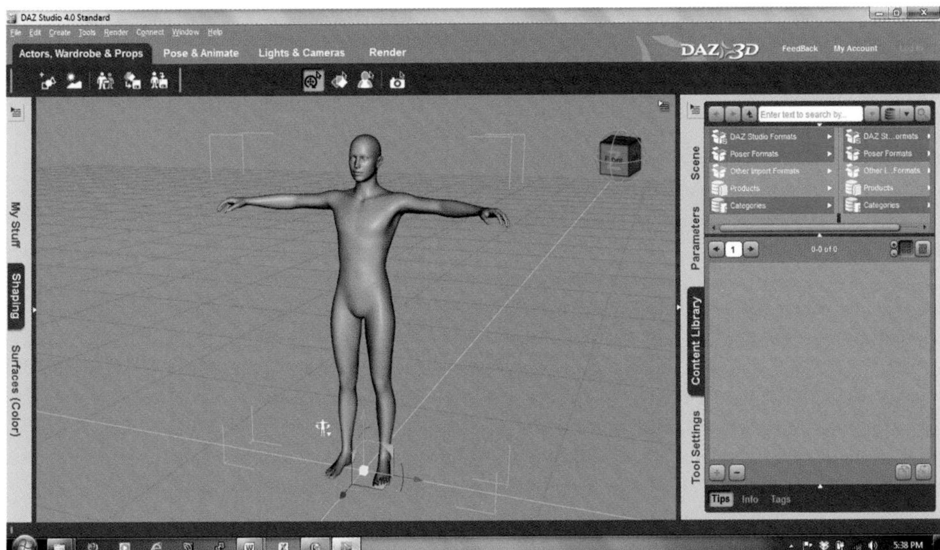

Figure 2.17
You can find models that are compatible with DAZ Studio in the Content Library.

Tool Settings

The Tools Settings panel tab is where you can change the settings for tools used in DAZ Studio. You won't need to worry too much about this tab as changing the tool settings is an advanced function. It is better to learn how to use the tools at their default settings before you start changing settings. See Figure 2.18 to see the Tools Settings panel tab.

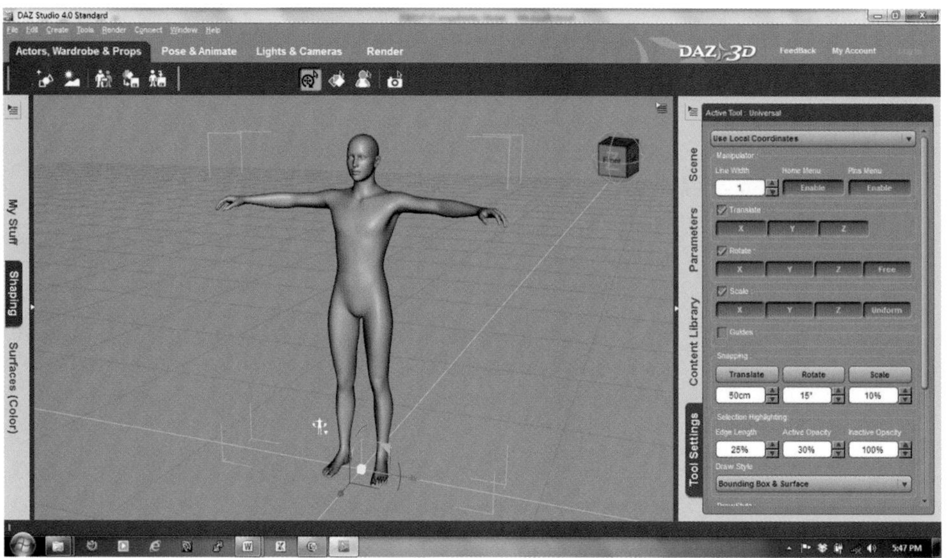

Figure 2.18
You can change tool settings in the Tool Settings panel tab.

Posing

Under the Pose & Animate activity tab you will notice that there is only one panel tab on the left side, titled Posing. This single tab contains a number of tabs useful in posing characters in a scene. See Figure 2.19.

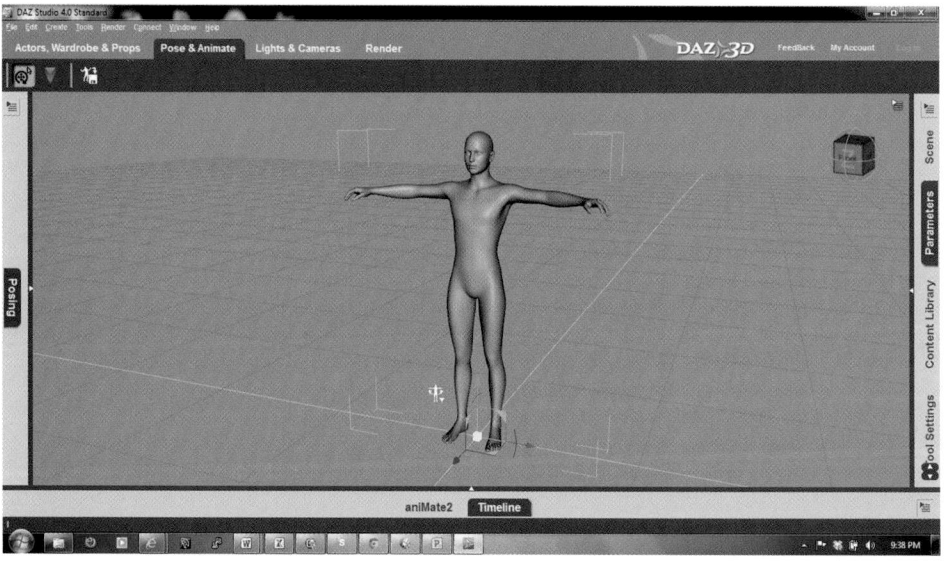

Figure 2.19
You can use the functions in the Posing panel tab to pose your characters.

aniMate2

At the bottom of the screen in the Pose & Animate activity tab there is a pull-up panel. This panel is along the bottom because the tools found here require lots of horizontal room and would be hard to use in a more vertical panel. The panel has two panel tabs. The first tab is the aniMate2 tab. The tools found in the aniMate2 tab are advanced animation tools that let you purchase animations from the DAZ 3D store and apply them to your characters. You can see the aniMate2 panel tab in Figure 2.20.

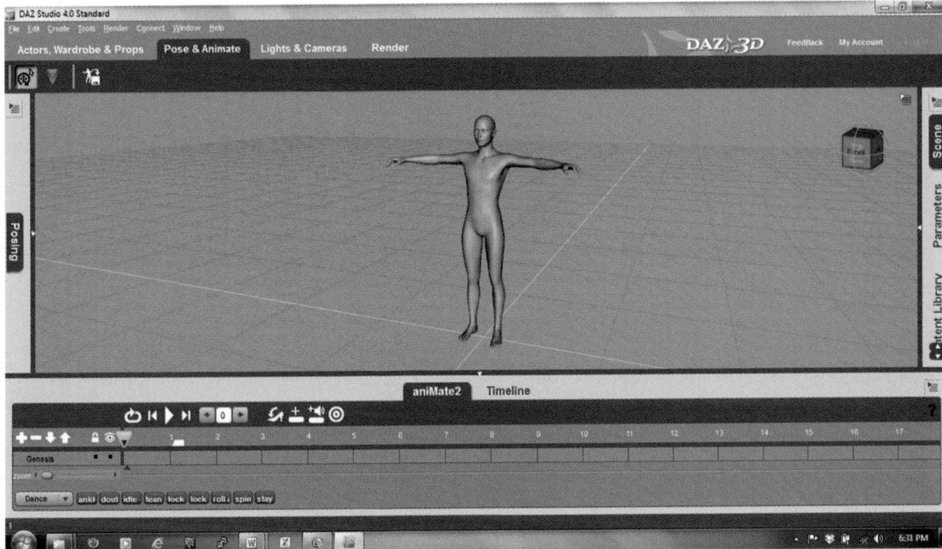

Figure 2.20 The aniMate2 panel tab lets you perform advanced animation.

Timeline

The Timeline is DAZ Studio's traditional keyframe animation tool. You can use it to custom build your own animations. It is also useful in non-character animation and when you need to move a character from one location to another. See Figure 2.21.

Lights

Under the left panel in the Lights & Camera activity tab you'll find two panel tabs, Lights and Camera. The Lights panel tab has two views, Presets and Editor. You can use Presets to load premade lighting for a scene. The Edit view allows you to edit lights once they are loaded into the scene. See Figure 2.22.

Camera

The Camera panel tab is similar to the Lights panel tab in function except that instead of adding lights, you are adding and editing camera views. Cameras are used to provide other views of a scene. It is useful to have multiple cameras when you want to see the same scene from several different angles. Figure 2.23 shows the Camera panel tab.

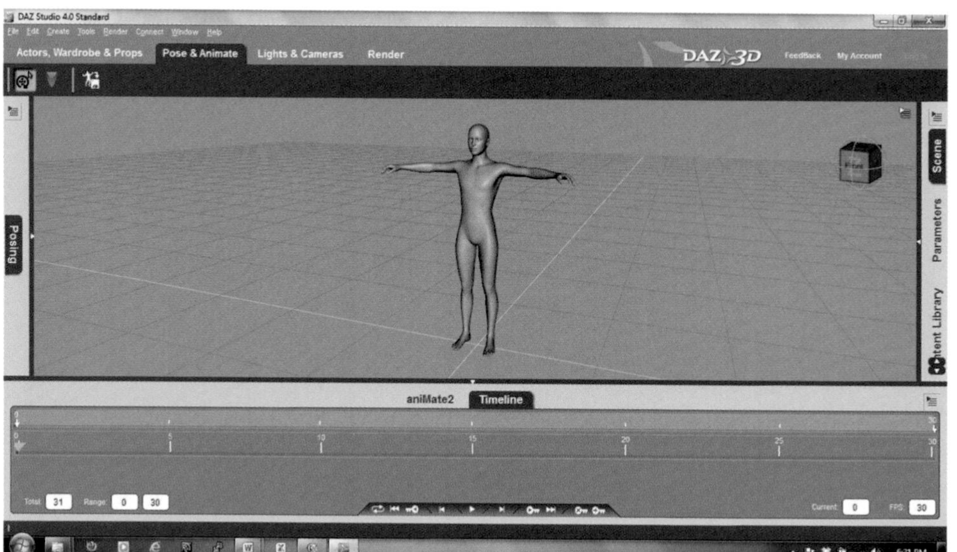

Figure 2.21
The aniMate2 panel tab lets you do advanced animation.

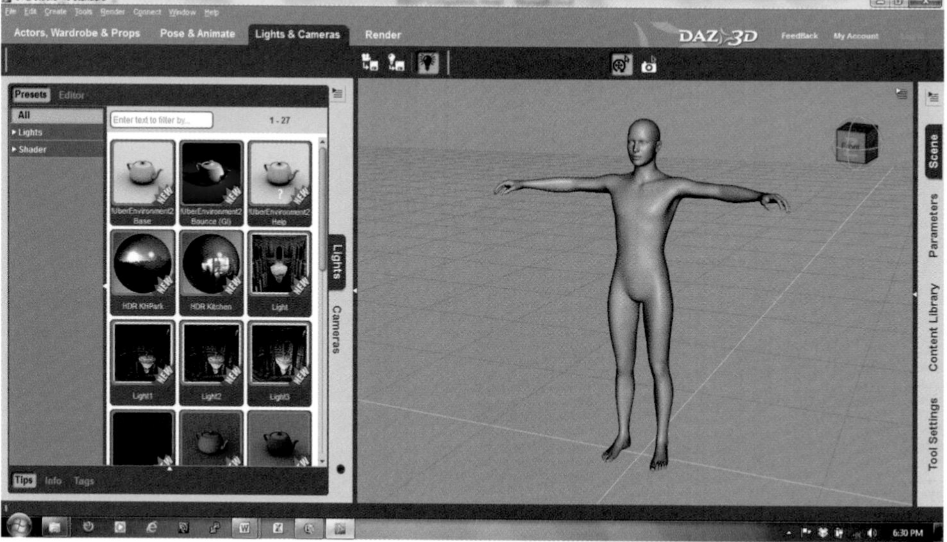

Figure 2.22
You can add and edit lights with the functions in the Lights panel tab.

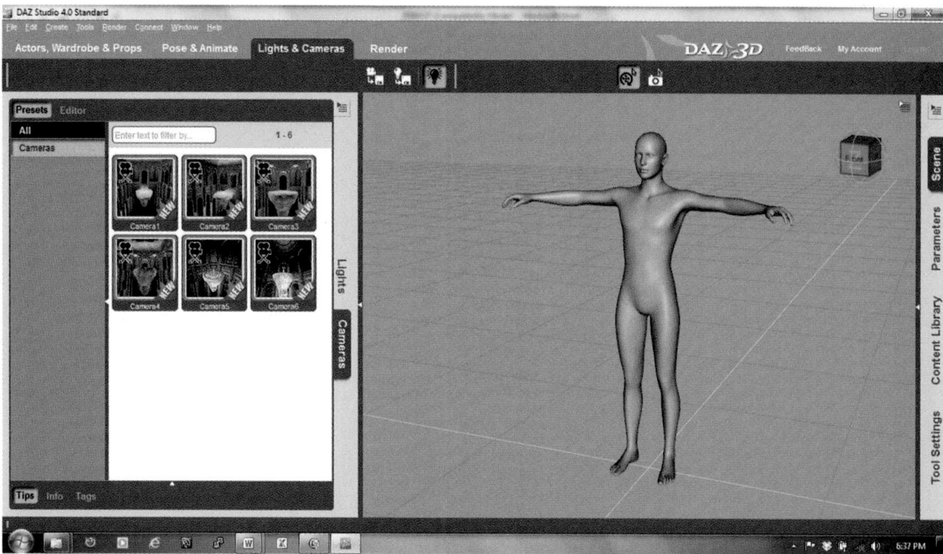

Figure 2.23 Work with cameras in the Camera panel tab.

Render Settings

Under the Render activity tab there are two panel tabs. The Render Settings tab lets you adjust the settings that control how your art will be rendered. See Figure 2.24.

Render Library

In the Render Library panel tab, you can organize your rendering. A test render of the current screen was placed in the library, as shown in Figure 2.25.

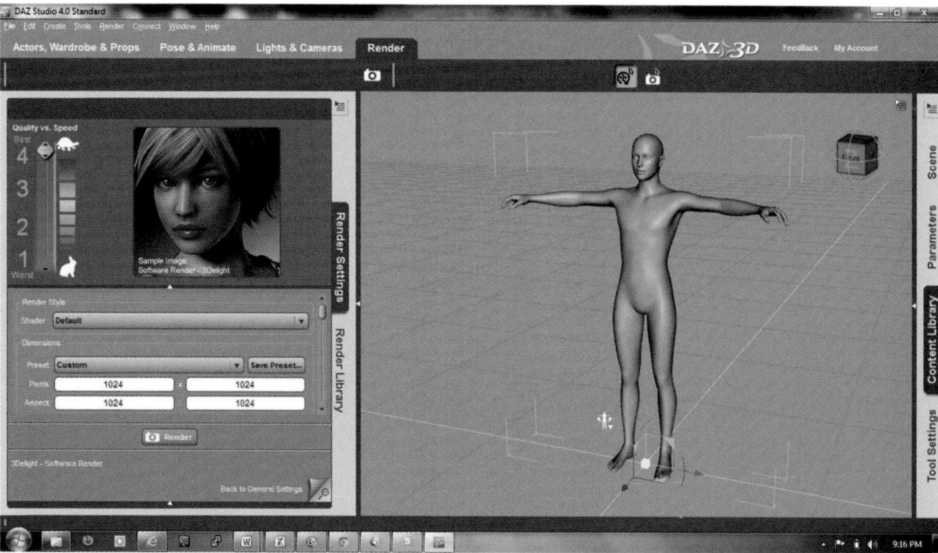

Figure 2.24 You can adjust the quality of your rendering in the Render Settings panel tab.

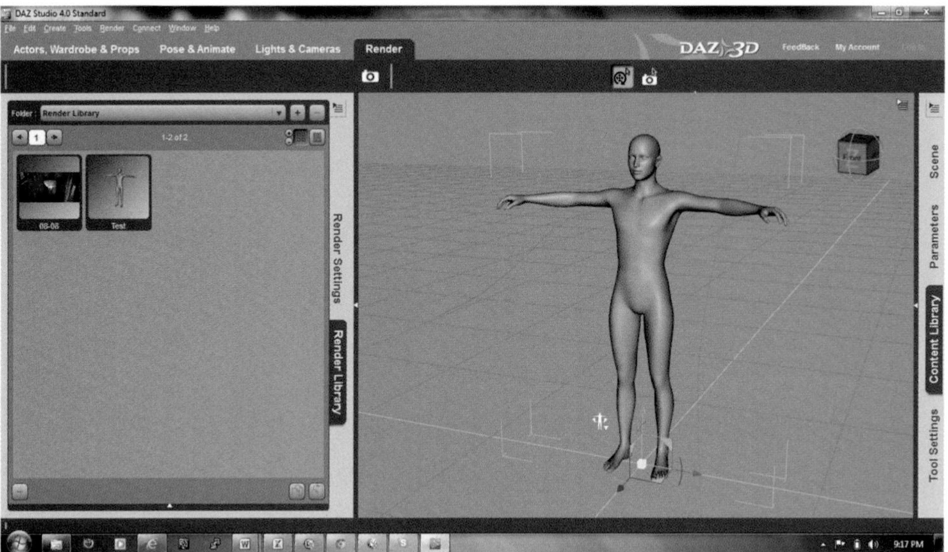

Figure 2.25
Use the render library to organize your renders.

The render library in your version will be empty until you render a scene. Once you have rendered a few hundred scenes, you will be thankful for this powerful tool.

Summary

Hopefully, this quick tour of the DAZ Studio screen will help as you start to tackle its many powerful features. In the rest of the book, we will go through each feature in more detail. The objective of this chapter was to give you an overall look at the interface so you can begin to get familiar with how it is organized and how it corresponds with the basic workflow of creating art in DAZ Studio.

3

The Scene

The *scene* is your 3D world. You can do with it what you want. It can be as large as your imagination and as small as your deepest thoughts. The scene is where you create your art. In this chapter, we take a look at how you can move about the scene and how you can put 3D objects into you scene. This will be your first step in learning how to use DAZ Studio for creating art.

Understanding Scenes

A scene in DAZ Studio is viewed in the work area where you will place your background objects, characters, and props. It can also contain lights, cameras, and anything else that you import or use to make up your art. The Scene tab in the right pull-out panel provides a complete list of all 3D assets you place in your scene. Let's take a quick look at the scene that loads with DAZ Studio. Click on the Scene tab on the right panel, as shown in Figure 3.1.

A quick look at the list in the Scene panel will show you what you have to work with. Right now you only have one 3D model in your scene, the Genesis model. Even though it is only one object, that doesn't mean that you see everything. Complex models like Genesis have many parts. Click on the arrow symbol next to Genesis. This should bring up the hip just below Genesis. If you then click on the hip, as shown in Figure 3.2, you will see that the scene changes. The hip is the origin point of the figure so it appears first in the list.

Each item you see in the list with an arrow symbol next to it has other parts that are connected to it. This means that you are not looking at a single item but rather a group of items tied together in what DAZ Studio calls nodes. For example, in Figure 3.3, part of the Genesis model's node structure has been expanded. You will notice that some of these are nodes within nodes. Nodes are hierarchal, meaning that if you select the first item in a node, all of the items below it are also selected. If, on the other hand, you select the bottom item in a node, only that item is selected. Think of the list like a tree. If you shake the trunk, all of the branches will shake as well. If you shake one of the end branches, it will shake by itself.

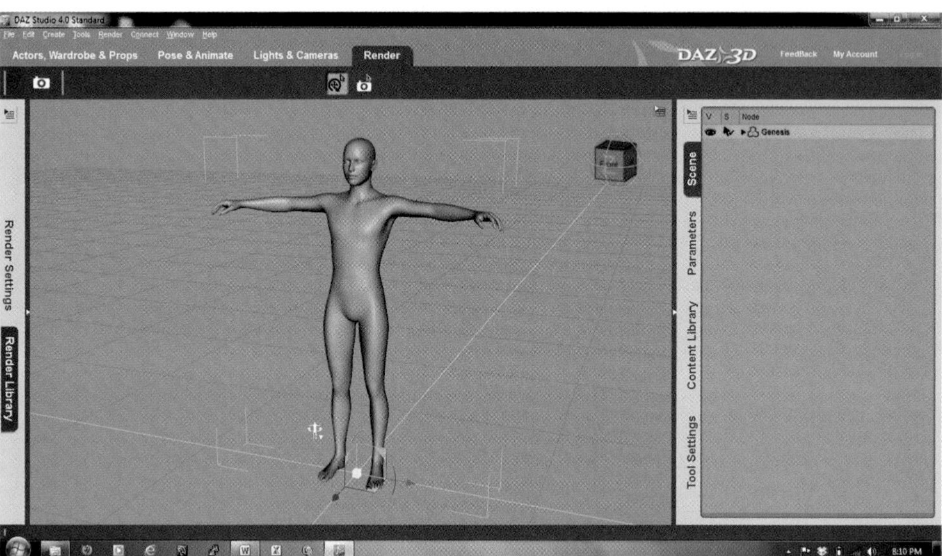

Figure 3.1
The Scene panel shows everything in the scene.

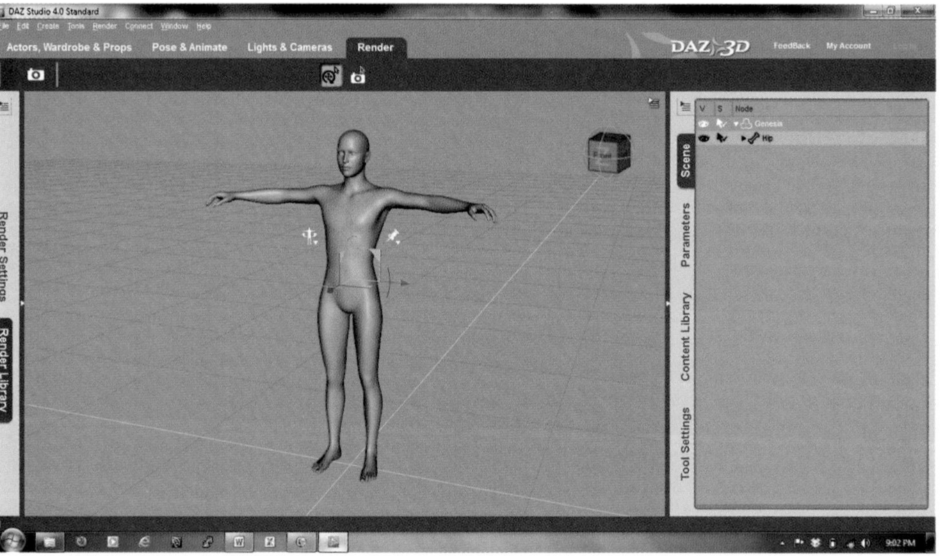

Figure 3.2
The scene changes when you click on the Hip.

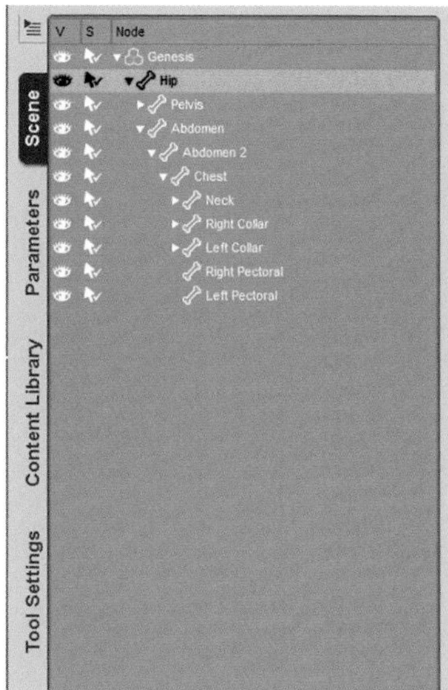

Figure 3.3
Items in the list are hierarchal.

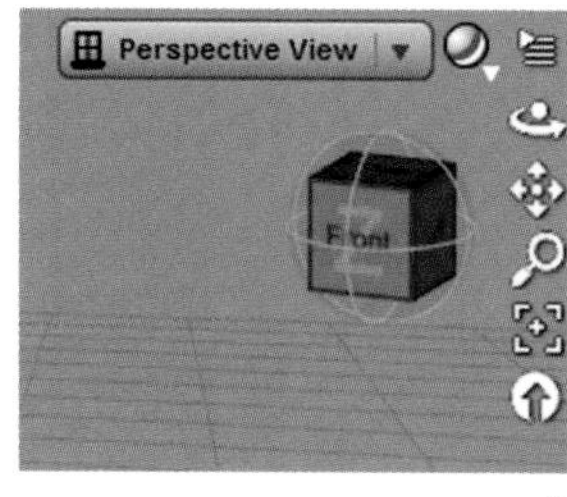

Figure 3.4
The toolbar in DAZ Studio.

The Scene list is an easy way to select specific items without having to find them inside the scene, which can be very helpful when animating a character or trying to find an object in a complex scene. However, items can also be selected by clicking on them in the scene. DAZ Studio allows for both types of selections.

Toolbar

In the upper-right corner of the scene is a set of tools that can be used to modify the scene. Let's go through each tool. Figure 3.4 shows the tools in the toolbar; they appear when you bring the cursor up to that part of the screen.

- **View Selection.** This is a drop-down list of available views of the scene. You can use this list to change the camera view or add new camera views to your scene.
- **Draw Style.** Changes the draw style of how you view your scene. These options are useful for working with complex scenes where draw times are slow, or to help place an object just right.
- **Viewport Options.** Displays the viewport option list.
- **Vantage/Orbit Cube.** This handy tool is always visible. You can use it to navigate to different views around your model.
- **Orbit/Rotate/Bank.** This tool lets you orbit, rotate, or bank with the camera view.
- **Pan/Dolly.** Pans the scene parallel to the camera view or dolly around the scene.
- **Dolly Zoom/Focal Zoom.** This tool lets you zoom in and out of the scene.

- **Frame/Aim.** This tool lets you frame the selected object in the scene or aim the camera at a selected object from any angle.
- **Reset.** Restores the default view.

The Vantage Cube and camera tools on the right are for the most part activated when you position the cursor over the tool and hold down the left or right mouse button. However, some of the tools require a mouse click. Hovering over the tool will bring up a tool tip window, if you ever need to refresh your memory of how to use them. It is very important for you to become familiar with the camera tools if you hope to be proficient in DAZ Studio. For those who prefer keyboard commands, hovering over the item will bring up a tool tip that identifies the keyboard command.

Orbit/Rotate/Bank

Many times when you are working in DAZ Studio, you need to view the scene from different angles. This is because you are working in a 3D world and the models are three-dimensional. The Orbit/Rotate/Bank camera tools are very handy for looking around your scene. To orbit around the center of the scene, place the cursor over the tool and press the left mouse button. Now drag the cursor to the left. Your scene should now look like Figure 3.5

You can also drag the cursor up or down or any angle for that matter, orbiting around the center and viewing the figure from any camera position. The orbit feature is kind of like tying a string from the camera to the center of the scene and then moving the camera on the end of the string around the center.

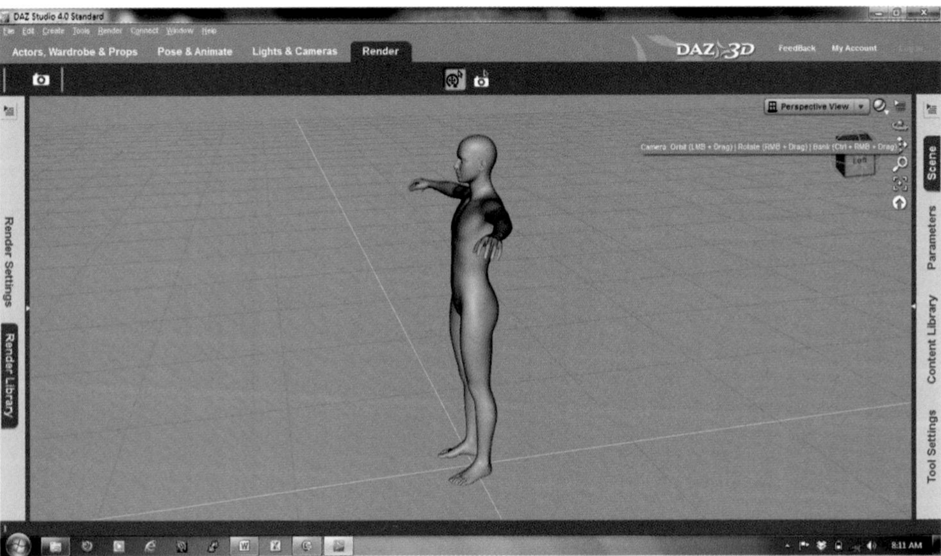

Figure 3.5
You can orbit around the center of your scene.

Rotating the scene is more like moving the scene around the camera than moving the camera around the scene. Think of it as standing in one location in a scene and looking around. Instead of pivoting around the center of the scene, the scene is pivoting around you. See Figure 3.6. To rotate, all you have to do is hold the right mouse button down over the tool and drag in any direction.

Banking is a little different from orbiting and rotating. Orbiting and rotating are like looking through a camera and holding the camera straight in front of you. Banking on the other hand, is like tilting the camera to the right or left, as shown in Figure 3.7.

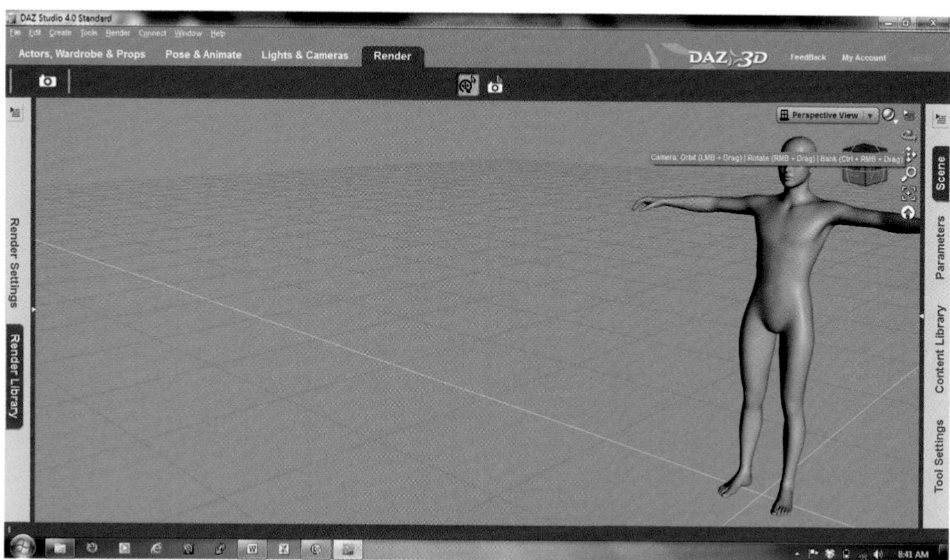

Figure 3.6 You can rotate the scene around the camera.

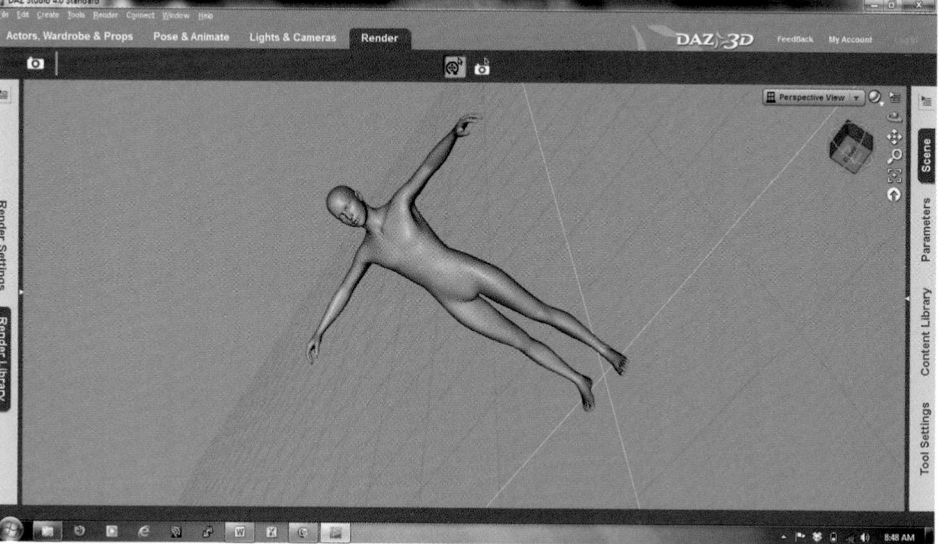

Figure 3.7 The Bank camera tool is like tilting the camera.

To bank you will need to use the right mouse button like you're rotating but also hold the Ctrl key on the keyboard down as well.

Pan/Dolly

Sometimes you want to keep the same orientation to the scene but want to move to the side parallel to the scene. This type of parallel movement is called *panning* in film terms. It is like holding a camera and stepping to the side without any pivots. The Pan camera tool lets you do this in DAZ Studio. Just hold the left mouse button down over the Pan camera tool and drag the cursor in any direction. See Figure 3.8.

Dolly is the other feature of the tool activated by holding down the right mouse button. The word *dolly* comes from the film industry. It is common when shooting a motion picture to place the camera on a cart on rails. The camera then can be moved along the rails smoothly. While we don't use a cart on rails in a virtual world, we still define the dolly-like movement of the camera as the Dolly feature.

The Dolly feature is similar to Pan when you move the mouse to the right or left, but when you move the mouse up or down the camera moves in and out of the scene. See Figure 3.9.

Dolly Zoom/Focal Zoom

DAZ Studio has two different zoom features: Dolly and Focal. The differences between the two are subtle but significant. With a Dolly Zoom you are actually moving the camera into and out of the scene. The Focal Zoom on the other hand, is more like the

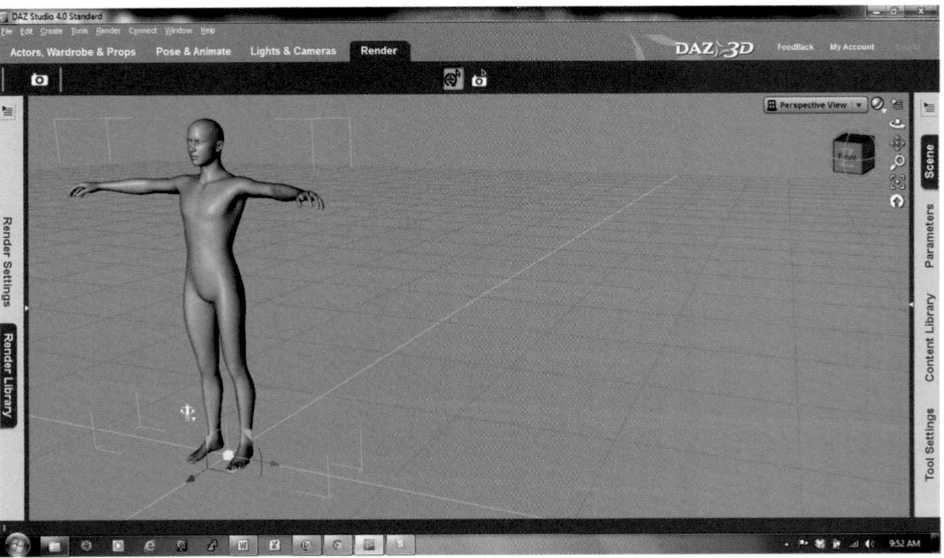

Figure 3.8
You can move the camera parallel to the scene.

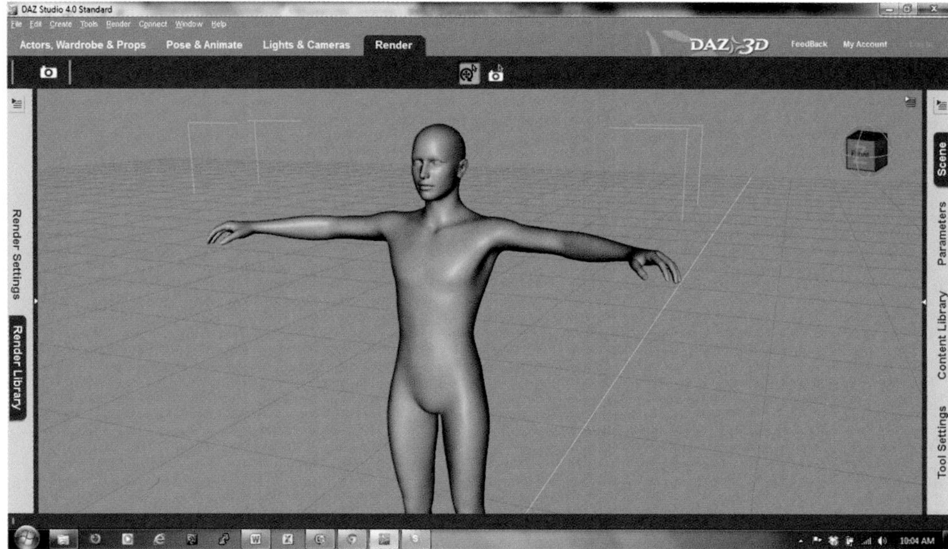

Figure 3.9 With the Dolly tool you can move in and out at the same time as moving left and right.

zoom lens on a traditional camera that uses telescopic lenses to take a close-up of an object. The camera stays in place but the telescopic lens makes the object appear to be closer. Take a look at Figure 3.10. In the top panel, a Dolly Zoom was used for a close-up of the model's face. In the bottom panel, the same thing was done using the Focal Zoom. Notice the difference in perspective between the two zooms.

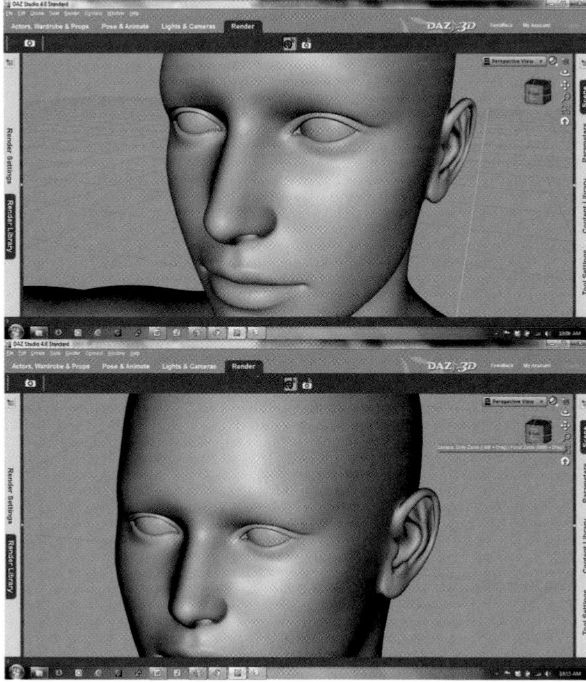

Figure 3.10 There are two types of zooms in DAZ Studio: Dolly and Focal.

The type of zoom you use is up to you, but knowing they are both there should help you when putting your scenes together. To perform a Dolly Zoom, hold down the left mouse button over the icon and drag left to zoom in and right to zoom out. Do the same thing for a Focal Zoom except hold down the right mouse button instead.

Frame/Aim

The next icon below the Pan/Dolly tool is the Frame/Aim tool. This is a convenient tool when working with complex scenes that contain multiple objects. You can also use the tool to see just a part of a model by using it in conjunction with the Active Node Selection tool. The Frame tool allows you to frame all objects you have added to your scene with one simple click of the left mouse button on the icon. To show you how this works I've imported a set that is much bigger than the Genesis model, as shown in Figure 3.11.

By simply clicking on the Frame/Aim icon, you can frame the entire scene in the view, as shown in Figure 3.12.

The Aim function is similar to the Frame function except that its purpose is to help you find specific objects in a scene. What the tool does is pivot the camera so it is centered on a selected object or selected part of an object. To show you how this works, I've selected the index finger of the model. I've zoomed in closer to the model so you can

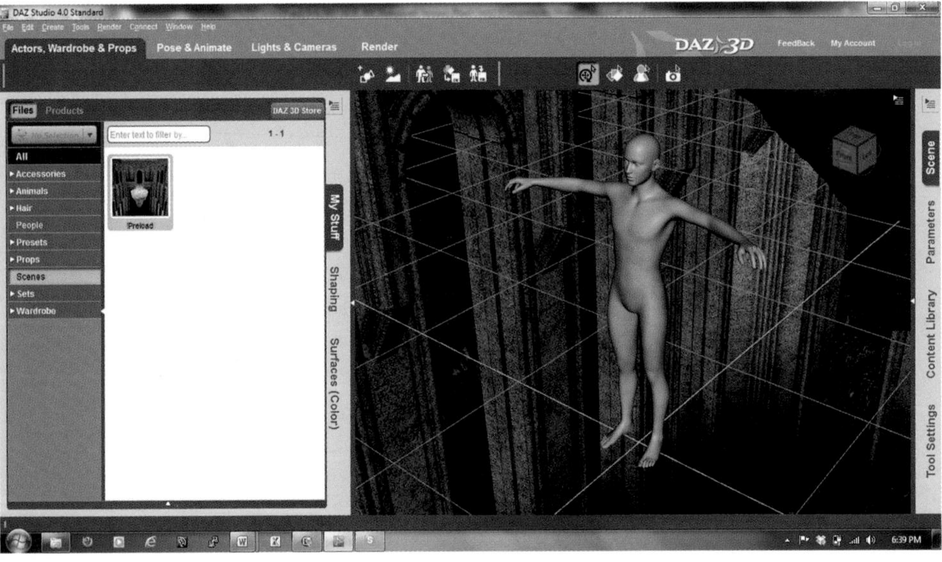

Figure 3.11
This scene is much bigger than the Genesis model.

see the selected finger in Figure 3.13. By clicking the right mouse button on the Frame/ Aim icon, the camera centers the scene on the finger.

Aiming the camera at an object also changes the scene pivot point to the center of the selected object. This means that the Orbit function now pivots around the object or part of an object that you aimed the camera at. See Figure 3.14.

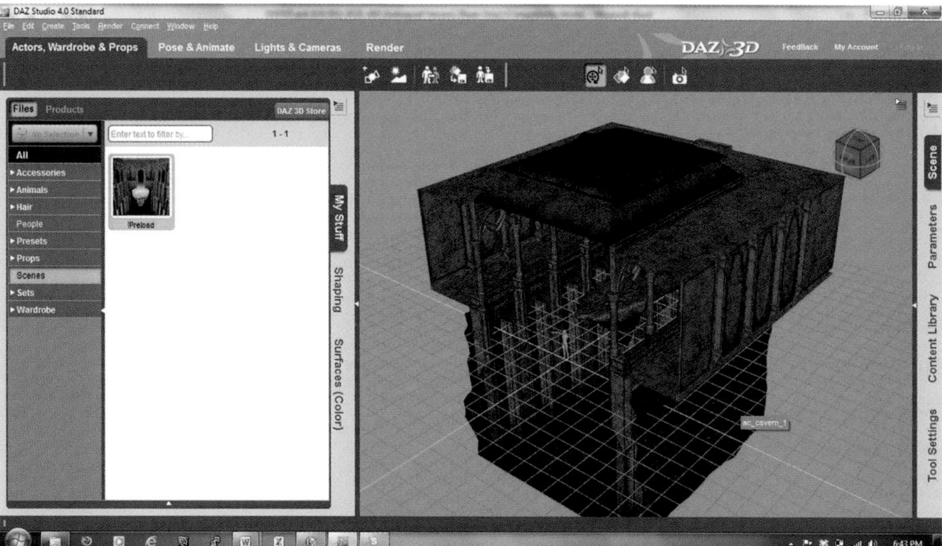

Figure 3.12
The entire scene is framed in the view.

Figure 3.13
Aim centers the scene on the selected object.

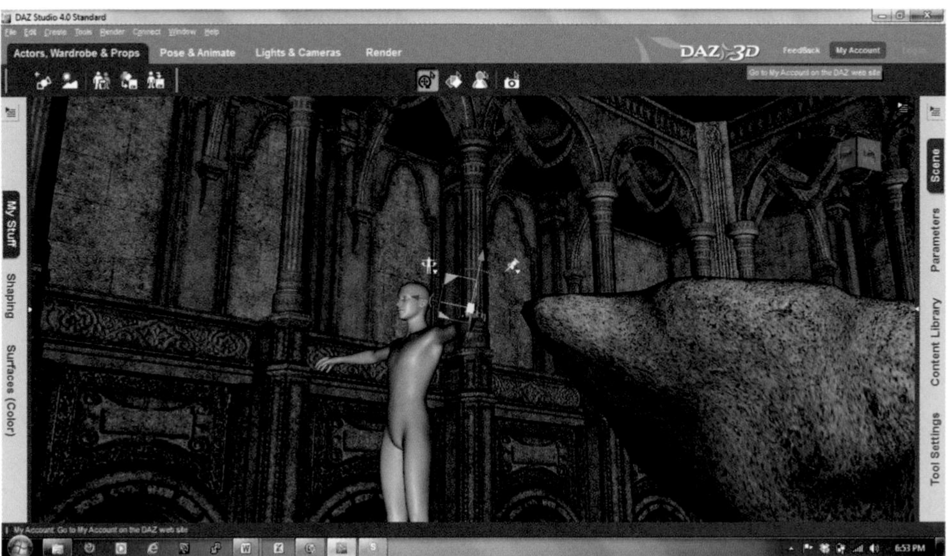

Figure 3.14
The pivot point changes when you aim the camera.

Reset

The last icon on the bottom is the Reset camera tool. Clicking on this tool resets the camera position to the default opening camera position, as shown in Figure 3.15. It uses either the left or right mouse button so it doesn't make any difference which button you use. Reset not only resets the camera but it also resets the pivot, which is helpful when working with the Aim feature.

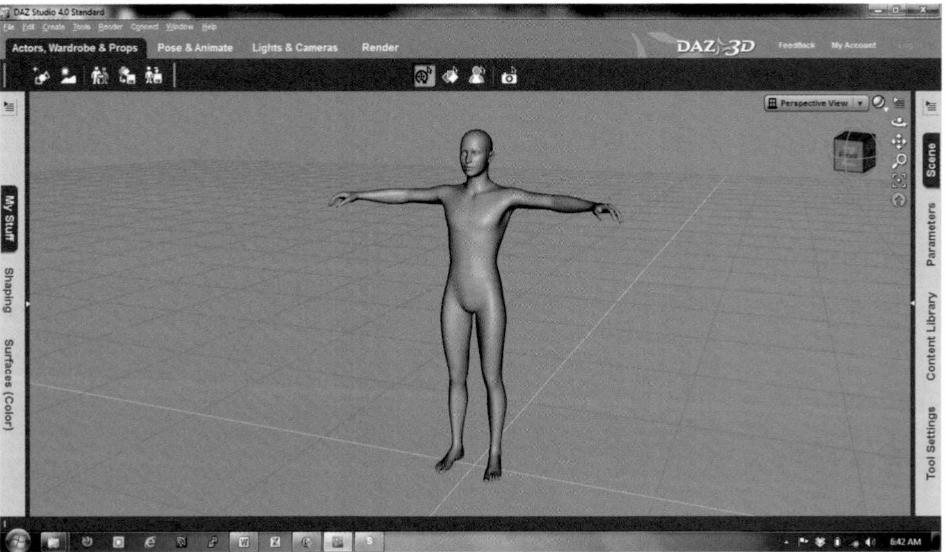

Figure 3.15
The Reset tool puts the camera back where it started.

Vantage/Orbit Cube

The Vantage/Orbit cube is always visible and is handy for quickly viewing your scene from different angles. The cube gives you quick access to the Orbit feature by simply clicking on it with your left mouse button. Then drag to orbit your scene. The labels on the cube faces can help keep you oriented in your scene. You can change your vantage of the scene by clicking on a part of the cube. The cube is broken into many parts. In Figure 3.16, the front panel of the cube was clicked.

In Figure 3.17, the back-right corner of the cube was clicked.

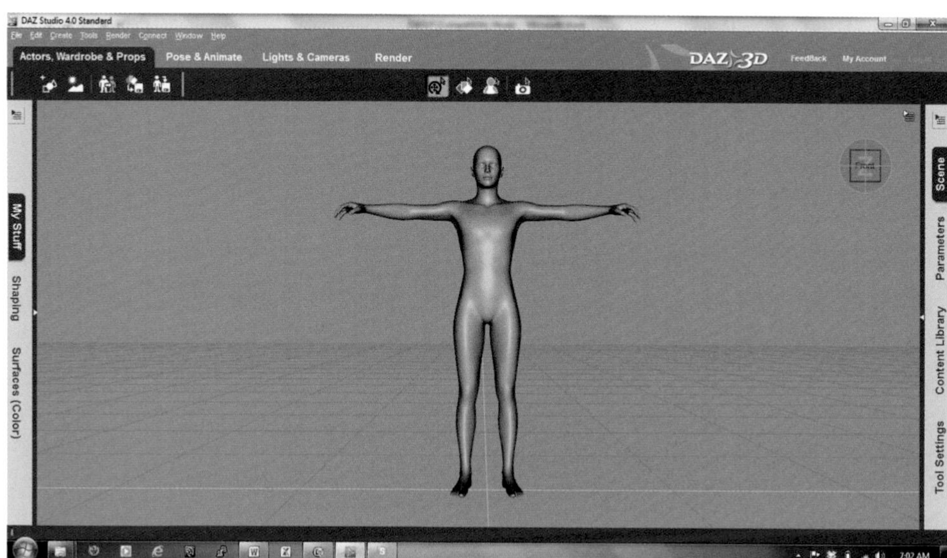

Figure 3.16
Use the front panel to go to the front view.

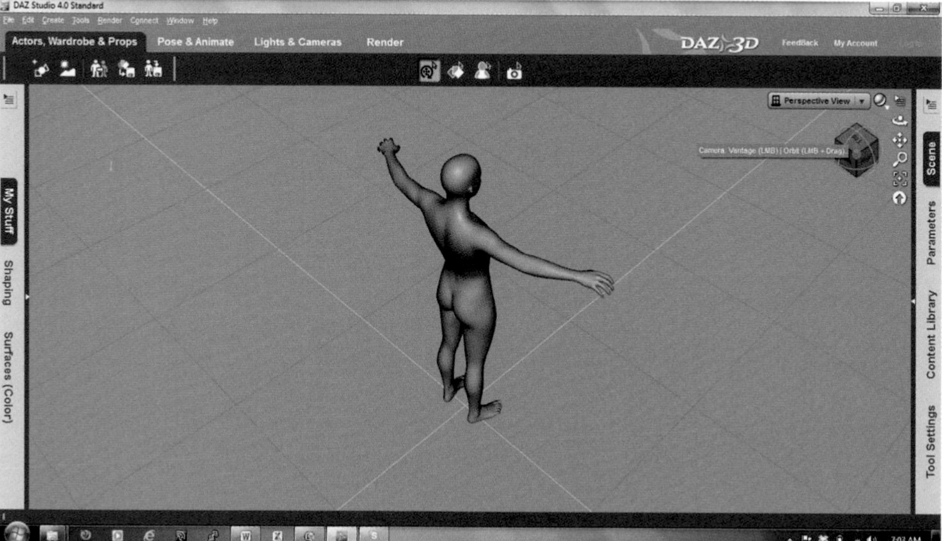

Figure 3.17
Use the back-right corner to go to that view.

You can quickly move all around your scene simply by clicking on different parts of the Vantage/Orbit cube. There are active hot spots on the cube for each face, edge, and corner.

It is important to note that the labels on the cube are set up in relation to the scene and not to you. That is why when you are in the front view, the right panel is on your left and the left panel is on your right. This is sometimes confusing to beginning users until they understand it is the same as looking at a person standing facing you. Their right hand is on your left and their left hand is on your right.

Wheel Mouse

With PCs, many mice have a wheel mouse button that acts as a third center button. If you have this type of mouse on your computer, you can use it to pan in and out of a scene. Rotating the wheel toward you will pan into the scene. Rotating the mouse away from you will pan out of the scene.

Loading

You add scene elements by loading them into a scene. This is done from the My Stuff or Content Library tabs. We covered these two tabs briefly in Chapter 2. Both tabs contain models that you can add to your scene and poses you can apply to those models. Let me show you how this is done. First, open the My Stuff tab and click on the Products button at the top of the panel. Make sure you don't have anything selected in your scene by clicking on a blank area. Now click on the All button on the left side of the panel. Your panel should now look like Figure 3.18.

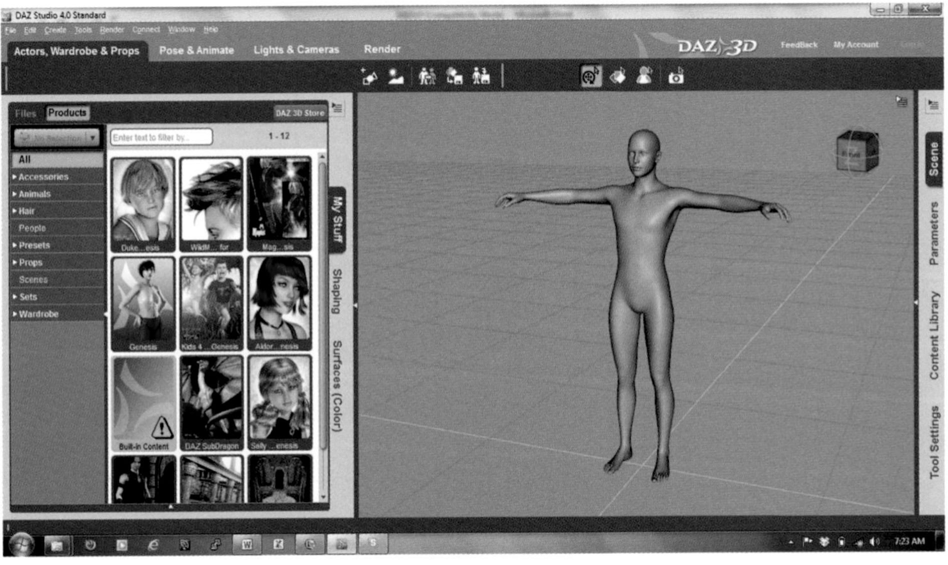

Figure 3.18
Bring up all your products in the My Stuff tab.

Now use the scroll bar on the right and scroll down to the Aikanaro panel and double-click on it. Your screen should now look like Figure 3.19.

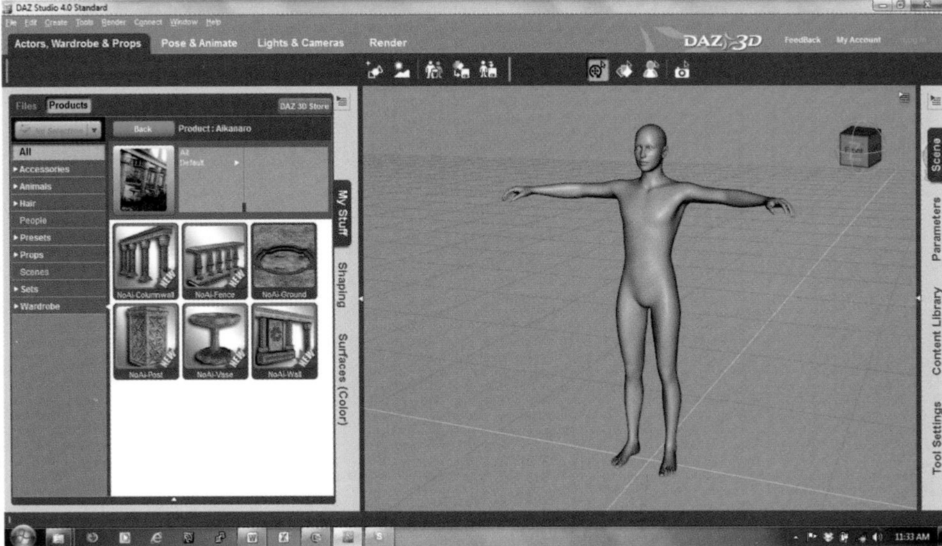

Figure 3.19 Bring up the Aikanaro object set.

On the top of the panel is the Aikanaro product panel. If you are connected to the Internet and click on the panel, it will take you to the product page on the DAZ 3D website. This is useful because there is a lot of information about the products there that might help you when you go to use them. To the right of the panel are two panels you can use to navigate to other objects. The actual objects themselves can be found below these panels.

Double-click on the panel labeled NoAi-Ground to load it into the scene. You can also right-click on the panel to bring up a menu that includes a Load It menu item to bring it into the scene. Your scene should now look like Figure 3.20.

You can try loading each of the objects into the scene, as shown in Figure 3.21.

You will notice that some of the objects are placed along the edge of the ground while others are placed in the center, right over the top of the figure model. Some artists will pre-place objects in a scene so when you load them they are already where the artist intended them to be. Other times the object is placed in the center so you can place them wherever you want. To move an object in the scene, just click on the object to bring up the Universal Manipulator tool, as shown in Figure 3.22.

This tool has many functions, which we will cover in a lot more detail in Chapter 4. For now just find the blue arrow, click on it, and drag the object forward, as shown in Figure 3.23.

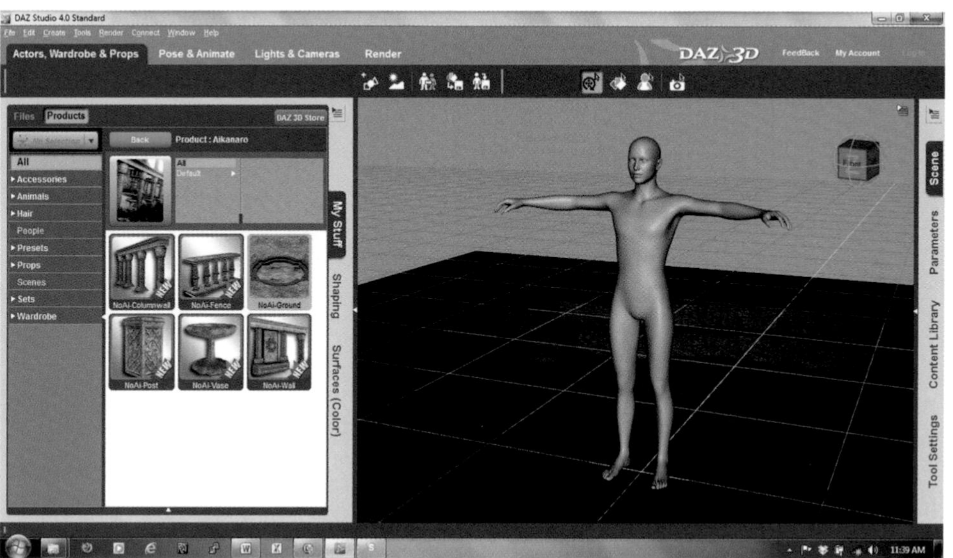

Figure 3.20
Load the ground into the scene.

Figure 3.21
Load all of the objects into the scene.

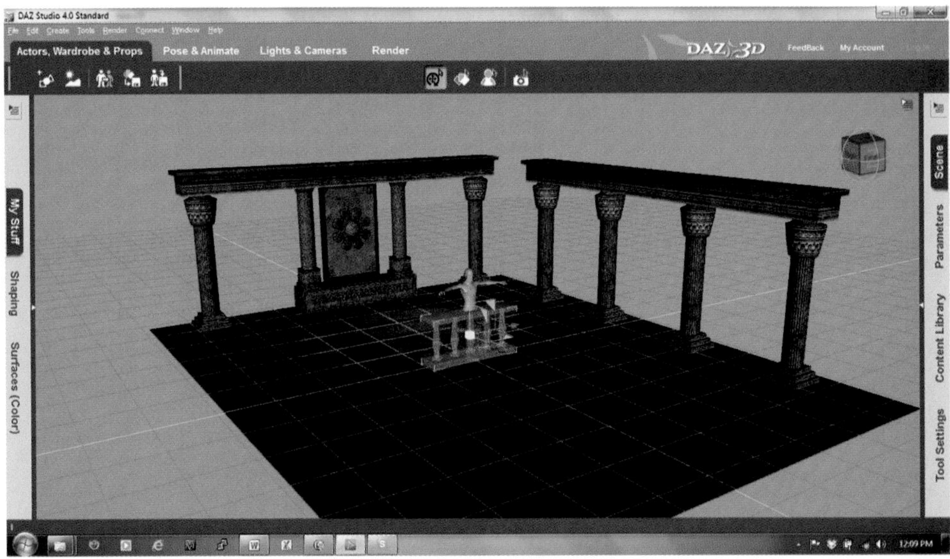

Figure 3.22
Select one of the objects in the scene.

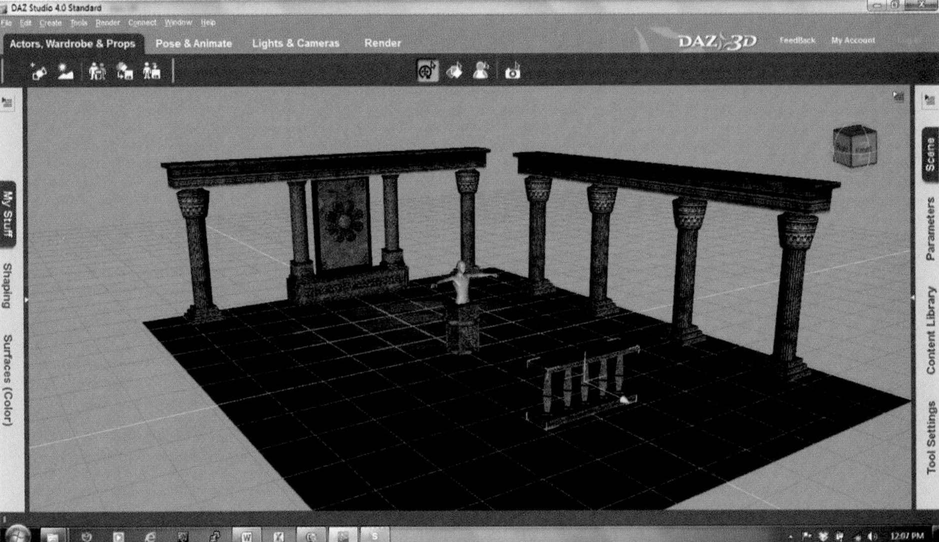

Figure 3.23
Pull the object forward.

Using the arrows on the tool, you can arrange the scene as you like by moving objects around. Go ahead and create your scene as you like.

Summary

In this chapter, we looked at the Scene tab and how models can be broken up into different parts. The Scene tab shows all elements loaded into a scene. We looked at DAZ Studio's Scene tools to understand how to view the scene. We also took a closer look at the toolbar tools so you are familiar with how to use them. These tools help you move about your scene and see it from any angle you like. We covered how to load objects into a scene and arrange them within the scene.

In the next chapter, we will cover what to do with objects once you get them into your scene.

4

The Figure

One of the most exciting aspects of DAZ Studio is the ability to load a character, put the character in an outfit, and then pose the character in any way that is needed for your final picture. This means that if you want to create a fantasy picture with dragons and heroes all in the act of confronting each other, you have complete freedom to express your vision. On the other hand, if you want to create a spy scene with your character sneaking into a building, you can do that also.

DAZ has gone to great lengths to create characters, sets, and props that are so lifelike that they are nearly indistinguishable from real life. Their library of 3D models is continually increasing, giving the 3D artist an ever-expanding source for creative development. In order to really understand how to use DAZ Studio and the great array of models you can use to create your artwork, you first need to understand a little about how 3D characters are put together. In this chapter we take a closer look at the 3D model.

Selecting Parts of the Figure

To begin with, let's take a look at our beginning scene with the Genesis model. Character models in DAZ Studio are made up of many individual parts. These parts are defined not by separate models but by how the body moves. In real life a body has many moving parts like arms, legs, hands, feet, head, etc. Our bodies provide us with a skeletal system powered by muscles to move around. In the 3D world, character models make use of a similar system called a Rig. 3D models of characters typically have a skeletal system very similar to our own. Each movable bone is designated in a hierarchal pattern similar to our own bodies. Select the Genesis model, as shown in Figure 4.1.

When you select the model, you should see the model framed in white brackets and the Universal Manipulation tool at the model's origin. Now open the Scene tab in the right pull-out panel and select Pose/Animate, as shown in Figure 4.2.

When any part of a 3D model in DAZ Studio is selected, it will appear highlighted in orange in the scene list. There are three easy ways to select parts of a 3D character in DAZ Studio. The first is by using the scene list. Open Genesis's list by clicking the arrow symbol next to the name in the list. This will bring up the hip. Click on Hip to

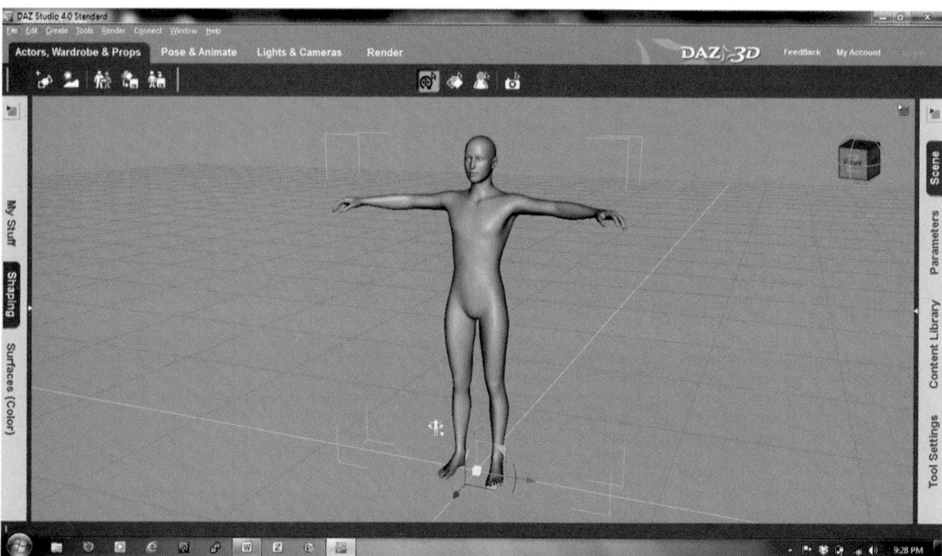

Figure 4.1
Select the Genesis model.

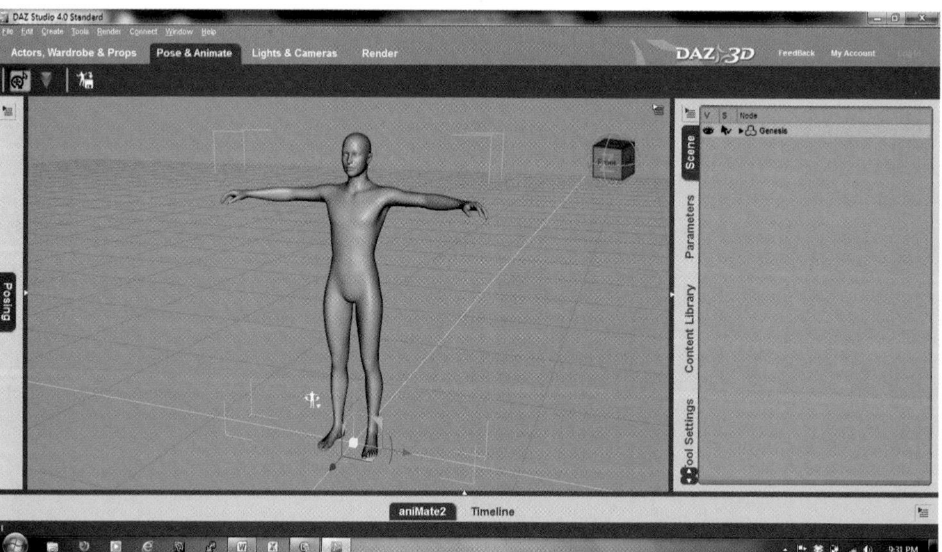

Figure 4.2
Select Pose/Animate.

select it, as shown in Figure 4.3. Notice that the Manipulator tool now is just over the hips in the scene.

A second way to select a body part is to select it directly in the scene. Move the cursor over the model. You will notice that as you move the cursor, the different body parts will turn orange. If you wait just a bit, a tool tip will appear describing the body part, as shown in Figure 4.4. To select the body part in the scene, just click on it in the scene. Notice that the list in the scene opens to show the same part selected there and the bones that connect that body part to the hip.

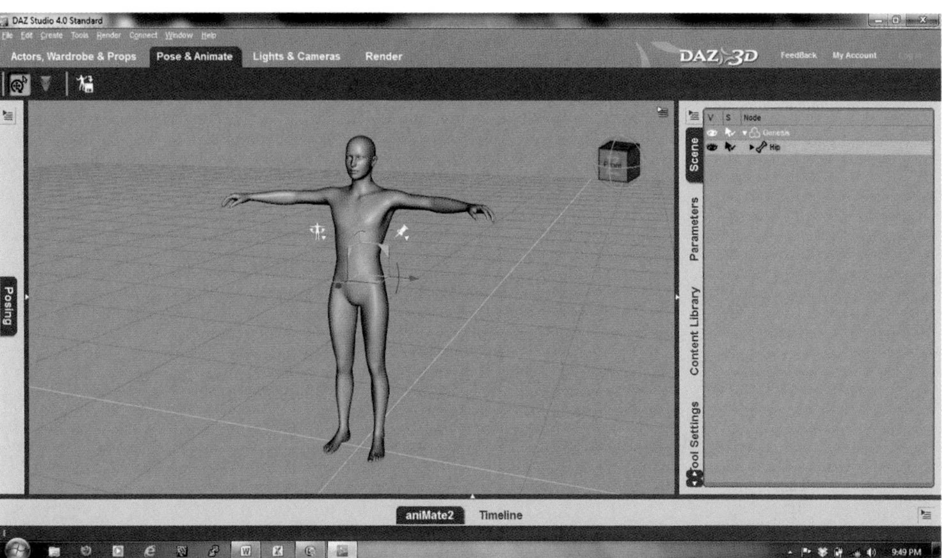

Figure 4.3
Select Genesis's hip using the list.

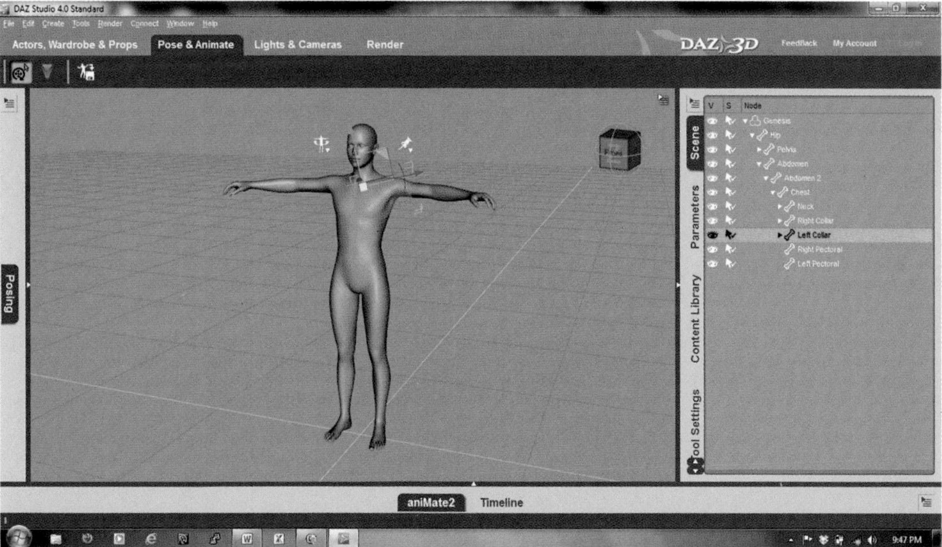

Figure 4.4
You can also select the body part directly in the scene.

The third easy way to select a body part is to select it in PowerPose. PowerPose is a special posing tool in DAZ Studio that speeds up the posing process. You can find it in the Tabs submenu in the Window menu, as shown in Figure 4.5.

These green dots are used for selecting and moving different parts of the body. Select the green dot over Genesis's left thigh, as shown in Figure 4.6. Notice when you select it, the left thigh is also selected in the scene and in the list.

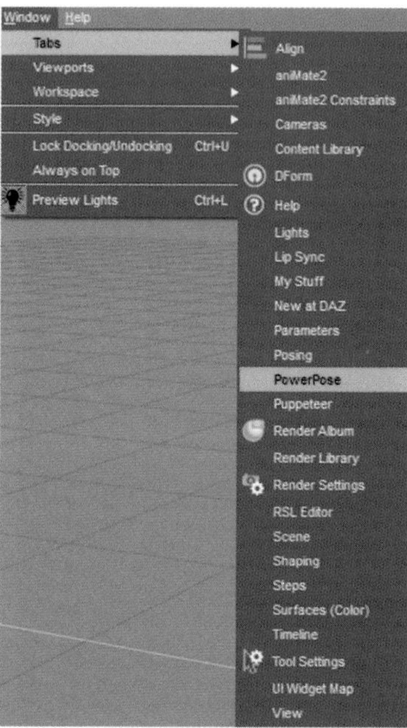

Figure 4.5
Find PowerPose in the Tabs menu.

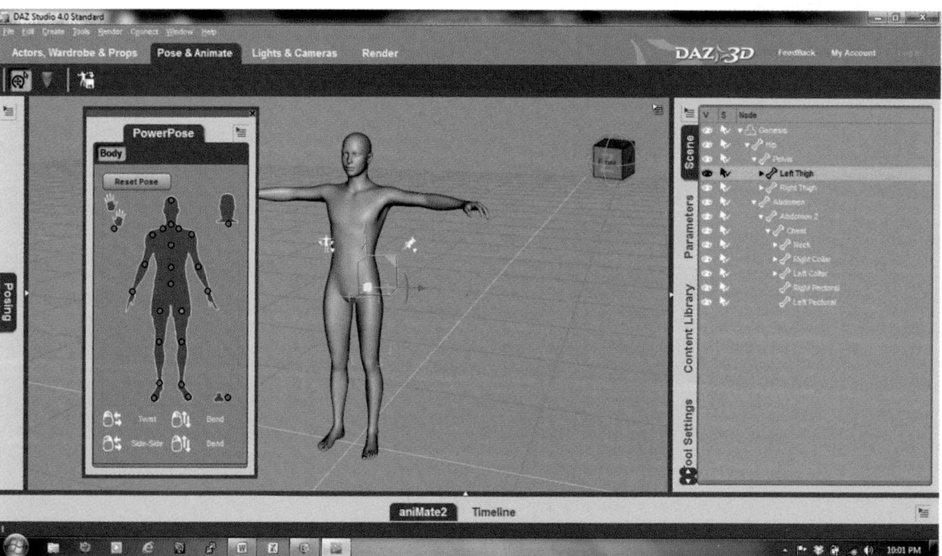

Figure 4.6
Select the left thigh in PowerPose.

You might wonder why there are so many ways to select body parts in DAZ Studio. Part of the reason is that some artists prefer one way and others prefer another, but the main reason is that while working on a pose, selections can become difficult. Having three different ways to select body parts speeds up the whole process.

Moving Parts

Now that you know how to select a part of the body, you need to know what you can do with it. The most obvious answer is to move it. You move parts of the model by selecting the part you want to move and then using the Universal Manipulator tool or PowerPose. You already have the thigh selected in PowerPose; hold the left mouse button and move the cursor upward on the screen. The leg should bend upward similar to Figure 4.7 in a kick-like motion.

You can also move the character by using the Universal Manipulator tool. Using this tool you can move the limbs directly on the figure. Select the left thigh again and then look for the red arc just below the green arrow. When you place the cursor over the arc, it should turn into a yellow circle. This is the rotate function of the tool. Click on the yellow circle and hold down the left mouse button as you drag the cursor around the screen. Notice how the leg moves with the mouse. See Figure 4.8.

Any position that can be achieved by a normal human being can be simulated in DAZ 3D models. The models are automatically set up to not bend past normal limits. For example, the elbow and the knee won't bend backward. It is best to pose all of your characters within these limits, but if you need to have more-than-human flexibility, the limits can be adjusted in the individual parameters. With the Thigh still selected, open

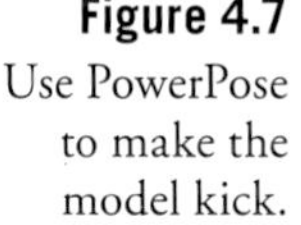

Figure 4.7
Use PowerPose to make the model kick.

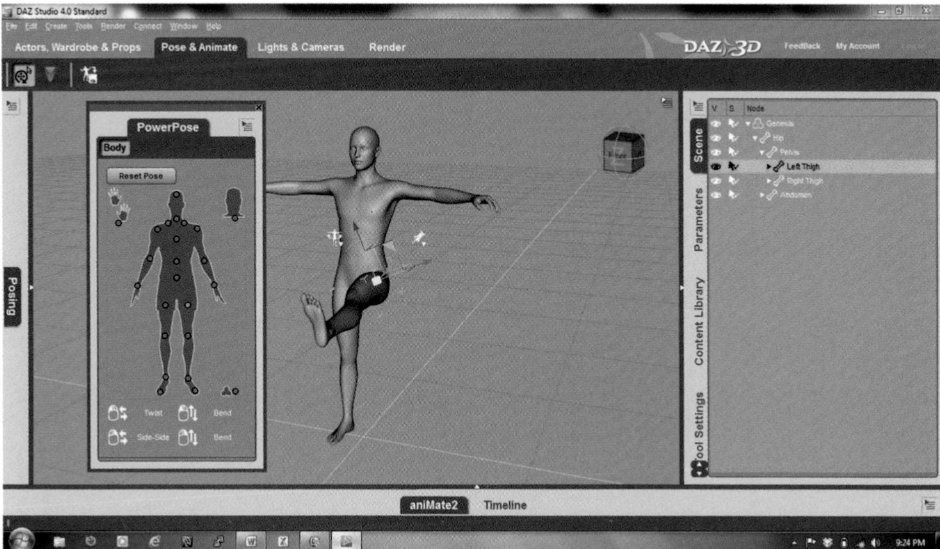

the Parameters tab. Under Transforms, click on the gear icon in the upper-right corner of the Bend slider bar box. This should bring up a menu where you can select Parameter Setting to bring up the Parameter Settings window, as shown in Figure 4.9. The Minimum and Maximum limits are defined in the settings.

Understanding the bone order is important because it makes up the moving parts of the body. The way they are connected to each other is important because it dictates how they all can move. For example, select the hip and rotate it in any direction. You will notice that the entire model rotates. This is because the hip is the root or beginning

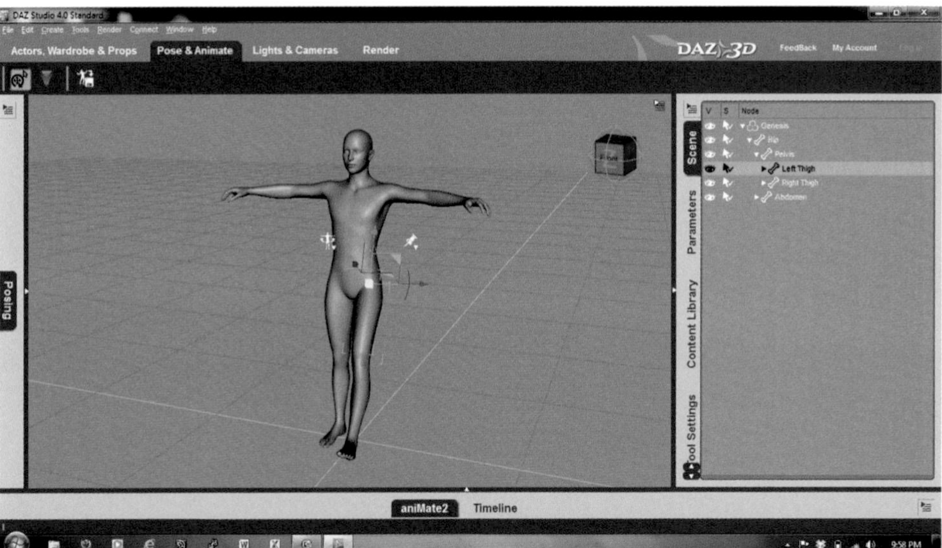

Figure 4.8
The Universal Manipulator tool can also be used to move the leg.

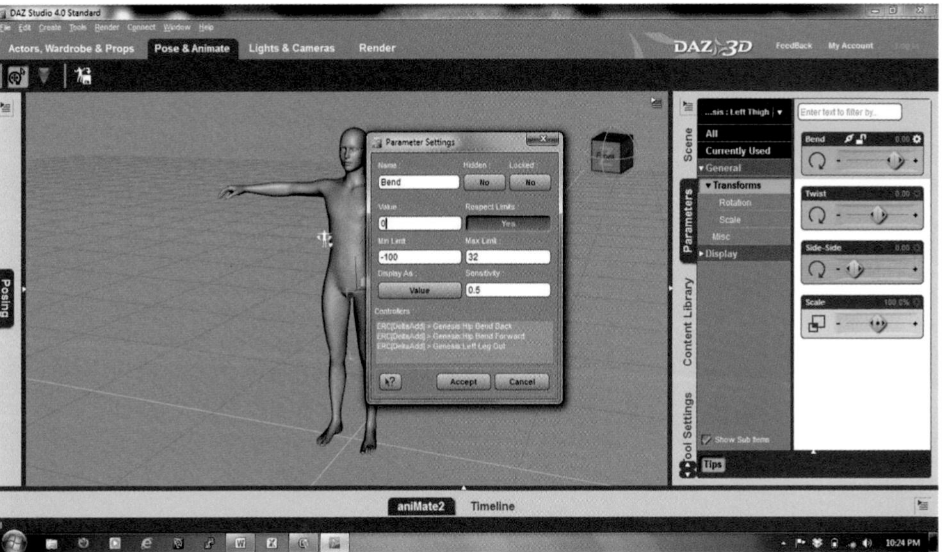

Figure 4.9
The Universal Manipulator tool can also be used to move the leg.

node for the model. On the other hand, select the abdomen and rotate it similarly to the hips and you will notice that the hips don't move but everything above the abdomen does.

Shaping the Model

Shaping a model is changing how the model looks. The change can be subtle, like a facial expression, or it can be a complete change of the model, like from a male figure to a female figure or an adult figure to a child.

Many DAZ models will have shaping options. Some models, like the Genesis model, will have extensive shaping options. Others will be quite limited. The older the model is the more likely that model will have fewer options for changing the figure.

The Genesis model was specifically designed to work with shaping. To see how it works go to the Actors, Wardrobe & Props activity tab, then in the left-hand pull-out panel, select the Shaping tab, as shown in Figure 4.10. Make sure you have the Genesis model selected and click the Editor button and the All button as shown.

You will notice several slider bars with pictures of characters on their left side. You can use these slider bars to change the shape of the Genesis model. Go down to the third slider bar labeled Basic Child and slide the bar all the way to the right, as shown in Figure 4.11. You should see the model getting younger and younger until it is a small child.

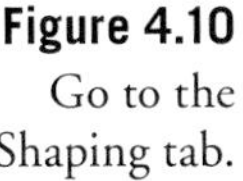

Figure 4.10
Go to the Shaping tab.

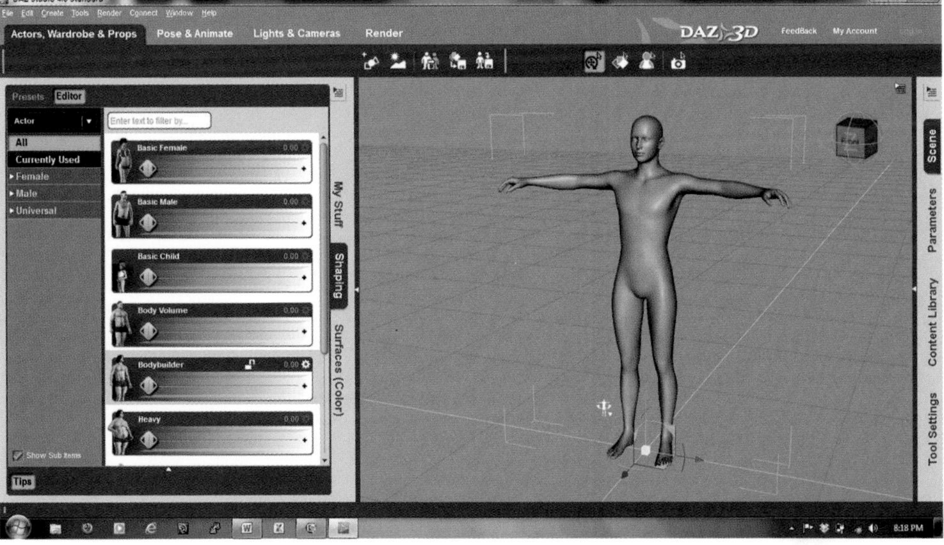

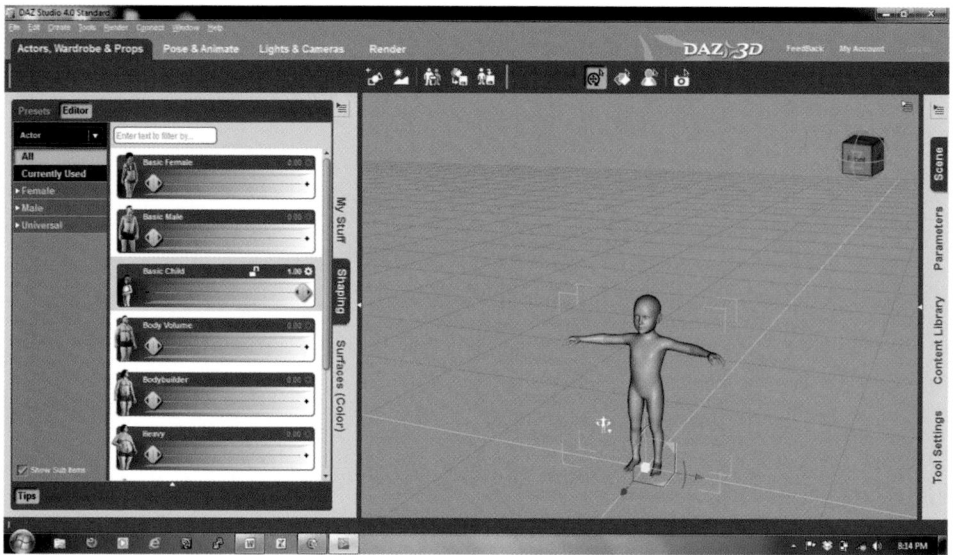

Figure 4.11
Change the model from an adult to a child.

When you shape a model in DAZ Studio you are not changing the number of polygons or vertices in the model; you are only changing their relative relation to each other. This means the model is basically the same from a component standpoint. Only the shape is changing.

Let's take a look at a few more shapes. Move the slider bar all the way back to the left on Basic Child and then go down to the fifth slider bar labeled Bodybuilder and slide it all the way to the right, as shown in Figure 4.12.

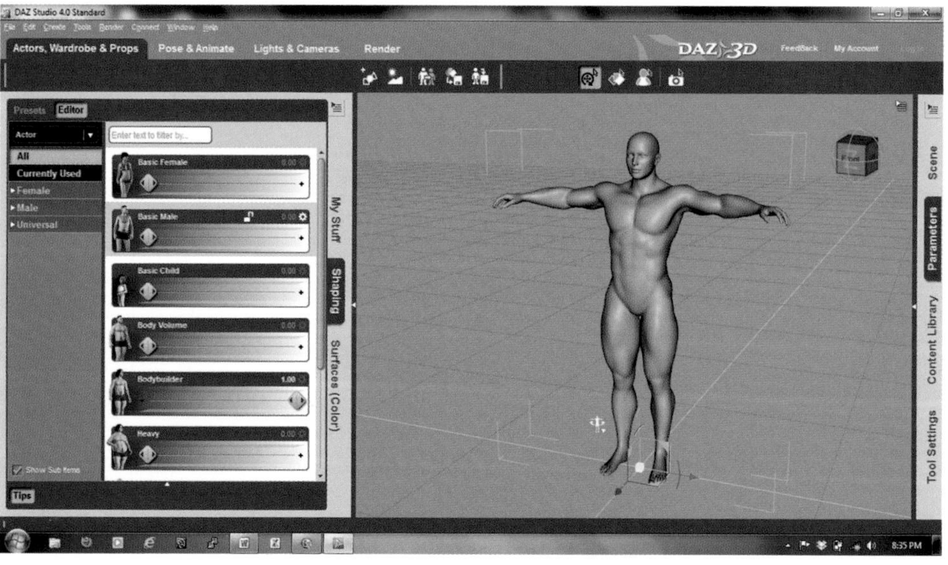

Figure 4.12
Change the model to a bodybuilder shape.

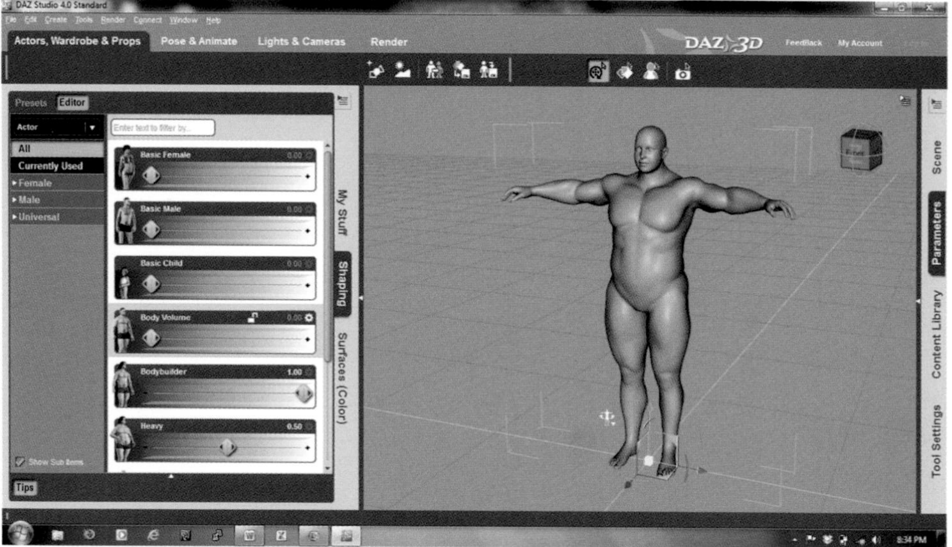

Figure 4.13 Change the model to a chunky ex-bodybuilder shape.

You don't have to always slide the slider bar all the way to the end. Often, less extreme changes are better. If we now go to the next slider bar labeled Heavy and pull the slider only about halfway across, we get a chunky ex-bodybuilder who has had a few too many donuts, as shown in Figure 4.13.

Shaping a model can be a lot of fun. Go ahead and experiment with a few of the shapes, seeing how they affect each other. You can adjust as many as you like.

You can also change the shape of your model in the Parameters tab on the right side of your screen. Open it and select Actor, as shown in Figure 4.14.

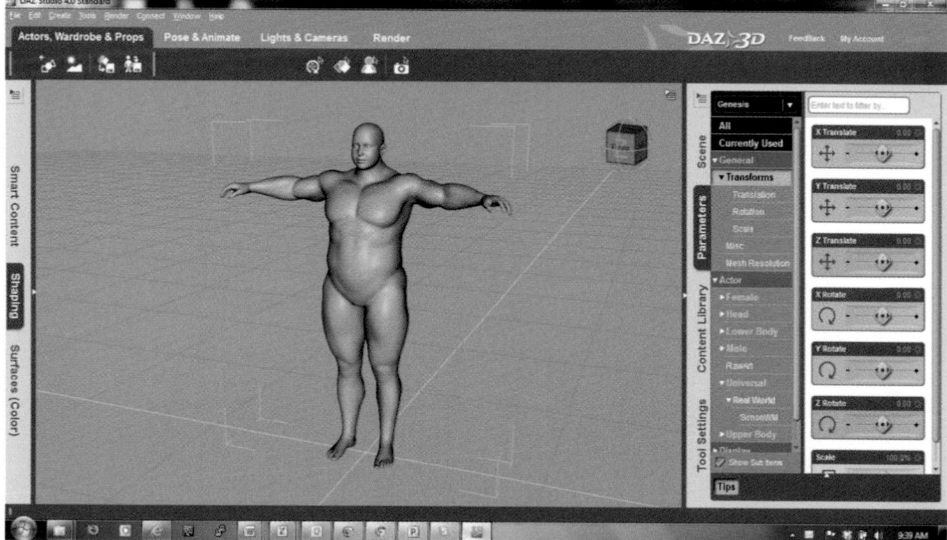

Figure 4.14 Select Actor from the Parameters tab.

As a general rule, the Parameters tab has a lot more controls than the Shaping tab, but because of that it is also more complex. In most cases, until you become accustomed to the program, using the Shaping tab will be easier. However, more advanced users will likely switch over to the Parameters tab because it gives them greater control over their characters.

As you look at the slider bars in the Parameters tab you will notice that many of them have the slider in the middle instead of the left side of the bar. The slider in the middle lets you change the shape in both extremes. For example, scroll down to Jaw size and slide the slider to the left. Notice that the jaw shrinks. Now slide it all the way to the right. The jaw grows huge. The natural default shape is somewhere in the middle.

If you want to push the changes in your characters even further than the slider allows, you can change the limits in the Parameter Settings window the same as the bend limits discussed earlier.

With all these options and a little creative thought, you can create almost any human shape you want to with the shapes available for the Genesis model.

Summary

In this chapter, we have taken a closer look at a DAZ 3D character model. It is very important for you to understand how models are put together so you can learn to pose them for your pictures. DAZ models are as flexible as our own human bodies. They can move into any position that a normal human can move into. DAZ uses a skeletal system similar to our own skeleton to control 3D character movement.

Also introduced in this chapter was DAZ Studio's Shaping system for changing the shape of the model. DAZ Studio can be used to change a character's body shape or give the character facial expressions or almost any other attribute the artist can imagine. Most of DAZ's models have morphs, but some of the older ones are less robust than others.

In the next chapter, we will cover dressing character models in DAZ Studio.

5

Clothing

One of the coolest aspects of DAZ Studios is the wide variety of character clothing. If you take a quick look at DAZ Studios' website, you will see some of the latest fashions along with many specialty outfits that range from uniforms to high fantasy. This variety allows an artist to create almost any type of character imaginable.

Until recently, clothing for models was created specifically for that model, which means that clothing created for Victoria will not likely fit Michael and vice versa. It is a little like the clothing you buy at the store. You try your clothing on and buy what fits. In DAZ Studio, the clothing was made to fit a specific model. When shopping for clothing for the earlier models, you had to make sure you bought the right clothing for the right model.

With the introduction of Genesis, DAZ models are starting to be more universal in the clothing you can use. Many of the clothing sets for Genesis will have the same shaping qualities as the main figure. This means that as you change the shape of the Genesis model, the clothing will change to fit the model. Let me show you how it works.

Go to the Actors, Wardrobes & Props activity tab and select the My Stuff tab. Click on the Genesis model, then click Files and Wardrobe. Your screen should look similar to Figure 5.1.

The clothing you see here is what comes with the base Genesis model. When you select the Genesis model, only those clothing items that are designed to work with the Genesis model will show up. If you don't have Genesis, those items will not show up. DAZ Studio presorts the items to only come up based on the object selected in the scene. You can dress Genesis with any of these clothing styles. Let's begin by giving Genesis some pants. You can load the pants into the scene attached to the Genesis model in two ways: either double-click the item you want to load and it will load the item onto the Genesis

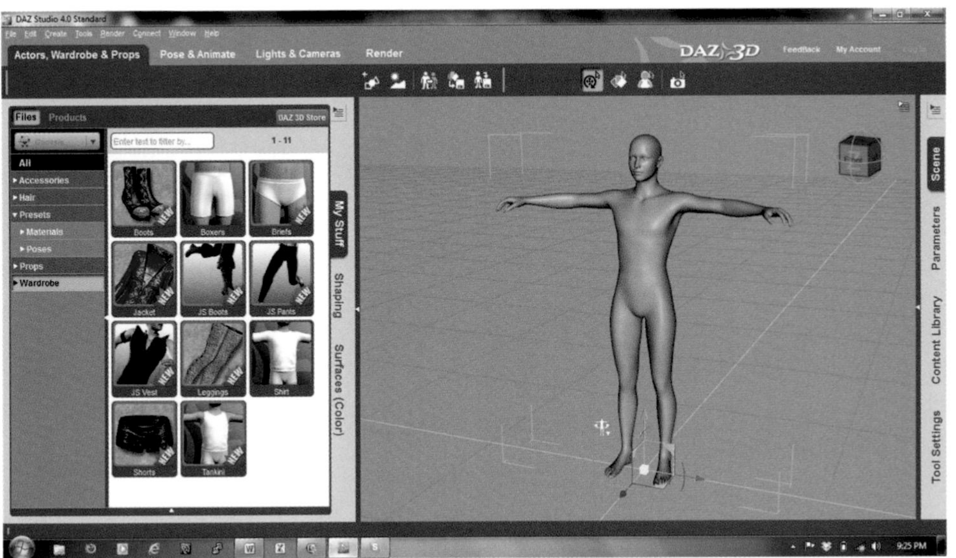

Figure 5.1 Open the wardrobe for the Genesis model.

model or right-click on the item you want to load then select Load It from the pop-up menu. Select the JS Pants and load them onto the model, as shown in Figure 5.2.

You can see that the pants come in attached to the figure. If you now go down to the shapes tab and play around with a few of the sliders on the Genesis model, you will notice that the pants change shape with Genesis. For example, in Figure 5.3 I've moved the slider on Heavy all the way to the right.

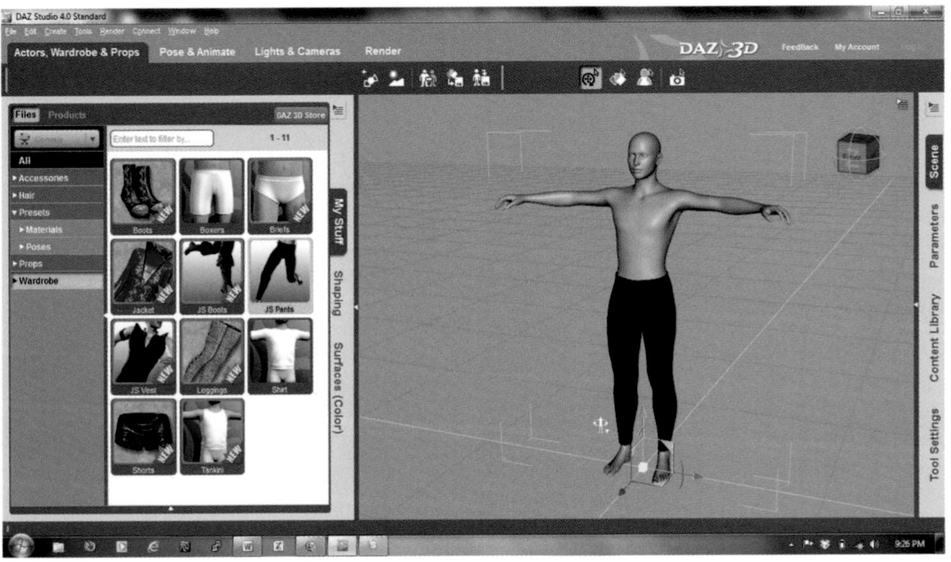

Figure 5.2 Load the JS Pants onto the Genesis model.

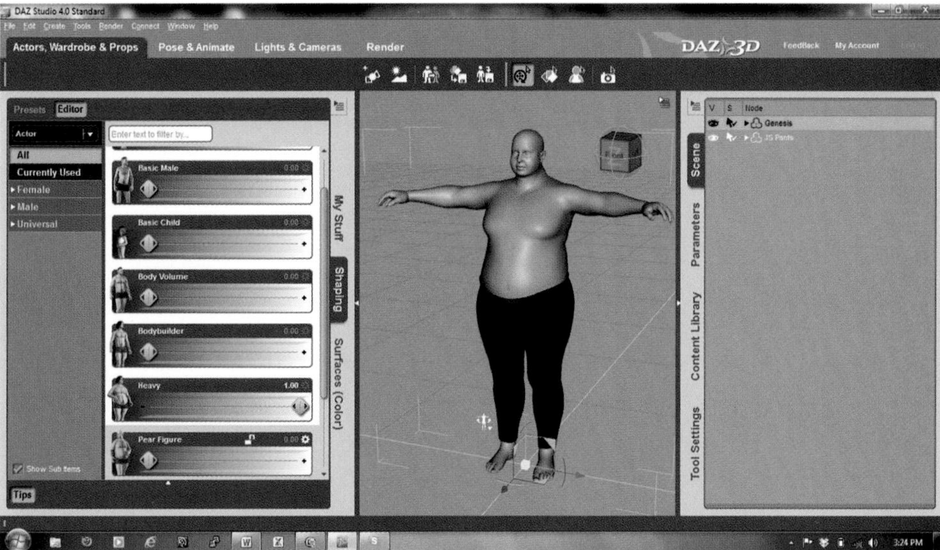

Figure 5.3 Clothing for Genesis changes shape with the model.

Not only will the Genesis clothing change with the shape of the Genesis model, it will also load in the correct shape if you have already changed the look of the model. Go back to My Stuff and load the vest. Notice that it comes in fitting the model. The same is true for the boots as well.

You will notice that the articles of clothing have a small arrow next to them in the scene similar to the Genesis model itself. When you expand these, you will see that they follow a similar pattern as that of the Genesis model. In Figure 5.4, the pants are expanded to show the hierarchal connections from the hip to each foot.

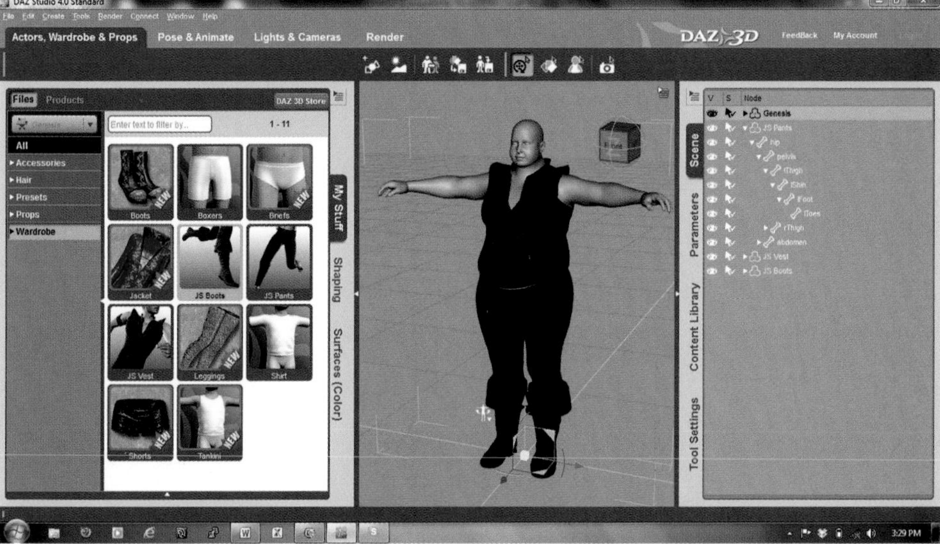

Figure 5.4 Clothing has bone structures similar to character models.

The bones from the hip to the feet of the pants match those of Genesis. In this way, the pants can follow Genesis's movements and shape changes. If even one bone is different between the clothing and the character, it can cause problems like the clothing not animating correctly or parts of the character's body showing through the article of clothing.

Applying Clothing to a Character

DAZ has a number of models that were created earlier than Genesis that have clothing and accessories created specifically for each model. While the clothing created for these models isn't as flexible, there is still a lot that you can do with it. Putting clothing on these models in DAZ is as easy as putting on a shirt yourself, except that the model doesn't have to button it up. There are several ways to add clothing; some methods require you to load the article of clothing and then fit it to your character while other methods fit it automatically. The easiest way to add clothing is to have it fit the character automatically.

Automatic Fit

Most clothing objects automatically fit to a character if two things are in place:

1. The model the clothing is to fit is already selected. DAZ Studio knows which character to fit the clothing to based on the model selected in the scene.
2. The clothing was created for that specific 3D model.

One of the most widely used models in DAZ history is Victoria. Do a search in your content library to find and load her, as shown in Figure 5.5.

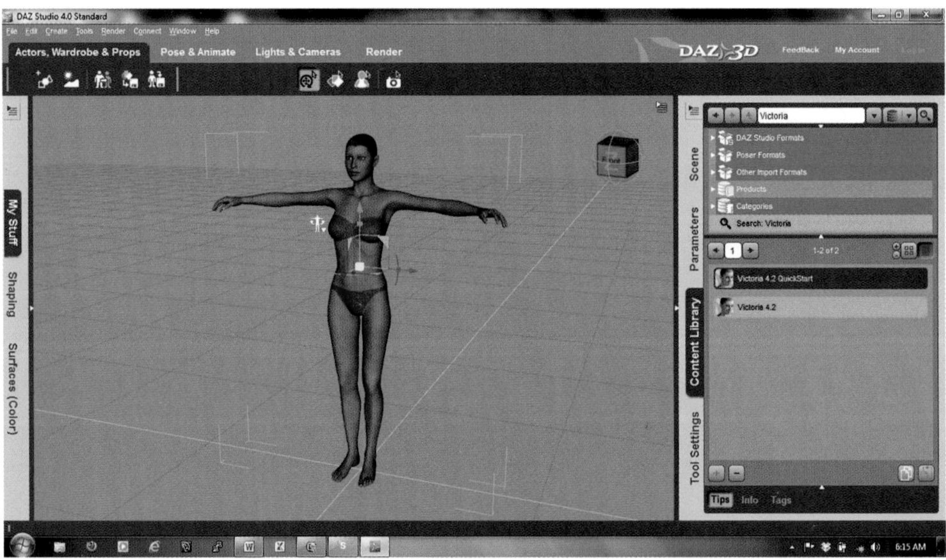

Figure 5.5
Load the Victoria model into the scene.

Victoria loads with her default texture, which is fine but not very useful for most situations you might want to use her in. She actually has quite an extensive wardrobe ranging from high fantasy armor to sci-fi suits. Let's put her into something she can wear about town. Bring up the Classic Casual set, which includes pants, top, and shoes, as shown in Figure 5.6.

Load each item into the scene by double-clicking on them with Victoria selected. There, that looks more sensible for leaving the house. You will notice that although she has on high heels, her feet are not rotated for them. You often will have to make minor adjustments to your models depending on the outfits you select for them. You can fix the problem by selecting Victoria's foot and rotating it to a more natural position, as shown in Figure 5.7.

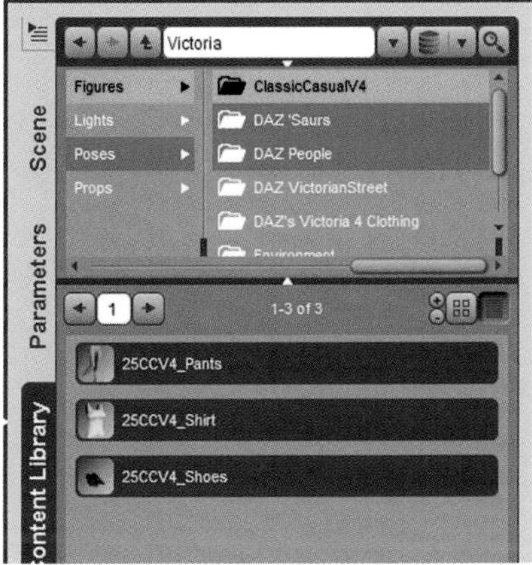

Figure 5.6 Victoria's Classic Casual set includes a top, pants, and shoes.

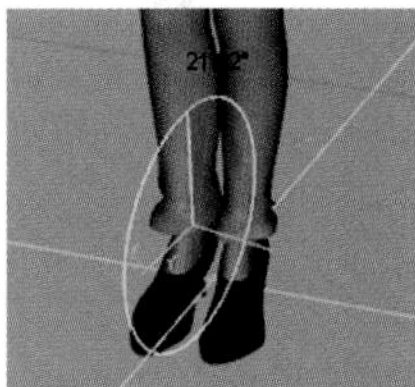

Figure 5.7 Minor adjustments are common when loading new clothing.

Now we need to do something about that hair. Victoria has almost as many hair types and styles as she has clothing. In this instance a simple straight hair style will look good, so choose Glamour Hair V4, as shown in Figure 5.8. Now she is ready to grab her bag and head out to the store.

As you can see, the clothing and hair comes in already fit to Victoria. Select the hair in the scene list then go to the Parameters tab. If you look under Misc in the Parameters tab, you will see an item titled Fit To. In the box below it reads Victoria 4.2. This means that the item is fitted to the Victoria model. You can check the status of any clothing item by looking at its Fit To status in the item's parameters. Also, if you made a mistake and didn't have Victoria selected when you loaded her top, you can select it using the Fit To pull-down menu.

There are several ways to add clothing to a character. Double-clicking the item over a selected character is just one of them. Another way is to simply drag the item from the Content Library over the character or you can right-click on the article and wait for the menu to appear. On the top of the menu will be an option to merge the item. This will put it into the scene but you will have to fit it to Victoria after it's loaded.

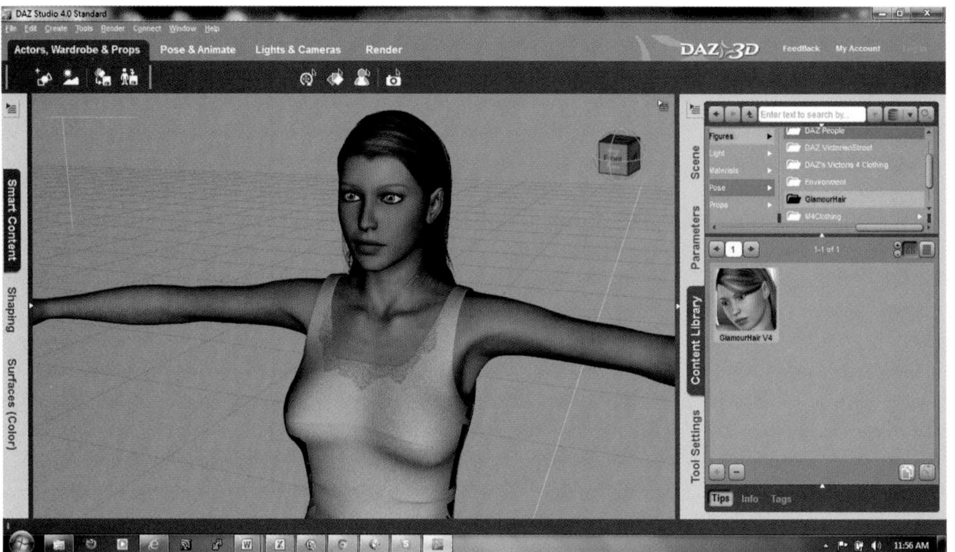

Figure 5.8
Give Victoria some hair.

Morphs

Morphs are different shapes that the model can assume, similar to the shaping we used earlier with Genesis. Morph is the common word among users for the different shapes that come with each model. In the program they are actually part of the basic parameters that you can adjust in the Parameters tab. In Figure 5.9, the Victoria model and the Morph/Shapes button are selected. As you can see, Victoria has a large number of morphs or shapes available.

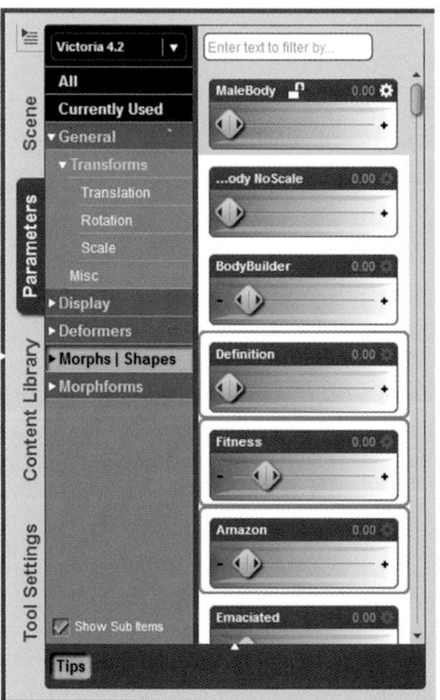

Figure 5.9
Victoria has a great number of morphs.

Usually if an article of clothing is fitted to a character, you can change the morphs and the clothing will change with it, but not always with great success, particularly with many of the earlier models. For example, if you use the Male morph you will notice that while Victoria changes into a male character, her clothing remains in the female shape, as shown in Figure 5.10.

Over the years the good people at DAZ 3D have worked hard to find a solution for the figure model clothing problem. They've made great advances. With the introduction of the Genesis model, the problem is solved for almost all situations.

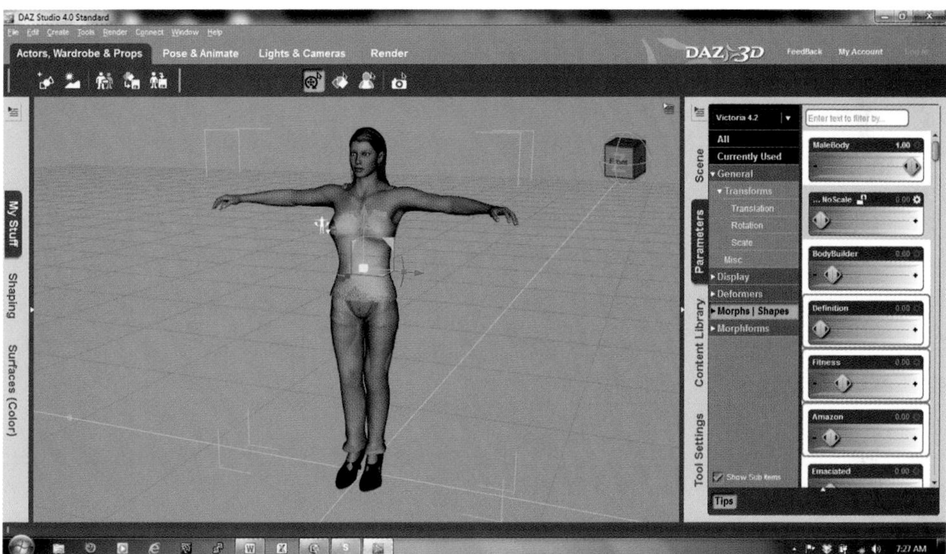

Figure 5.10 Victoria male grows out of her/his clothing.

Magnetize Pose

For Victoria, DAZ Studio has a feature that adjusts clothing morphs with any adjustments to the character morphs. It is called V4 Morph Magnet Fit. It automatically adjusts the clothing to match any morphs used in the character, if the clothing has a morph that corresponds to the same morph on the character. For example, Figure 5.11 shows the same set of clothing on three different figures with different morphs. As you can see, it handles the different body morphs very well.

Even though you may only have one character model and just a few outfits for that character, by using the morphs, you should be able to create an extensive variety of characters. You can find the feature on the DAZ 3D website as an add-on to use with Victoria, as shown in Figure 5.12.

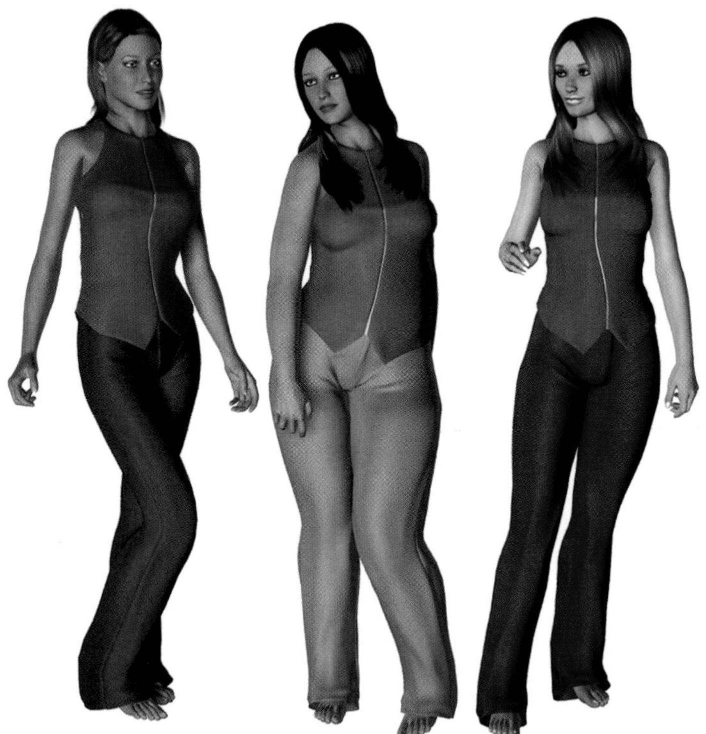

Figure 5.11
The clothing is conforming to the shape of the character.

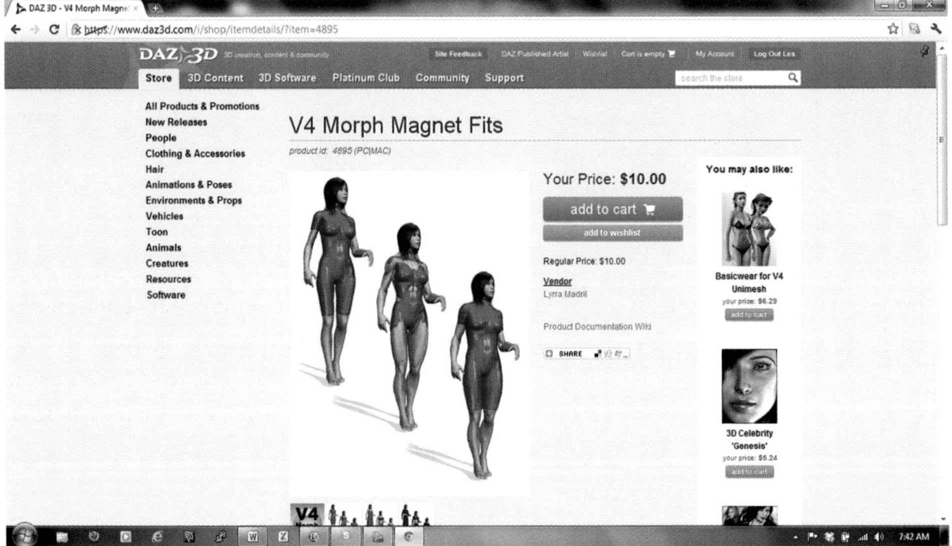

Figure 5.12
V4 Morph Magnet Fit is available from the DAZ website.

Surfaces

Every model in DAZ Studio will have surface qualities or attributes. Just like in real life, surfaces have qualities. For example, you can tell the difference between a shiny metal car and a wooden fence just by the surface properties. The car's surface is smooth and reflective, while the wooden fence has a rough surface. DAZ Studio gives you some control over the surfaces in your scenes in its Surface tab found in View > Tabs > Surfaces, as shown in Figure 5.13.

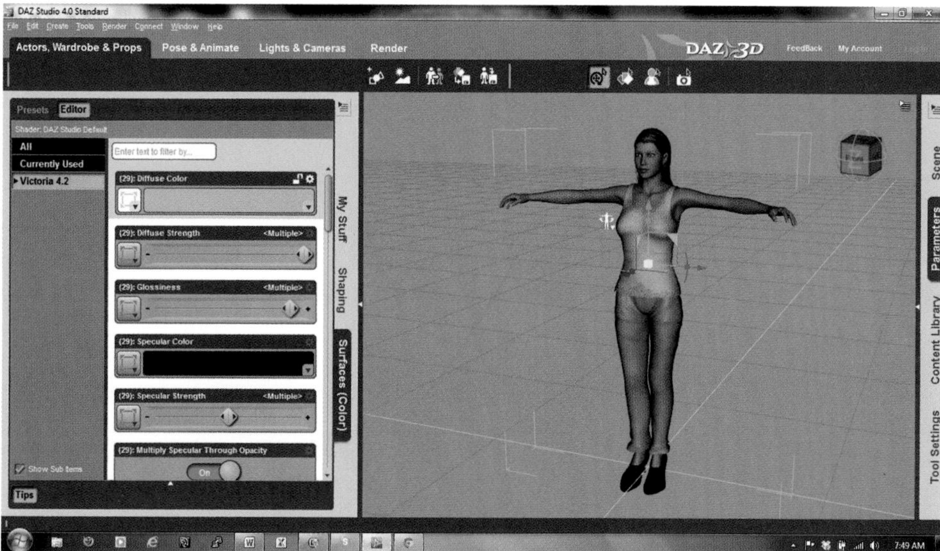

Figure 5.13
The Surfaces (Color) tab has a number of settings.

For a first-time user, the sheer number of settings can be a little intimidating. Adjusting surface qualities is an advanced feature meant for advanced users; therefore, it was designed with these users in mind. I'll touch on it briefly to give you an idea of how powerful of a feature it is.

Depending on the setting DAZ Studio uses different controls. Some settings are adjusted with slider bars and some have color swatches or on/off switches. Each one is specific for the type of setting it is. Each Surface is a material zone that isolates an area on the model such as the Skin, Head, Fingernail, Iris, and more. These in turn have a multitude of parameters that combine to give the overall appearance of that particular surface.

Diffuse Color

Diffuse Color is the color of your object. In most cases it will be a texture or several textures, which are 2D pictures that are applied to the surface of the model. Sometimes it can be just a single color. The Victoria model currently loaded has a detailed skin texture already applied to the model. You can change the color of the model by replacing the texture with a color or new texture in the Diffused Color settings. You can also tint the texture using the color palette. On the left of the settings there is a box. Clicking on the box will bring up a list of currently used textures and a browse option for locating a texture that is not on the list. You can also choose none to remove any texture already placed on the model. On the right of the setting is an arrow. Clicking on it will bring up a color palette for changing the color of the model.

Complex models like Victoria have many parts that use different textures or colors. Select Victoria's hip in the Scene tab. You will notice that Victoria's many parts are now displayed in the Surface (Color) tab, as shown in Figure 5.14.

You can adjust each surface attribute individually. Some surfaces will have a texture attached to them. If the surface has a texture it will show up in the loader box on the Diffused Color attribute on the top of the list and you can see a larger view of the texture by scrolling over the box. Clicking on the loader box brings up a menu where you can change the texture by loading a different one. This comes in handy if you want to adjust a texture map and load the new map in the place of the old one.

Below the Diffuse Color is a slider bar for Diffuse Strength. This setting gives you control of how strong you want the diffused color to be. It is usually set for 100% but sometimes you may want to adjust it a little to change the effect slightly.

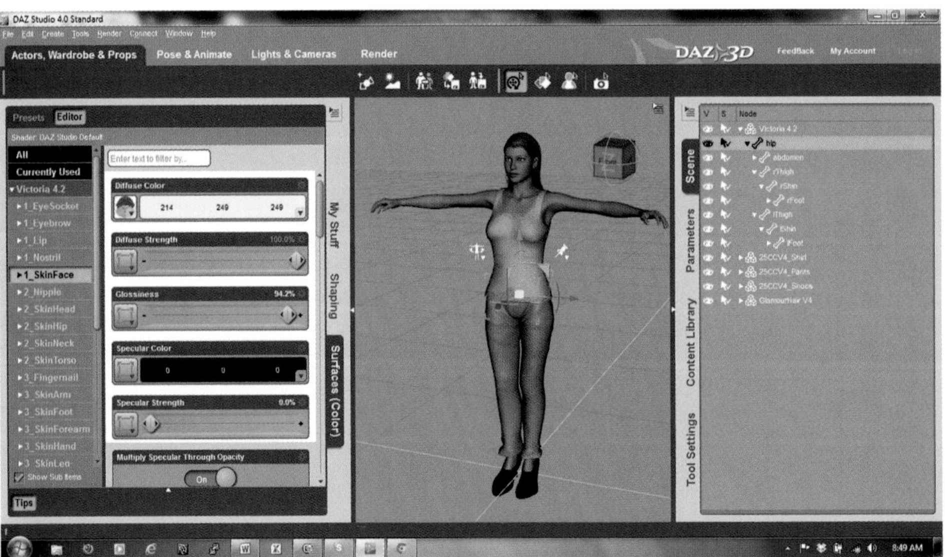

Figure 5.14
Complex models have many different surfaces.

Glossiness

The next several settings control the shininess of a surface. They include Glossiness, Specular Color, Specular Strength, and Multiply Specular Through Opacity. You will notice that some of the settings have the word Multiple in them. This means that instead of one setting for the entire model, the artist created different settings for different parts of a model. On a character model like Victoria, the eyes will be shinier than the skin. If a setting includes the word "Multiple," it is usually a better idea to adjust individual parts than it is to do an adjustment of the entire model.

Ambient Strength

Ambient strength is a control to indicate how bright the surface will appear in a scene. Full ambient strength takes full advantage of light in a scene. Lowering ambient strength will reduce the brightness of an object in a scene even when it is lit by a strong light. Ambient only works if there is a light in the scene and Ambient Strength isn't set to black.

Opacity

Next, let's take a look at Opacity. Opacity controls how transparent a surface is. Opacity can be used in a number of ways, like creating transparent-like veils or sheer material. Any surface in DAZ Studio can be made transparent as a whole just by using the slider bar, but the Opacity controls are more powerful than just a simple blanket opacity setting. You can also add an opacity map to any object. An opacity map is a 2D grayscale image or Alpha Map that tells DAZ Studio what parts of the surface should be transparent and to what degree. This gives the artist the ability to have very fine control over any surface.

In an opacity map, DAZ studio reads white as 100% opaque and black as 100% transparent. Ranges of gray are partially transparent. Figure 5.15 shows a black-and-white opacity map. The top of the map is white and the bottom of the map is black.

By applying this map to the character's pants, you can change what she is wearing from pants to shorts, as shown in Figure 5.16.

Figure 5.15 This opacity map is split into completely opaque and completely transparent.

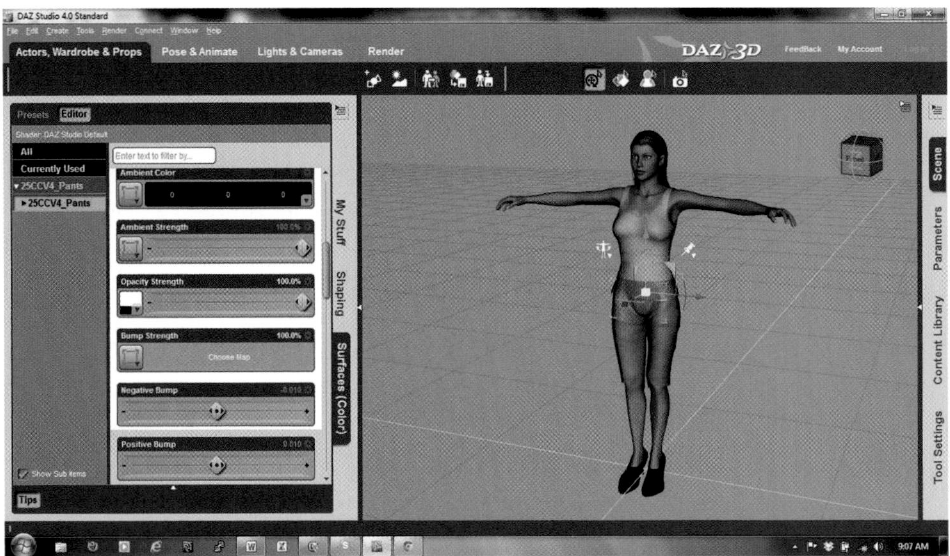

Figure 5.16
The character is now wearing capris.

Bump, Displacement, and Normal

Bump, Displacement, and Normal settings control the appearance of fine surface detail. The detail can simulate a rough surface like a graveled road or the fine weave of a delicate fabric. Most of these surface settings require a texture map to work, which will be included with the model if there are any.

Bump settings and normal settings change the appearance of a surface to make it appear rough but don't actually change the geometry and should only be used for more distant objects where tight scrutiny of the surface is less likely. Displacement, on the other hand, changes the actual geometry of the surface and should be used in close-up scenes where detail is important. It is a good idea to use displacement only when you absolutely have to because it adds significantly to the render time and slows performance while setting up a scene.

Reflection, Refraction

Reflection and Refraction deal with the way light bounces off an object. A reflective object like a mirror reflects light in direct relationship to the angle of the surface and the light source. Refraction, on the other hand, is the scattering of light that changes the angles the light travels. A shiny flat surface like a mirror shows a clear reflection of the object's surroundings. A rough surface like denim jeans scatters the light showing no clear reflection.

Tiles

The next several settings deal with tiling. Tiles are repeatable textures. Think of floor tiles in real life. Like these tiles you can create a surface that is really just one small texture repeated multiple times over it. Tiling a texture is very useful because it reduces the render time of an object and makes it easier to manage in the program while setting up a scene. Tiles are often used for building surfaces like brick walls and even organic surfaces like a larch patch of grass.

Lighting Model

The lighting model is a set of preset lighting systems that light the model in different ways. They can be used to change the way your surfaces look in a scene.

UV Set

UVs are the coordinates of the textures and other surface attributes on a model. By changing the UVs you can change the position of surface qualities on a model. Usually the artist sets up the UVs and there is very little call to change them. Some models will have multiple UV sets. You can change a UV set with this feature.

Smooth

3D objects are usually made up of flat polygons. The Smoothing function blends the flat polygons so they appear to be a rounded surface rather than multiple flat surfaces. Smoothing is on by default. To better see the effect of smoothing, just turn it off. Figure 5.17 shows the pants with smoothing turned off.

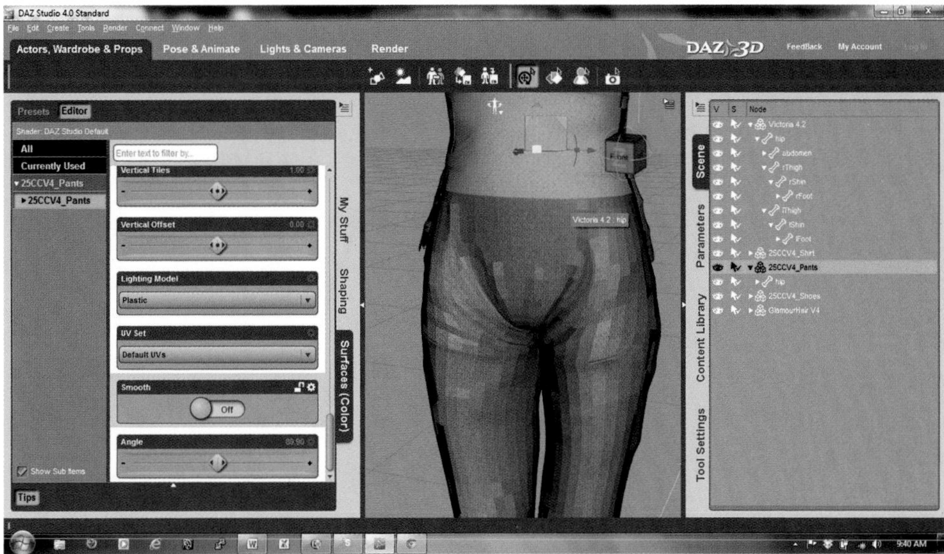

Figure 5.17 When smoothing is turned off, you can see the flat polygon shapes.

As you can see, without smoothing, the flat polygons of the pants are noticeable. It would take millions of polygons to give a rounded look without smoothing. Even though DAZ models are quite detailed, they still need to have some smoothing done to give them a completely natural look.

Angle

The angle of the smoothing will determine the amount of smoothing between polygons. The default is 90 but it can go up to 180 and down to 0. If you need greater smoothing of an object, you can increase the number, and if you need less smoothing, you can decrease the number. For almost all instances, 90 works fine and should only be adjusted in small increments so as not to cause huge shifts in the surface.

Summary

This chapter was about clothing your characters in DAZ Studio. It covered two major topics: clothing objects and surfaces. Surfaces were included here because the clothing is the most common objects for which surface variation is used.

The Genesis model is DAZ's most advanced model with regard to clothing and shaping. Clothing designed for use on Genesis will automatically change with changes to the figure.

Clothing objects in DAZ Studio are 3D objects similar to characters. They are made for specific characters and have bone structures that match those characters. Sometimes clothing objects need to be adjusted to fit properly. Usually adjustments are made by using morphs.

DAZ Studio has a number of functions that affect the surface qualities of an object in the Surface tab. These surface functions allow the artist to have a great deal of control over the look of any 3D object in DAZ Studio, including color, texture, shininess, opacity, and smoothness.

In the next chapter, we will take a closer look at character faces.

6

The Head and Face

If you put people in your art, you need to pay extra attention to the placement and orientation of each person's head. If there is a person in a picture, the most likely center of attention will be the head of that person. If there are many people in a picture, the head of one of them will likely be the center of attention, and the other heads will be secondary centers of attention. While this rule is not 100% true; it is generally the rule.

It is natural for us to look first at any face that appears in a picture. In life if we want to know how a person feels, we don't look at his feet, we look at his face. Even small children train themselves to know when mom and dad are happy or angry by looking at their parents' faces. Even small movements of an eyebrow or lips can have a major impact on conveyed feelings. Therefore, one of the first places we focus on when meeting someone in the real world is her face.

In this chapter, we will look at the many possibilities available to the artist when using models in DAZ Studios for expressive art with a character's head.

Parts of the Head

The head is a complex structure containing many smaller structures, called features, that in themselves are also complex. To help make things simple and easy to understand, we will first look at what you can do with the face as a whole and then take a closer look at individual features.

Head Construction

In real life, the human skull is comprised of a number of bones. These bones can be split into two groups: the skull and the jaw. The skull is the rigid bone structure that makes up the majority of the head. It has no moving parts and is designed to give structure to the head and protect the many delicate organs of the head.

The jaw is the only movable part of the face, and it is hinged to the skull just below the ears. Because the jaw has a simple hinged motion, its functions are very broad in nature and the only subtleties are those of how far open or closed it is.

The majority of facial expressions don't come from the movement of the jaw but rather movement of the many muscles that cover the skull and head. For example, the muscles around the mouth are very flexible and can control a wide range of expression. Other muscles in the cheek and brow can have a wide range of subtle motion.

Models in DAZ Studio are made to mimic how our bodies work. If you look at the bones of the head, as shown in Figure 6.1, you can see that there are only bones associated with the head itself. Most of the bones are connected to the model's tongue. Because most of the facial expressions are better animated using morphs than using bones, there are no bones for that part of the face. Bones work better for large body movements but are not as effective for small surface changes like those of facial animations.

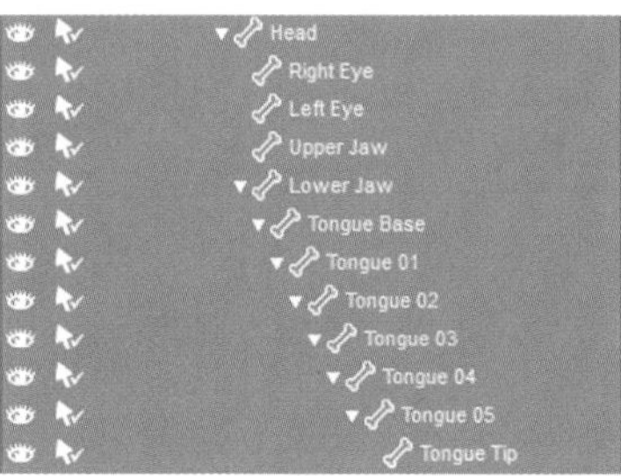

Figure 6.1
There are few bones that are used in animating the head.

Working from large motion to small, an animator will generally position the head first and then work on the expression. General movements of the head are controlled by animating either the head or neck bones. The head bone pivots at the base of the skull and has a wide range of motion, as shown in Figure 6.2.

The pivot point for the neck is right at the base of the neck and has a wide range of motion, as shown in Figure 6.3.

Because it is easy to move the head and there is such a wide range of motion, the animator has to be careful not to overdo it and pose the head to a greater angle than what might look natural.

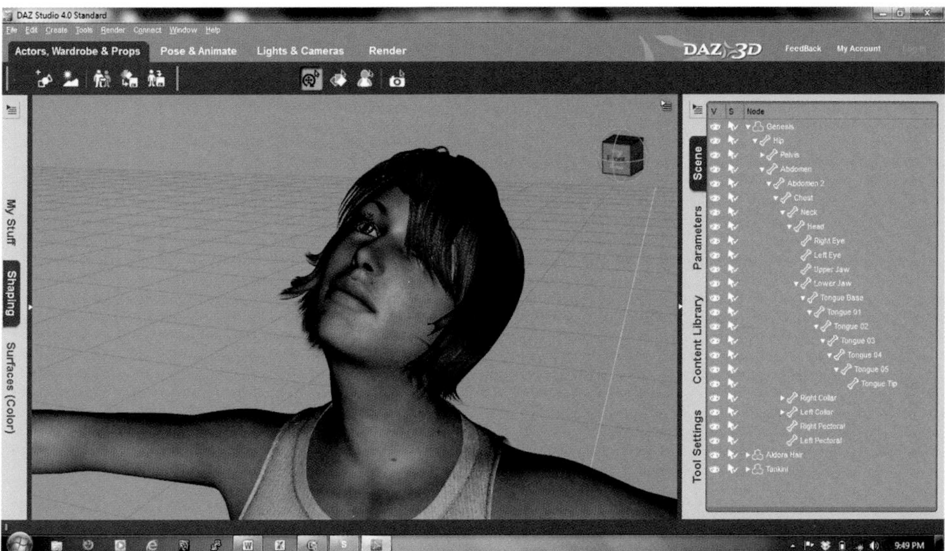

Figure 6.2
The head pivots at the base of the skull.

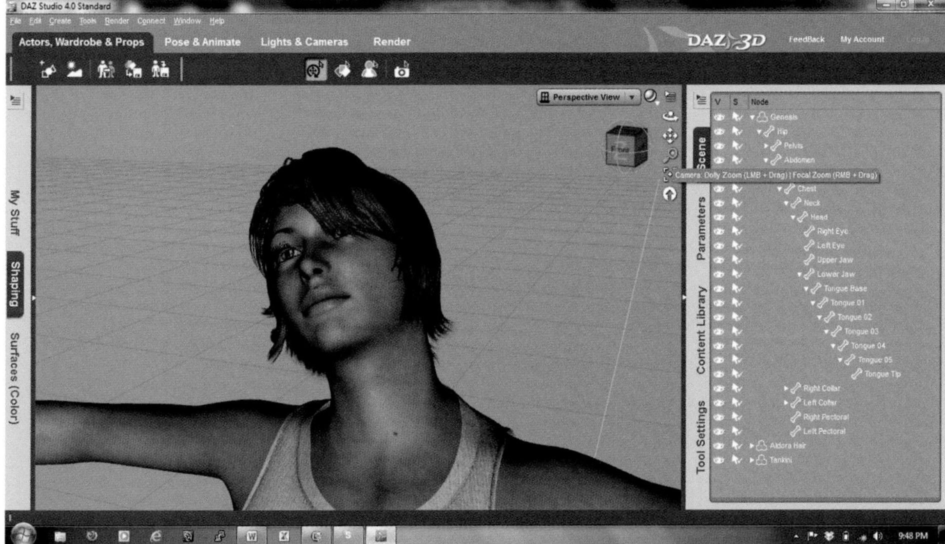

Figure 6.3
The neck pivots both the neck and the head.

The eyes are actually separate objects inside but attached to the head. They both can move independently or you can move them together using the tools in PowerPose. This freedom of movement allows for extreme variation, like making the character cross-eyed, as in Figure 6.4.

Even though the eyes are separate objects from the head, they still influence the eyelids around them. Try rotating the eye and you will see that the eyelids adjust to accommodate the movement of the eye.

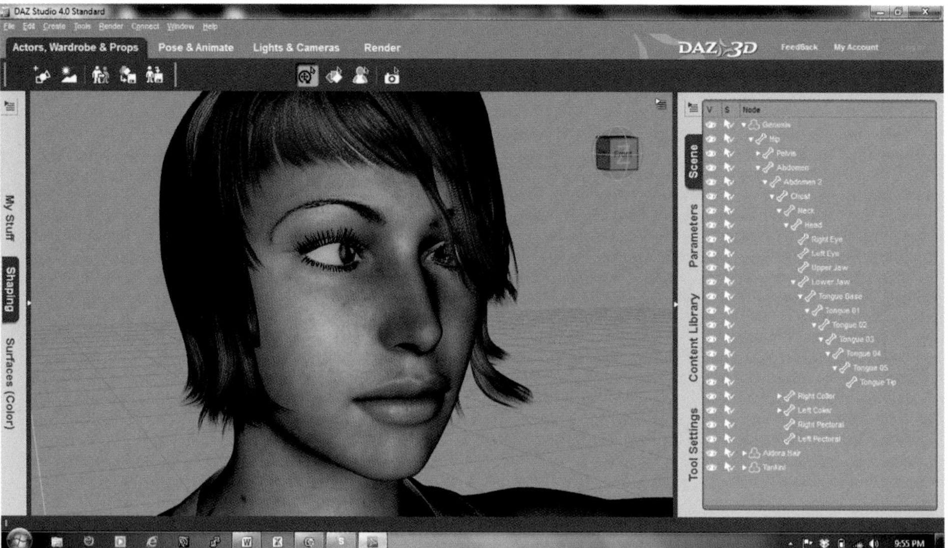

Figure 6.4
The eyes can move independently.

Head Morphs

The head has a number of morphs attached to it for creating facial expressions and lip-sync animation. You can find these morphs in the Parameters tab when you have the head selected. Select Head from the list on the left. You will see a number of morphs on the left as shown in Figure 6.5.

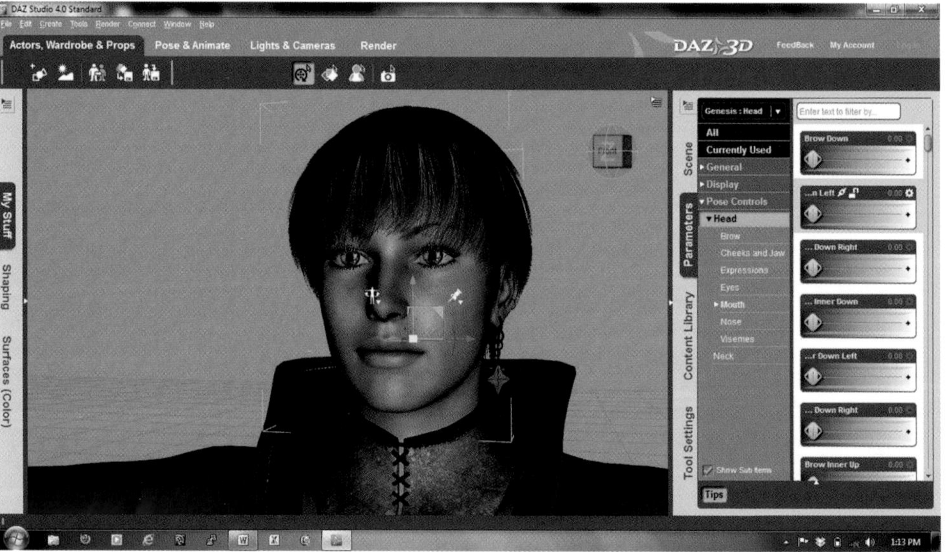

Figure 6.5
The head has a number of morphs.

To apply any of the morphs to the model, all you have to do is select one of the slider bars on the right and move the slider left or right along the bar. For example, in Figure 6.6 the top slider is moved to the right to lower the model's brow.

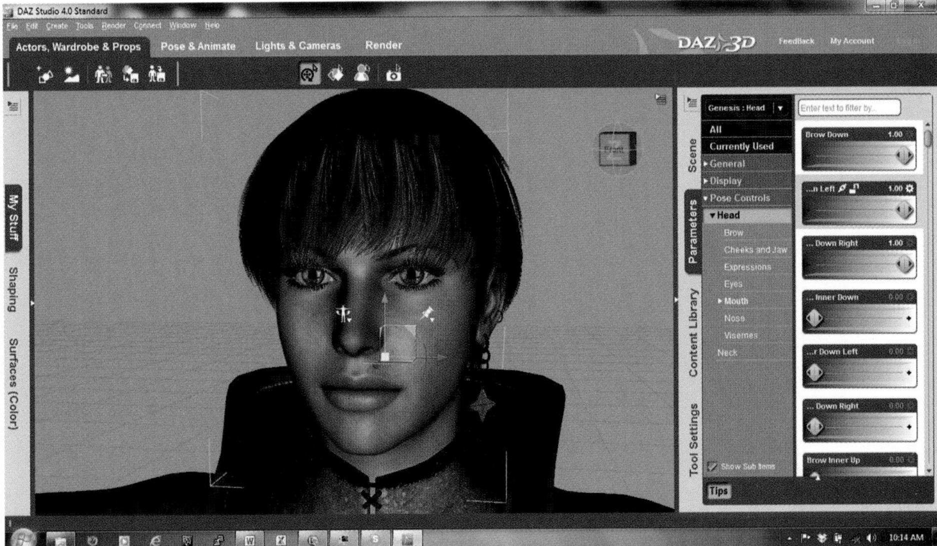

Figure 6.6
Move the slider to the right to lower the brows.

Morph Groups

Trying to figure out how to deal with all of the morphs available for a model like Genesis can be a little overwhelming. It is a lot easier to work with head morphs, if you use the morph groups. Click on the arrow by the head to open the head sub-groups. Each model may be a little different, but for the Genesis model they are Brow, Cheeks and Jaw, Expressions, Eyes, Mouth, Nose, and Visemes. Mouth also has a lips sub-group.

Brow

The brow can be very expressive, denoting all kinds of emotions. A slightly raised brow can mean surprise. A lowered brow can mean anger. Genesis has 20 separate morph controls for the brow to give an almost endless variety to the different emotions that might be expressed. Figure 6.7 shows a combination of inner brow up and outer brow down. The result is a slightly worried expression.

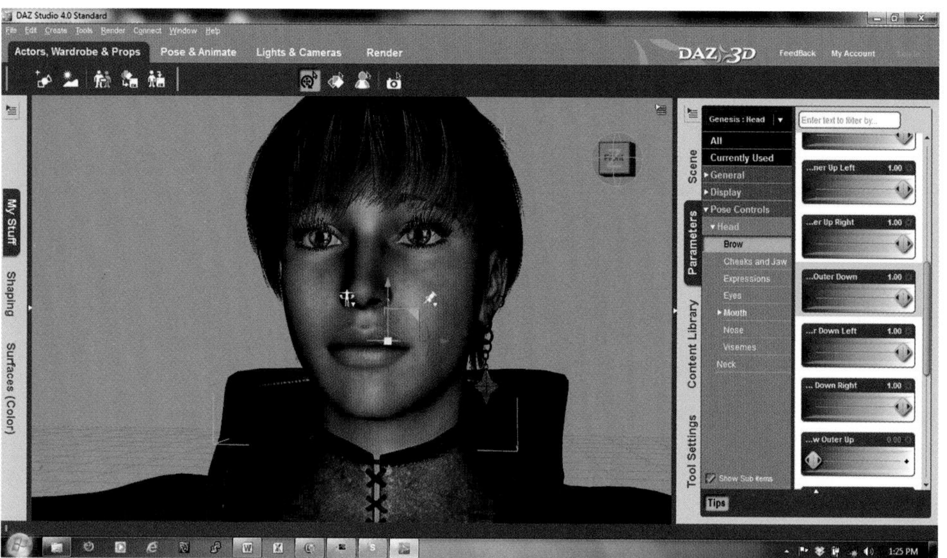

Figure 6.7 Changing the brow can add emotion to your characters.

Eyes

As noted earlier, the eyeballs are separate objects that are animated using DAZ Studio's bone system. They also have some influence on the eyelids and the area around the eye. The areas around the eye can also be animated using morphs. There are 20 different morph sliders for the eyes on the Genesis model. These morphs can be used to make the eyes blink, squint, wink, etc. Like the brow, there are morphs that control both eyes at once and others that only work on one lid of a single eye, allowing for great flexibility in posing and animating the eye, as shown in Figure 6.8.

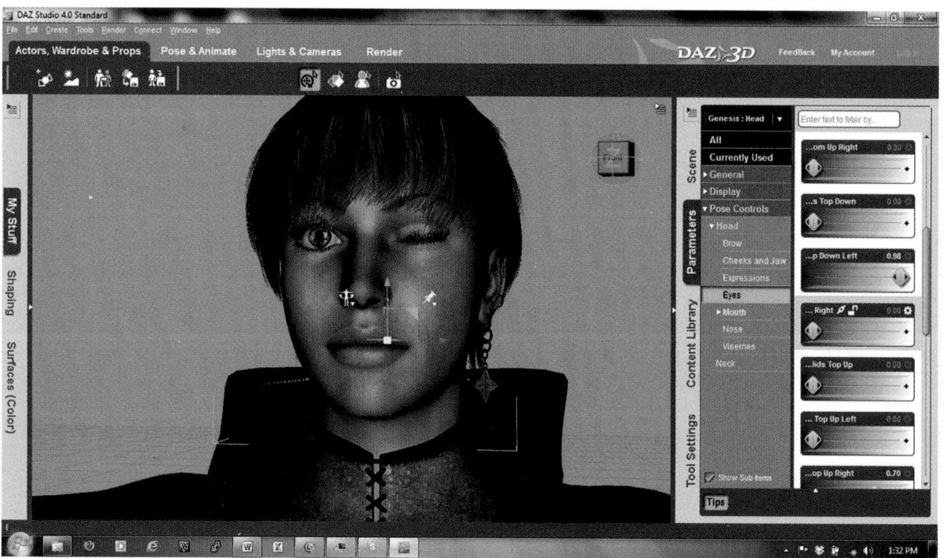

Figure 6.8 This is an example of an eye morph.

Nose

The nose only has two different morphs: NoseWrinkle and Nostrilsflare. These two morphs work best in combination with other facial morphs, but an example of them without other morphs is shown in Figure 6.9.

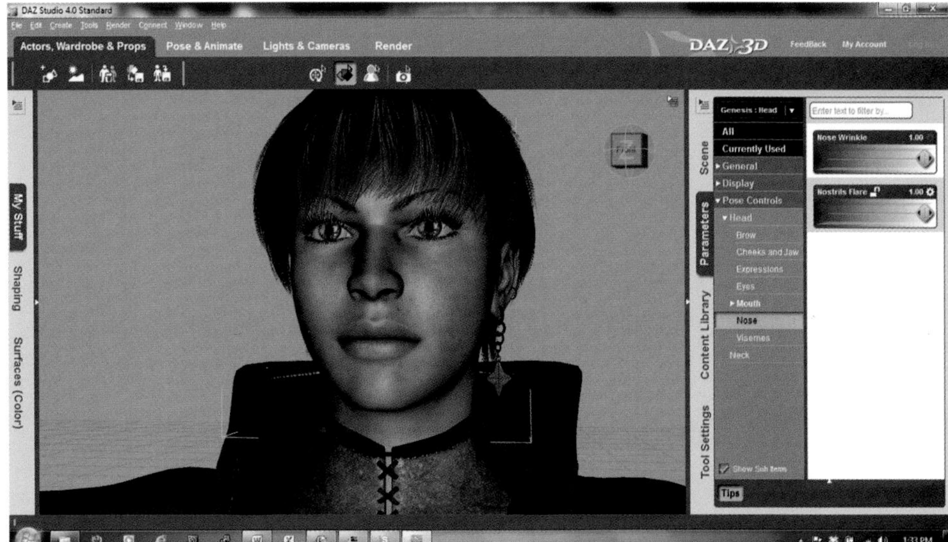

Figure 6.9
The nose only has two morphs.

Cheeks and Jaw

The cheeks are the major fleshy parts of the face and house many of the muscles that affect other facial features. Because of their location and the muscles they house, they often change shape when other areas like the mouth or eyes are animated; however, they do have significant personality of their own. There are 11 cheek morphs and two jaw morphs on the Genesis model. The two jaw morphs move the jaw in and out and from side to side. They do not animate the mouth open and closed. For that you will need to select the Mouth group. Figure 6.10 shows a pucker morph for Genesis.

Mouth

The mouth is the most flexible feature on the face. It is capable of great ranges of movement because it is connected equally to the skull and the jaw. The mouth group has far more morphs than any other facial feature, totaling 37. An example of the mouth morphs is shown in Figure 6.11.

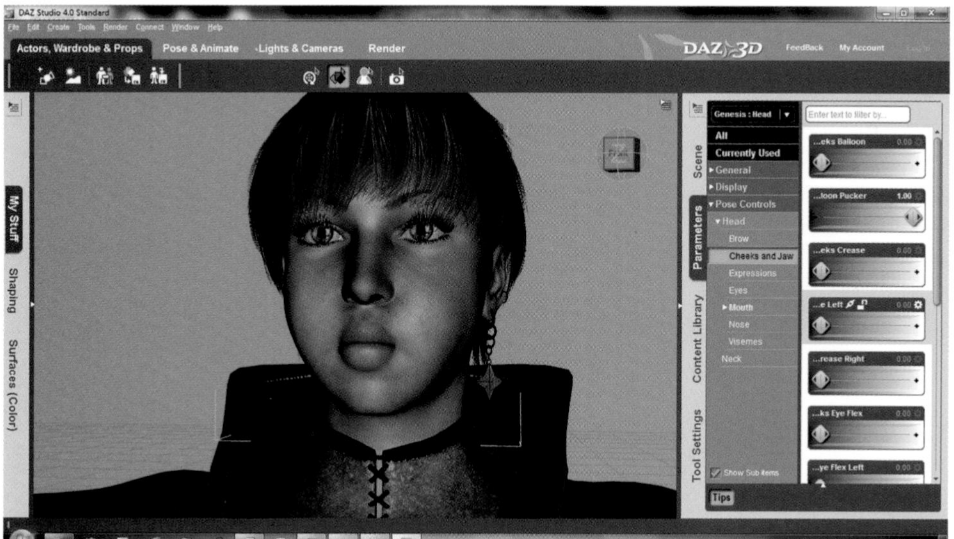

Figure 6.10
The cheeks have 11 morphs including a pucker morph.

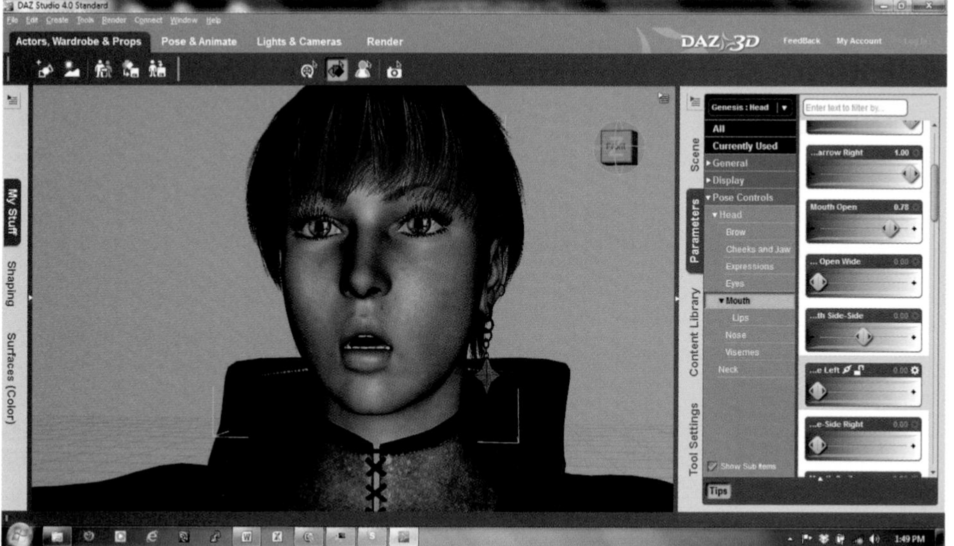

Figure 6.11
There are several morphs for the mouth.

Lips

Although the lips are a part of the mouth, DAZ Studio has a set of 22 different lip morphs. They are part of the mouth but are more focused on the lips themselves, like the ones shown in Figure 6.12.

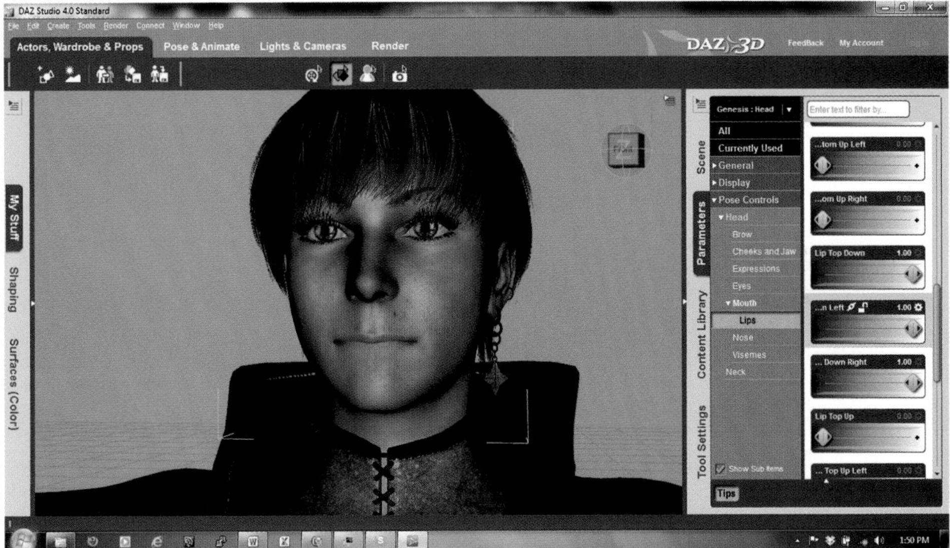

Figure 6.12
The lip morphs focus specifically on the lips.

The long list of facial morphs can become confusing, but having such a huge variety of morphs for the face does give the artist extreme control. While there are many morphs for the head, it is important to understand that facial animation requires that the artist think of the face as a whole and not just several separate parts. Movement of one part of the head affects other parts of the head. Seldom can you achieve the full impact of an expression with just one morph. Usually you will need to adjust several to get the right look.

It is common for an animator to have a mirror handy, and you can often find animators making faces into the mirror. They do this because they are studying facial expressions. It might seem a little funny at first but it is one of the best ways to really see how face muscles work on a human head.

Expressions

DAZ 3D has created collections of facial expressions that you can buy and use. They were created by professional artists and are great for quickly plugging in an expression to give your artwork more emotional impact. By studying each of the four expressions, you should be able to see how the individual morphs were used to create these more general morphs. Figure 6.13 shows anger fully morphed.

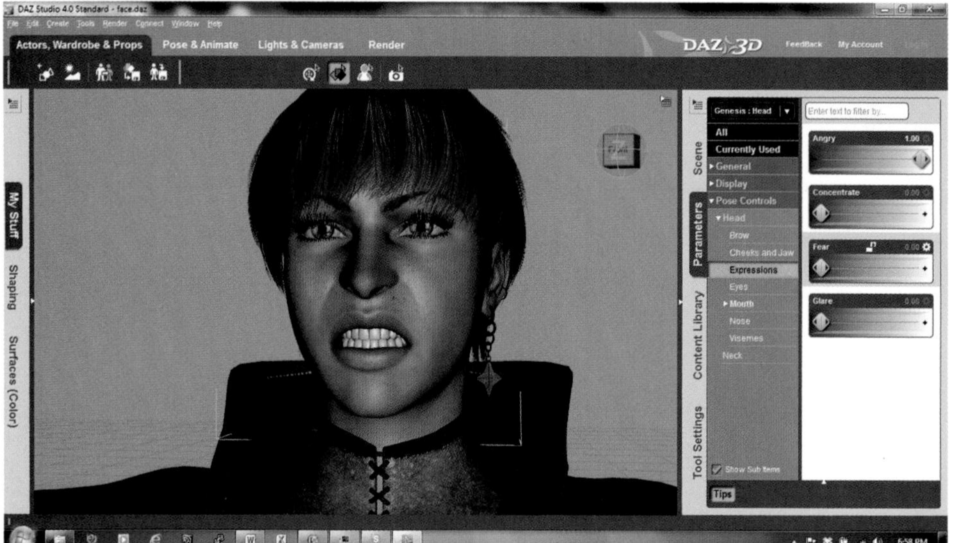

Figure 6.13
The anger morph uses several of the smaller morphs.

The Anger morph uses morphs from all over the face. Notice how the lips, mouth, and eyes all change. Slide the slider back and forth to see the changes. Anger is a major emotion and changes the face in a dramatic way. The next expression concentrate is a lot more subtle. Slide the Anger slider back to the left and then slide Concentrate all the way to the right. Notice that the changes to the face are much smaller. See Figure 6.14.

You can mix expressions. Figure 6.15 shows Concentrate with a little bit of Fear added.

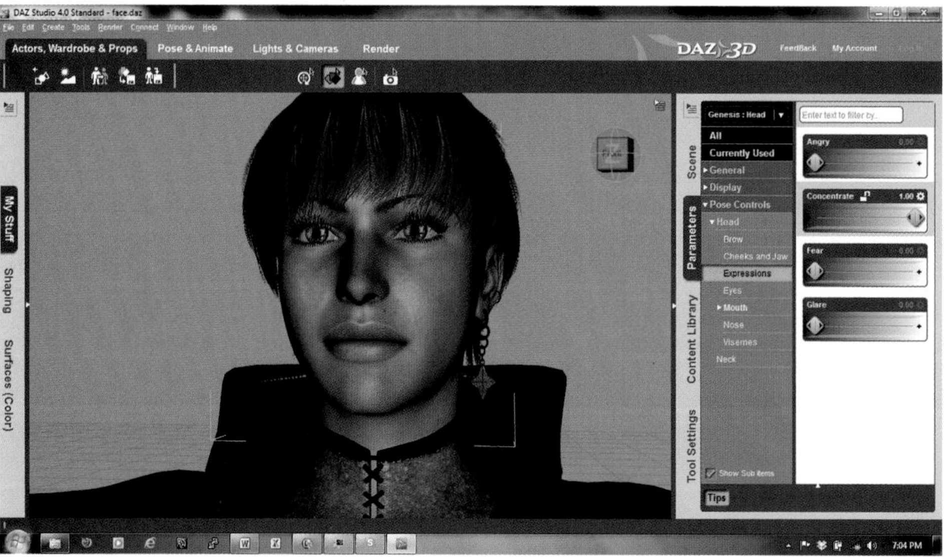

Figure 6.14
Concentrate is more subtle than anger.

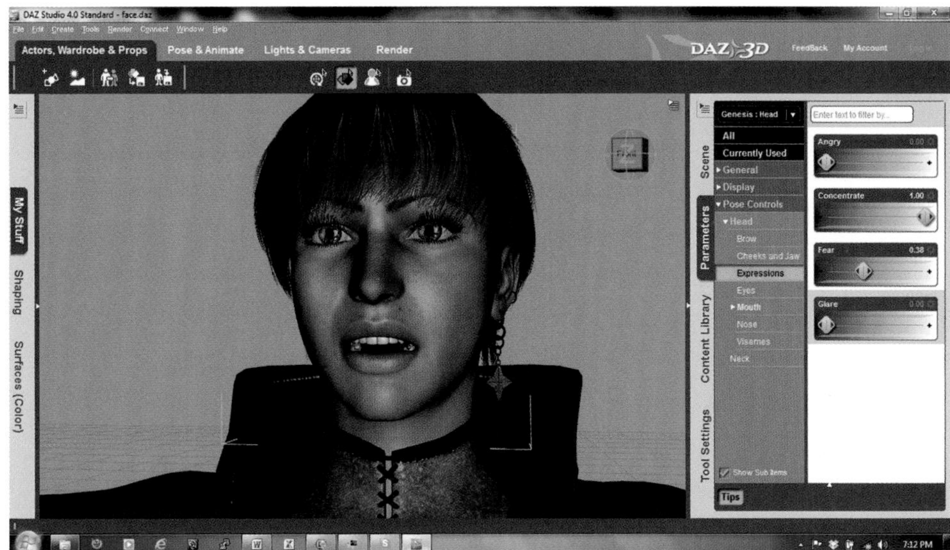

Figure 6.15 You can change the expression by mixing two morphs together.

Have some fun and experiment with the different emotions you can achieve by mixing the expressions together or using the other head morphs.

Summary

In summary, DAZ Studio gives the artist a lot of choices for changing and animating the head. These choices include bones that move the head and the eyes along with a number of morphs that can be used to change facial expressions. Morphs can be used to change small aspects of the face such as large lips for small thin lips, or they can be used to change facial expressions.

7

Posing the Figure

One of the most important skills you will develop by using DAZ Studio is how to pose a character. Posing a character is a means of communication. It even has a language that everyone is at least a little fluent in: body language. We can tell if a person is happy, sad, angry, or pleased just by his stance and posture. As an artist, understanding body language will be one of the most powerful ways of conveying emotion in your work.

Whether you just want to create still pictures or make animated movies, learning how to pose a character will be essential to your artistic development. In a still picture, you have to capture all of the emotion of the character in a single pose. In an animated movie, you create a series of poses called key frames that guide your character through his actions.

In this chapter, we will examine how to pose a character in DAZ Studio and then we will look into what makes a good pose. As with anything artistic, it is important to understand the basic principles so you can better express yourself.

Posing a Character

So far, you have learned a great deal about how DAZ characters are built and how to modify them by adding clothing or morphs. Now it is time to make your character move. Figure 7.1 shows the same character in two different poses. The first one is the standard open arm pose that the characters are imported in. The second pose has the character in a more animated pose. Do you see how dramatic the difference between the two poses is?

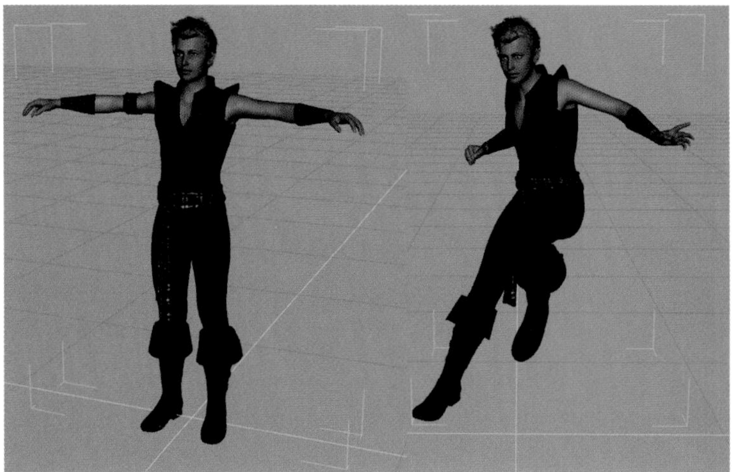

Figure 7.1
Posing the character can have a dramatic effect on the picture.

Movement

Moving a character in DAZ Studio basically requires the movement of one or more bones. When we examined the scene in Chapter 3, we saw that a character has many bones and those bones are connected in a hierarchal manner. In 3D language, these bones have parent-child relationships, as shown in Figure 7.2.

A parent is hierarchal above a child; therefore, when a parent is moved, so is the child attached to it. In Figure 7.3, only the shoulder was moved, but as you can see, the rest of the arm moved as well. That is because the other joints in the arm are attached as children to the shoulder joint.

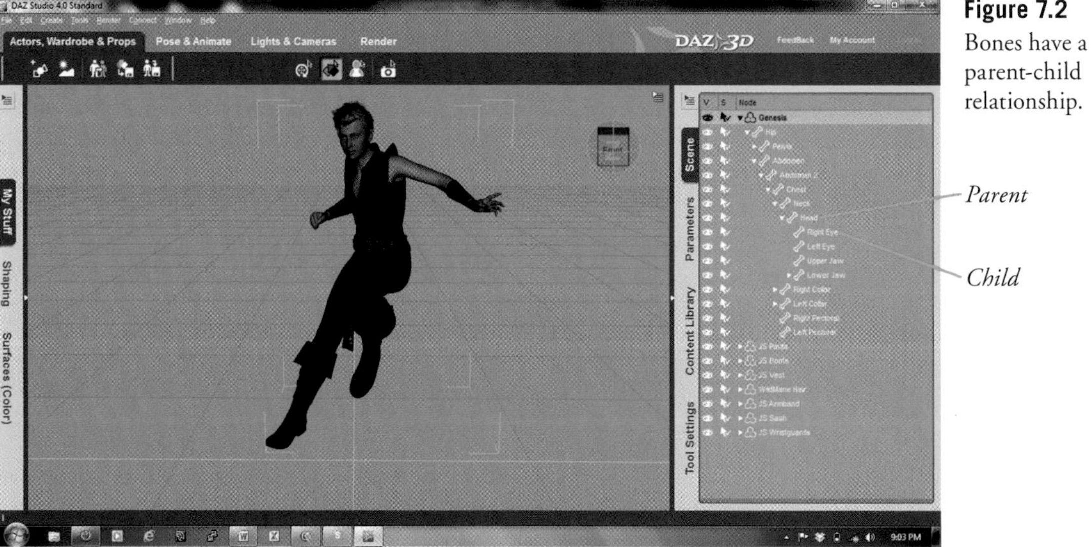

Figure 7.2
Bones have a parent-child relationship.

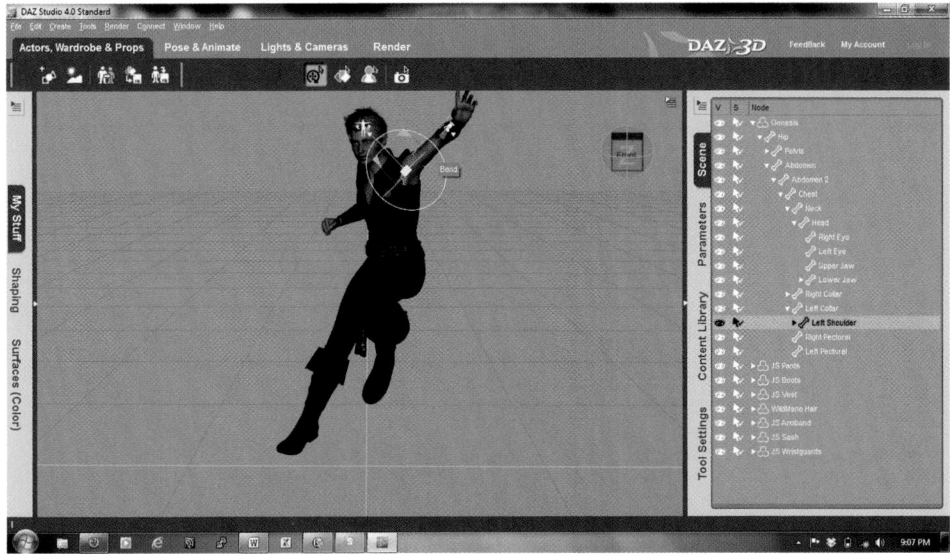

Figure 7.3 When the shoulder is moved, the rest of the arm moves too.

This parent-child relationship is very important to understand when posing characters in DAZ Studio because often it is easier to start from a parent and flow out to the children when posing.

Posing and Positioning in the Work Area

DAZ Studio allows for direct manipulation of a character in the work area. This means that you can select bones directly on the character and move or adjust them as necessary for your pose. The main tools for manipulating the character directly are the Active Pose and the Universal Manipulation tool found in the Toolbar, just below the main tabs, as shown in Figure 7.4.

Figure 7.4 The pose tools are located just below the main tabs.

Active Pose

The most advanced way of manipulating a character is to use the Active Pose. Active Pose isn't so much a tool as it is a way of using the selection function of the Universal Manipulation tool and moving the model by dragging the end of a bone chain. The Active Pose is a child-to-parent system that allows the user to move a child affecting the up-line parent bones in a string. For example, Figure 7.5 used the system to pull the hand to the side. Notice how the up-line bones of the arm and torso are affected. Also, notice how the down-line bones of the fingers react as normal.

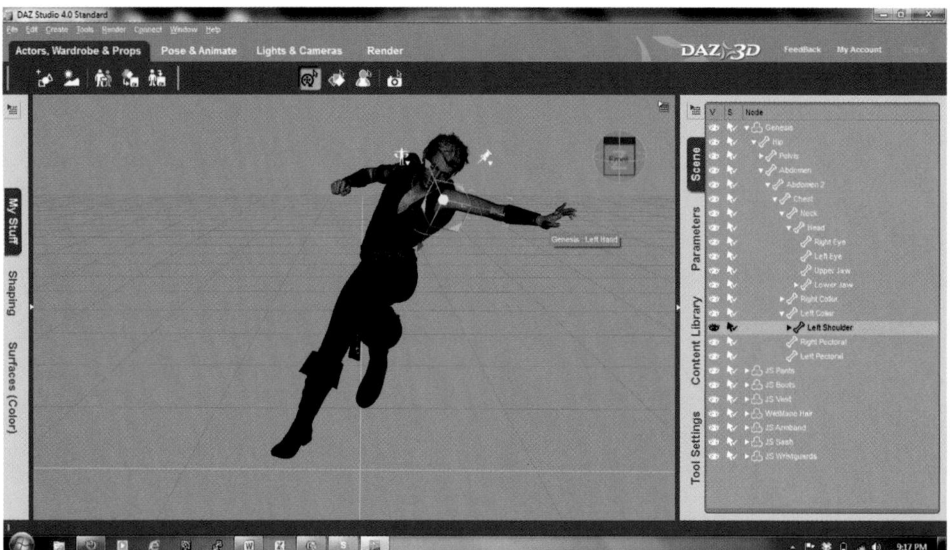

Figure 7.5
The Active Pose system is a child-to-parent manipulator.

To get the same type of pose movement working from parent to child would take the adjustment of several bones. By using the Active Pose, you can do it with just one selection. Active Pose is ideal for roughing in the basics of a pose because of its freeform nature; however, it is often difficult to get exactly the pose you want. This is why many artists will start by setting up the basic pose using the Active Pose tool and then refine it using small adjustments in parent-to-child rotations using the Universal Manipulation tool.

> **Note**
>
> As you move the character using the Active Pose system, you will notice that many of the joints will only move so far. The models in DAZ Studio have constraints on their joint movement to coincide with our own bodies. These constraints keep knees and elbows from bending backward, making the body move in a natural way.

Rotate

The most common tool used for posing in DAZ Studio is the Rotate tool. This is because almost all joints in the body are rotation joints. Some joints like the hip are ball-and-socket joints; others, like the knee and elbow, are hinge joints. No matter what kind of joint, it will have a pivot point around which it rotates. For example, in Figure 7.6, the Thigh joint is rotated moving the model's leg to the side.

You will notice that when the Rotate tool is selected, a yellow circle appears around the pivot of the joint. This tool has three handles in different colors. Each color represents

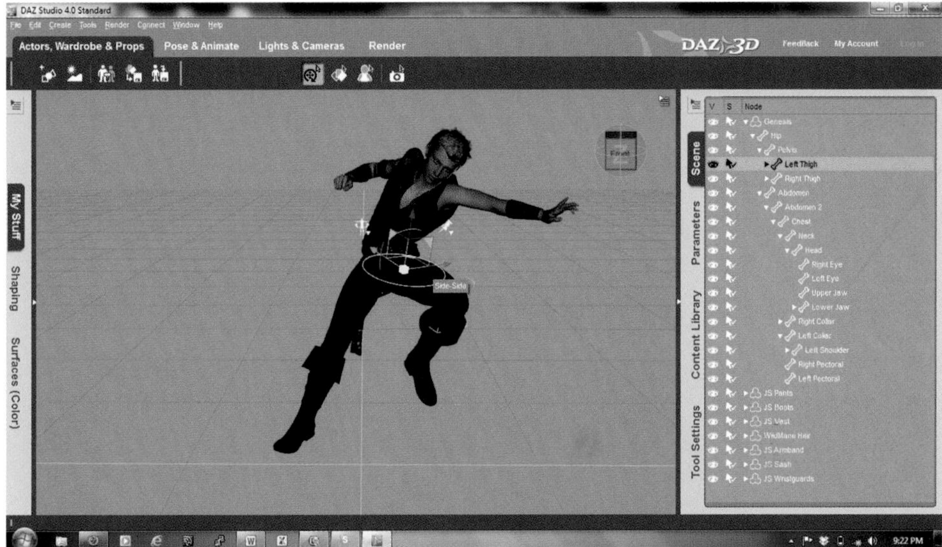

Figure 7.6 The Thigh joint is rotated to the side.

an axis. If you click on one of these rings, you can limit the rotation of the joint along that specific axis.

Translate

The Translate tool is seldom used to manipulate body parts. The main purpose for the Translate tool is to move the entire model. If you wanted your character to crouch like in Figure 7.7, the hip bone is lowered, then the feet are positioned in the crouch. The main purpose for Translate is to position the character rather than moving body parts.

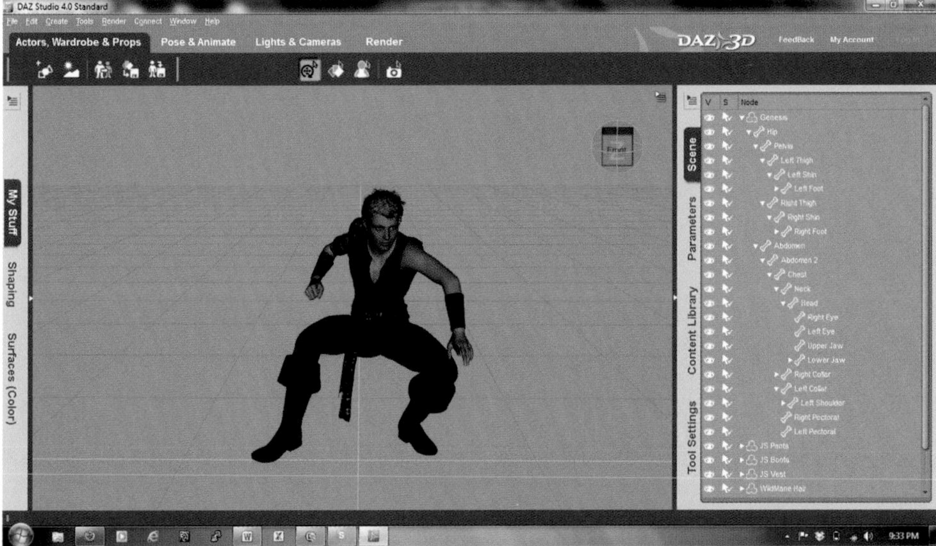

Figure 7.7 The Translate tool is used to position the character.

Scale

The Scale tool is very seldom used in posing except for exaggeration. It is more of a character set-up tool. In real life, our arms and legs don't suddenly get longer or shorter, so there is really little need for that to happen when posing a realistic model. Figure 7.8 shows part of the model scaled smaller. Notice that it tends to make the model look deformed. Scaling is an advanced animation technique and should only be used after you become familiar with squash and stretch animation techniques. While it is an animation technique, it can cause problems if it isn't understood by the animator. You are welcome to experiment but be careful.

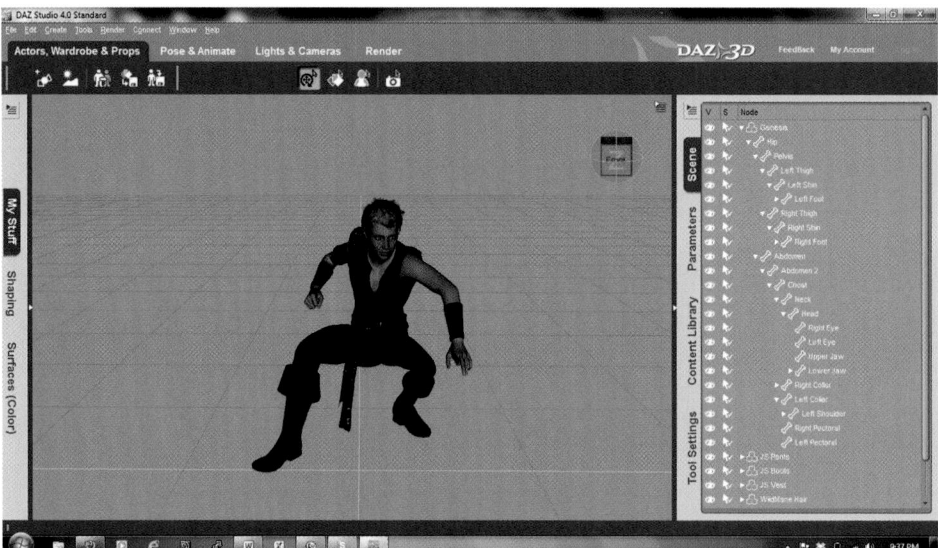

Figure 7.8
The Scale tool scales the character bigger or smaller.

Creating a Pose

If you are ready, let's create an original pose. Rather than starting with the model's default position, it is often easier to start with a predefined pose that is close to the desired finished pose. In this example, we will start with a pose that has the model with his hands to his side in a relaxed standing pose. Our objective will be to have him sit down in a chair. Figure 7.9 shows the start pose with the model and a chair.

1. Rotate the model to the side and lift the feet so the legs are in a sitting position, as shown in Figure 7.10.
2. Now, select the Genesis node in the Scene and move the model to the chair, as shown in Figure 7.11.

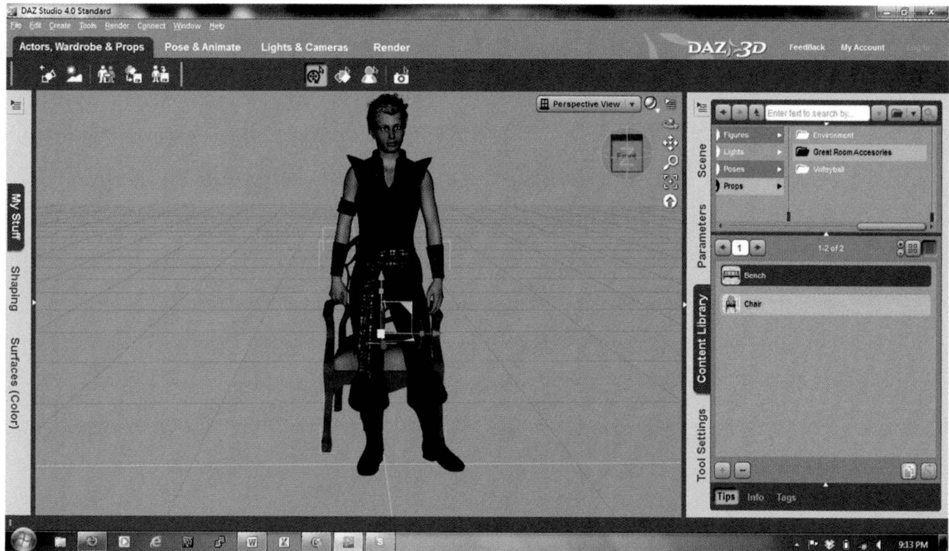

Figure 7.9
We begin with a predefined pose and a chair prop.

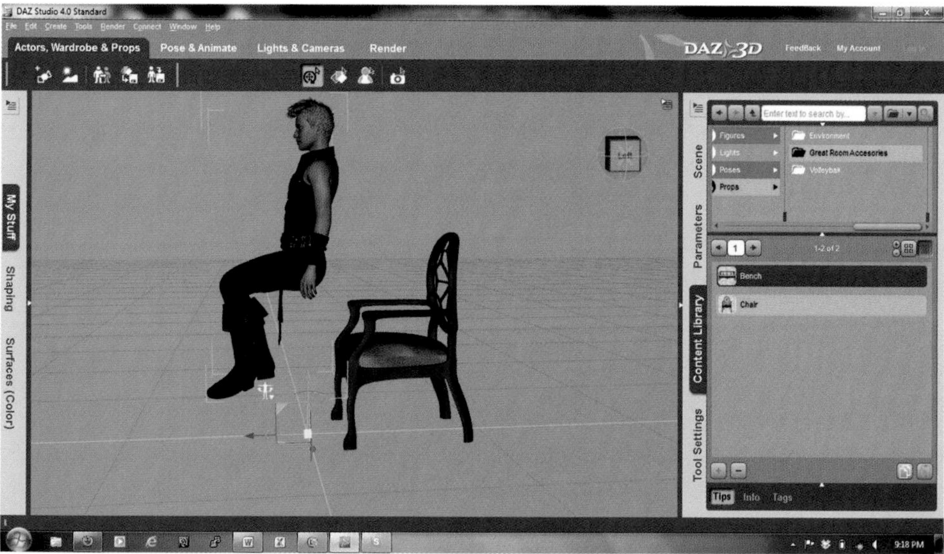

Figure 7.10
Lift the legs to a sitting position.

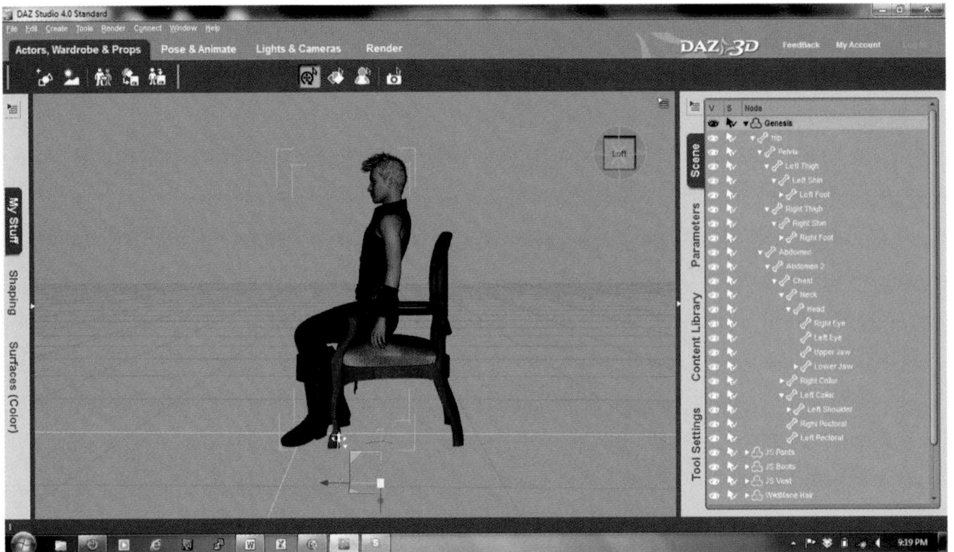

Figure 7.11
Move the model to the chair.

3. The model is sitting but he looks a little uncomfortable. Start with the abdomen and rotate the bones going up the spine forward just a little.
4. Next, rotate the neck and head so the model appears to be looking straight ahead instead of down at the floor, as shown in Figure 7.12.
5. Move the hands up to about where the arm rests are, as shown in Figure 7.13.

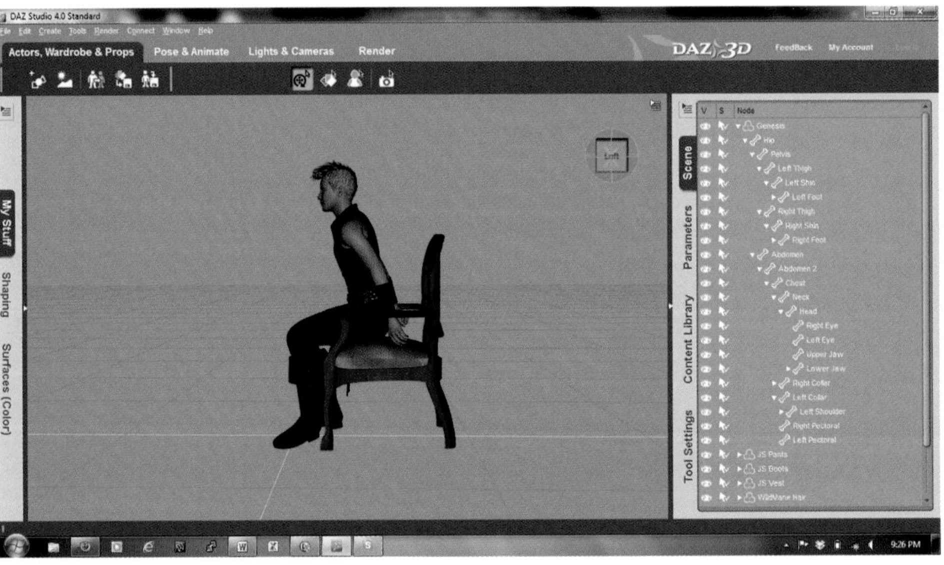

Figure 7.12
Rotate the bones along the spine to the head.

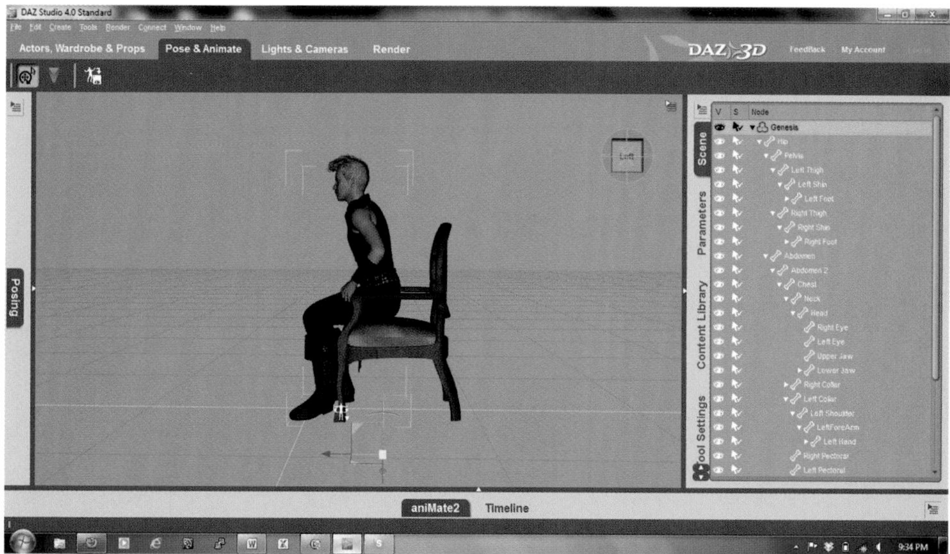

Figure 7.13
Move the hands up to the arm rests.

6. To get the hands on the arm rests, you will need to rotate the scene back to the front and then place the arms on the arm rests, as shown in Figure 7.14. Never assume your model is posed when only looking from one view. Always check the model's pose from multiple views.

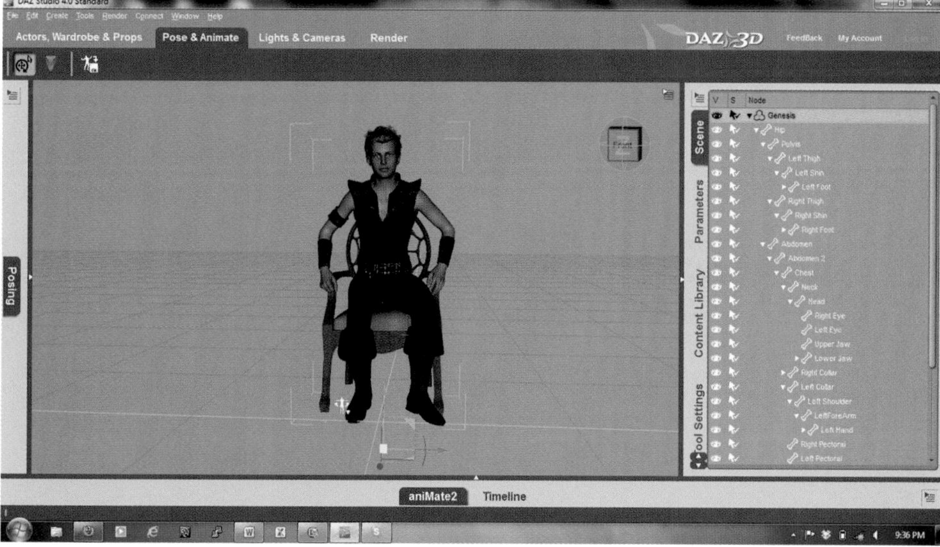

Figure 7.14
Adjust the hands and arms in the front view.

As you can see, posing a character is easy and takes very little time. Learning the controls allows you to select and move body parts quickly and effectively. You can take the pose further, giving the character a more relaxed look and adding other touches that really give the character the feeling you want to portray. Experiment a little and see what you come up with.

Puppeteer

Puppeteer is an effective open system for creating animation and developing new poses without having to go through a lot of individual posing. It is especially effective if you want to use predefined poses for your art and have your character move between them. Puppeteer is one of the tabs in the Windows menu. See Figure 7.15.

There are three modes in Puppeteer: Edit, Preview, and Record. Figure 7.16 shows the Puppeteer tool next to the Genesis model. The three modes are shown in the top of the tool. Below them is a grid. This is where you will set up your pose points, or key frames as they are called in animation.

Puppeteer is an animation blending system that blends between two or more poses. In Edit mode, you set up your poses. In Preview mode, you can see how the poses blend. In Record mode, you can make a movie.

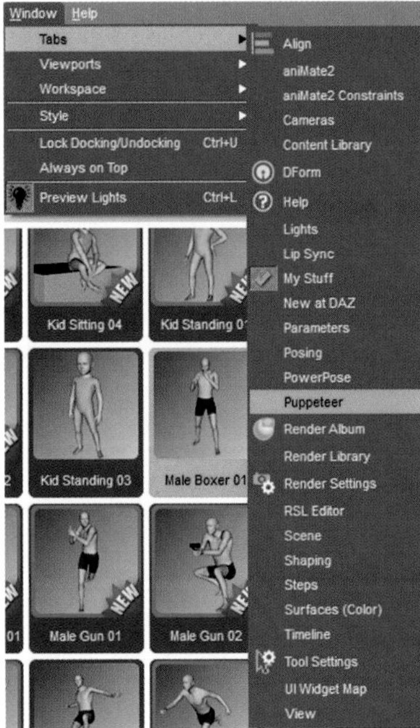

Figure 7.15
Find Puppeteer in the Tabs menu.

Figure 7.16
Puppeteer has three modes.

Edit Mode

In Edit mode, you can place pose points or key frames in the Puppeteer grid simply by clicking inside the grid. Figure 7.17 shows the model with a pose point set in Puppeteer.

To set a pose, just pose your character and then with the character selected, click on any location on the grid. An orange dot will appear on the grid where you clicked. This dot is a pose location on the grid and stores the pose data from your pose.

In Figure 7.18, a second pose is set for the model.

Figure 7.17
Genesis pose set in Puppeteer.

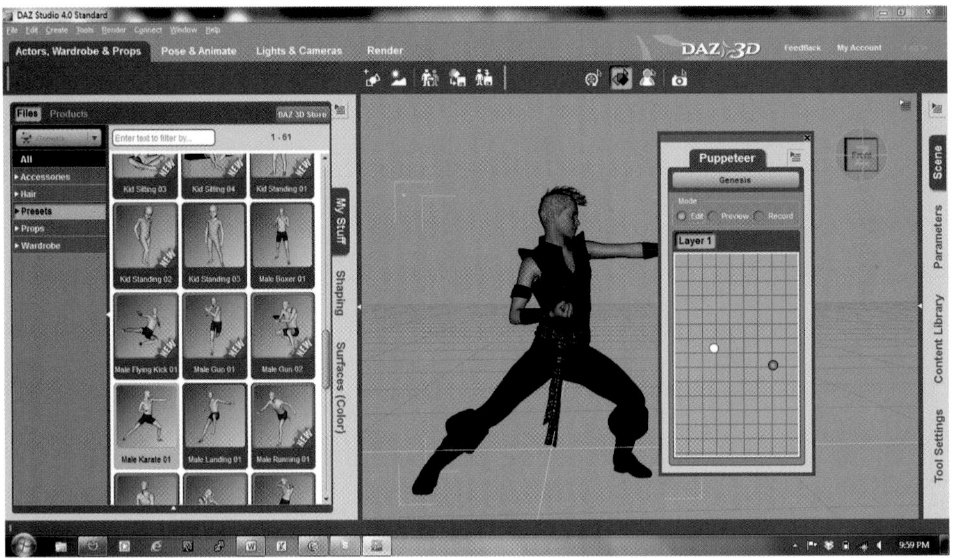

Figure 7.18
A second pose is set.

Preview Mode

With two poses set, you can preview how Puppeteer blends between the two poses. Change the mode to Preview and slide the cursor between the two poses, as shown in Figure 7.19.

That is pretty cool and easy don't you think?

Figure 7.19
Slide the cursor between the two poses in Preview mode.

Puppeteer goes beyond just blending two poses. The program blends between every pose on the grid. In Figure 7.20, a third pose is added.

Figure 7.20
Set a third pose.

Now when you slide the cursor in Preview mode the blending takes place between all three poses, as shown in Figure 7.21

Figure 7.21
Puppeteer blends between all three poses.

Record Mode

In Record mode, you can record the character's animation based on how you move the cursor. It is very similar to Preview mode with the major exception that you are recording the character's movements. In this way, it is very easy to make a movie of your character.

Puppeteer is very useful for creating quick movies of your character and is only limited by your imagination. It is also very useful for creating a series of still images where you want your character to change poses in the same background. All you need to do is set up the background and then place your character in each pose. As you pose your character, you can save your poses in Puppeteer. Then you select the pose point in Puppeteer to get the right poses for your picture.

Pose Sets

In addition to posing a character yourself, there are a number of pose sets available with some of the models or from the DAZ store. These pose sets contain many common poses that can be used right away. In the last section, we used three poses from the poses that come with the Genesis figure. Figure 7.22 shows a number of poses.

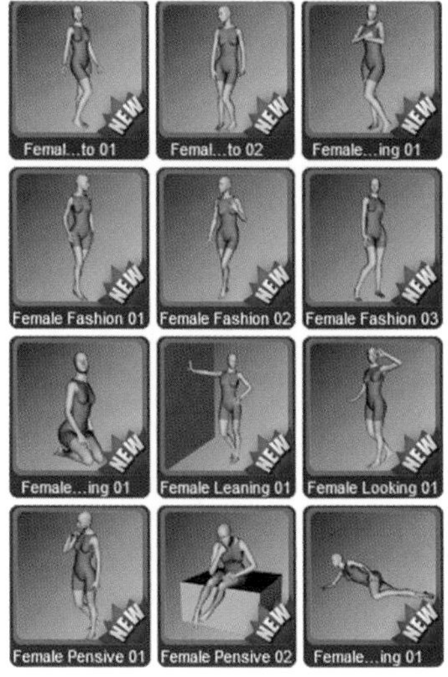

Figure 7.22
There are a number of ready-made poses available for many DAZ models.

Using a ready-made pose is very easy. All you have to do is find the pose you want to use in the My Stuff tab and then import it into the scene with the target model selected. When you create a pose, you can start with a premade pose then adjust it to exactly what you want. By starting with the premade pose you save time in your art development process.

Now that you have some idea of how to pose a character, let's move ahead into what makes a good pose.

Getting the Right Pose

The human body has an expressiveness that communicates through an unspoken language often referred to as body language. As an artist, you have to learn this language and become as expressive with it as the writer is with words.

How you want to pose the figures in your art is determined by the purpose or goal you have in mind. It begins with the creative germ of an idea that is developed sometimes well before a scene is created. Sometimes the idea is developed wholly by the artist, although many times the artist has influence from outside sources like in the case of commissioned work or commercial art.

Another aspect of posing a character that is very important is the physical association of the body with the environment. Because we live in a physical world, our bodies are subjected to a number of physical forces, not the least of which is gravity. A pose that is off balance or ignores the effects of gravity can often make for an awkward-looking picture.

Maybe the most difficult aspect of posing the figure is also the most important. That aspect is the expression of emotion. Being able to express a feeling or emotion simply by how you pose your character is the difference between a want-to-be artist and an artist.

Purpose

There are many elements that go into determining the pose for a picture, but they all begin with the artist's purpose. The fundamental question is "Why am I creating this piece of art?" The purpose might be to make a beautiful scene or it might be to promote a product. Whatever the purpose is, it will form the foundation for developing the work to completion.

Having a purpose for your pictures gives you direction. It gives you a goal. A goal will give you a starting point for judging your work.

Natural

One of the great advantages of a software program like DAZ Studio is that it has almost unlimited possibilities for posing figures. Not only can you pose the figures in almost any position possible with the human body, but you can change the figures themselves for a huge variety of looks from fat to thin, from muscular to frail. A variety of costumes and facial expressions for these virtual characters are also available. But with all of this freedom, there is also a danger that the figure may not look natural or like it fits into its environment.

In a real-world situation, we have to follow natural laws like gravity. In a virtual situation, the artist has to remember these laws and simulate their effects. If the artist doesn't plan for the effects of natural laws, then the pose can look odd or even uncomfortable to the viewer. For example, in Figure 7.23, the seated figure is not in the same perspective as the chair, making the pose seem very out of place.

Balance and Weight

For a character to look right with its surroundings, it needs to have balance and look like it has weight to it. It's easy to pose a figure that looks slightly odd or out of place. The perspective could be off, or the lighting might be wrong.

Balance

If the character is off balance, she may look like she's about to fall. In Figure 7.23, the character is leaning to one side. The viewer may feel the need to try to catch her.

Because artificial environments don't have gravity, you have to compensate by learning how to keep your characters balanced. You do this by locating the center of mass of the body and then determining if it is supported by the figure. To find the center mass, look to the person's hips. Even though the chest or upper torso of some characters may be larger than the hip area, the hips are what really determine the balance of a figure in most cases because they are connected to the legs, which are the primary support system.

Once you've examined the relationship between the hips and the rest of the torso, then you can move on to looking at how they relate to the legs to see if the torso is balanced between the legs or any artificial support like a wall or chair. If you have your character leaning against anything in a scene, make sure you have that object in the scene before you finalize the pose.

It is worth mentioning that you need to examine the character from several different angles. Characters exist in virtual 3D space. From one angle, it may look like your character is in balance, but from another it may not. Rotate your model to see it from multiple angles.

Being off balance is not always a bad thing. If you are working on an action picture, you can use balance as a way of emphasizing that action. Say, for instance, you are working on a picture of a person running, as shown in Figure 7.24. When a person runs, her weight is shifted forward in an off-balance position. Standing still in that position would likely cause the runner to topple over. The viewer recognizes the off-balance position of the person and interprets it as part of the running motion.

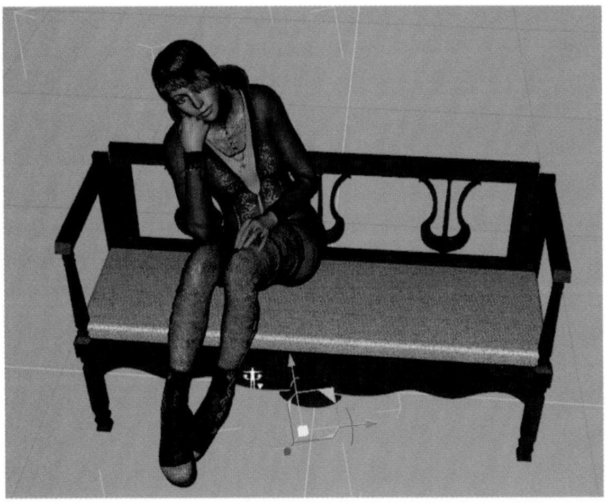

Figure 7.23 The character looks awkward in this pose.

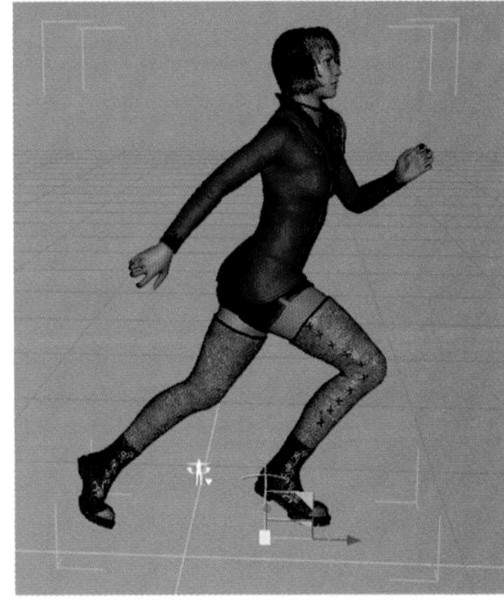

Figure 7.24 Some poses are off balance on purpose.

Weight

Every figure in life has some weight unless it is floating in outer space. Weight is closely related to balance in that without weight, balance is not an issue. A character's weight is a combination of mass and gravity. Gravity is constantly pulling a figure toward the ground. The figure's skeletal and muscular systems work to help the figure stand, move, and, in essence, fight the effects of gravity. When working with a virtual figure in a virtual setting, the model often appears weightless. This can be a problem if you are working toward a realistic picture.

A common problem that you see in poses is that the artist gets a figure set up and in balance, then adds a prop to the scene that the figure is holding. The prop may be a large gun or some other device that looks like it should weigh a lot. However, in the picture the gun looks almost weightless because the posed figure is not reacting to holding that extra weight. In the real world when we carry something heavy we shift our body to compensate for the weight and balance the weight of our body with that of the heavy object.

Emotion

Our emotions are often expressed through our body language. Close observation will reveal unique characteristics to almost any emotion. When we react to an emotion, our reaction takes on these characteristics. As you explore the different characteristics of each emotional reaction, you will start to notice a flow or overall directional movement. This is very important to be aware of because the major flow of the body is the most likely aspect of body language for emphasizing an emotion.

Let's take a quick look at a few of the more common emotions and how to you might try to depict them in your work.

Anger

One of the most powerful emotions that an artist has to depict in a character is anger, as shown in Figure 7.25. Anger is also one of the easiest emotions for the audience to interpret.

Anger is indicated by a stiff gesture, with many muscles straining against each other. The stance often looks like two upward pointing arrows, one over the other.

Some general characteristics of anger are as follows:

- The joints in the legs and arms are locked, and the muscles of the limbs strain against one another.
- The feet are firmly planted on the ground, and the hands are tightly clenched.
- The head is often lowered forward, with the shoulders raised.

Surprise

Surprise, as shown in Figure 7.26, is a common emotion in animation. It is used often because it involves a lot of drama and has an impact on the audience.

Surprise is an open gesture that recedes from the object of the surprise. It is characterized by a very strong curve in the character.

Some general characteristics of surprise are as follows:

- When a person is in the midst of recoil from a surprise, the hands are opened with the palms forward, and the fingers and thumb are bent back.
- The arms and sometimes one of the legs are bent.
- There is a strong action line that curves dramatically from the foot through the body to the head.
- The eyes are usually locked on the object of surprise.

Happy (Joy)

Joy is a happy expression of gleeful contentment, as shown in Figure 7.27. It is a strong contrasting emotion from anger and dejection.

Animators often exaggerate happy emotions to emphasize the character's feelings to the audience. It is a sweeping gesture that pulls the eye upward from the feet to the head.

Some general characteristics of happiness or joy are as follows:

- The arms often form a diamond shape, with the elbows spread wide.
- The hands are either laid flat against the body or clasped.

Figure 7.25 Anger is shown by tension in the limbs.

Figure 7.26 Surprise is seen often in animated productions.

Figure 7.27 Animators often exaggerate happiness.

- Sometimes, the arms are brought in, and the hands are clasped just below the chin. However, this could be confused with the action of pleading.
- The feet and legs are usually close together.
- The head is almost always at an angle following the arch of the body.

Sad (Dejected)

Sadness, as shown in Figure 7.28, is another powerful emotion. It resonates with the audience because it is a common emotion that promotes sympathy for the sad character.

The general action line of a sad character is hooked with the head down turned.

Some general characteristics of sadness are as follows:

- Drooping shoulders characterize sadness.
- The arms and legs are held close to the body as if the character wants to recede into itself.
- The head is down cast.

Authoritarian (I'm the Boss)

The animator will often want to show that a character is in charge by putting a character in an authoritarian posture, as shown in Figure 7.29. This type of stance is filled with pride and arrogance.

Figure 7.28 The head turned down often shows sadness.

Figure 7.29 This character seems very arrogant.

The arrogant character has a strutting posture with strong lines leading to the person's head emphasizing a "look at me I am important" kind of feeling.

Some general characteristics of an authoritarian or arrogant character are as follows:

- Strong directional motion toward the character's head.
- Chest puffed out with the hips tilted forward.
- Head slightly tilted back so the character is looking down his nose.

Only a Sampling

These are just a few of the many emotions you might use when posing your characters. This book is not long enough to list every emotion. The emotions presented in this chapter were meant as examples only and are not the only way that a particular emotion can be expressed. We have so many ways to express emotions that there are no hard-and-fast rules. Your best aid in understanding emotions is to observe natural reactions in real life.

Summary

Posing characters in DAZ Studio is easy with the many tools available. We have only touched on a few, but with the basic knowledge from this chapter, you should be able to create about any pose you can dream up.

An important thing to remember when posing your characters in DAZ Studio is that they need to look right for the purpose you have in mind. Characters need to have weight and they need to be balanced. Expression of emotion in body language is also important.

In the next chapter, we will take a break from human characters for a moment and show how DAZ Studio deals with backgrounds and props.

8

Props and Sets

Props and sets are used to enhance your pictures. A *prop* is any non-character object that is used by a character and includes things like chairs, cars, umbrellas, and swords. The main difference between a prop and a set is that a prop is something that the character can use. A *set* is a setting or environment in which the character will be placed. Sets in DAZ Studio can be a simple backdrop similar to those found in a photography studio or they can be a complete 3D model of an environment.

In this chapter, you will learn how to import and use props with your characters. You will also be introduced to several different types of sets. To finish the chapter, you will learn how to create your own sets using another great tool from DAZ Studio called Bryce. This program is specifically designed for the creation of incredible 3D environments.

Props

Sometimes the distinction of what is a prop and what isn't is somewhat vague. Technically, anything other than clothing can be called a prop, including hair; however, for this book we shall define props as items used by a character, like a gun or cane, or objects in a scene that are not fit to the character.

Character Props

Character props are props that a character carries either in her hand or attached to her body or clothing. A jewelry prop is shown in Figure 8.1.

Character props can also be things like weapons, as shown in Figure 8.2.

Figure 8.1
Jewelry items are character props.

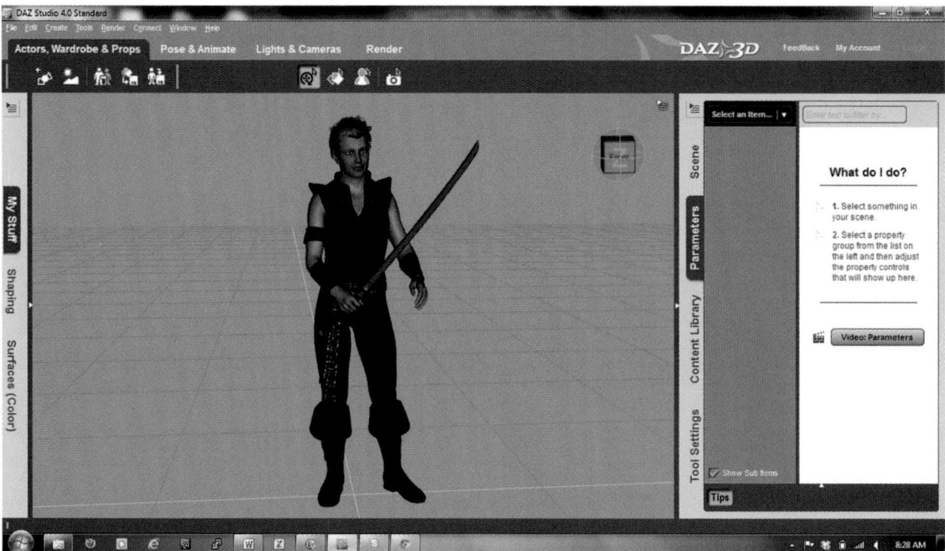

Figure 8.2
Weapons are also props.

Weapons like guns, staffs, swords, and so on can be carried in a holster or sheath, but often they are held in the hand, as shown in Figure 8.2. To get a weapon to fit in a character's hand and to move with the character, you need to follow these steps:

1. Many props will already be set up to work with a specific model. For example, the katana shown in Figure 8.2 was designed to work with the Genesis model. If it is loaded into the scene while the Genesis model is selected, it will automatically load attached to the model's right hand.
2. If you don't want the katana in the right hand or you want to use the katana with an older DAZ model, then you will need to attach the prop manually. Just move the prop into the right position in your scene.
3. Next, open the scene and move the object to be a child of the joint you want it attached to, as shown in Figure 8.3.

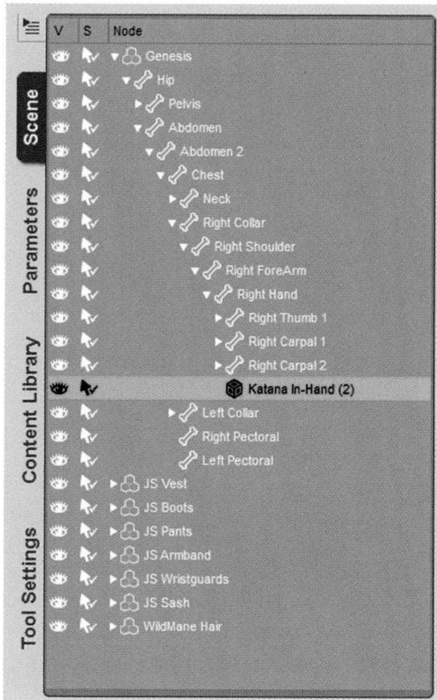

Figure 8.3
This prop is for use in the character's right hand.

Environment Props

Environment props are part of an environment and not carried or held by a character. Some examples of environment props include things like park benches, lampposts, furniture, and so on. Figure 8.4 shows some of the variety of environment props available for DAZ Studio.

Unlike character props, environment props are not attached to a character but rather are placed in a scene. Props will load into the scene centered and scaled to work well with most DAZ characters. Once in the scene, they can be adjusted using the Rotate, Translate, and Scale tools located on the toolbar along the top of the screen.

Many sets available for DAZ Studio come with a number of extra props that you can place in the scene as you like. For example, in the scene shown in Figure 8.5 there are several prop objects like traffic cones, fences, and other objects that help make the scene seem more realistic.

You can also add other props that don't come with the scene, as shown in Figure 8.6. DAZ Studio lets you mix and match props with total freedom.

The beauty of DAZ Studio is that as you extend your library of objects, you increase the options for creative opportunities. As your library grows, your options for picture content grows as well.

Figure 8.4 There are many types of environment props.

Figure 8.5 Many of the environment props in this scene came with the scene.

Figure 8.6 The car in this scene came from another model set.

Backdrops and Settings

A setting in DAZ Studio is the stage upon which you create your artwork. It can be as simple as a backdrop like in a photography studio or as complex as a full 3D environment like a city block replete with alleys, warehouses, and city lights. Regardless of how detailed the setting, it will be limited because 3D environments are limited by the speed and power of your computer. It you put too much into a setting, you will start to notice a performance hit. However, just because you are limited by technology doesn't mean you can't make your pictures seem like they go on forever. The trick is not to let the viewer see the edge of the scene.

To have success when working with settings you have to be aware of where the set ends and plan your pictures of animation so you stay within those edges. Figure 8.7 shows a set pulled back so you can see the edges.

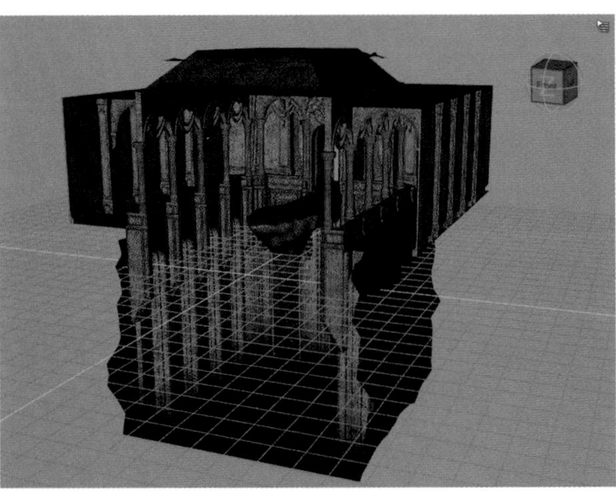

Figure 8.7 The set has edges.

Notice how the set is made specifically for the camera, pointing to the center, as shown in Figure 8.8. The set only works if viewed from looking into the scene. It is truly like a stage where the audience is in the front.

Figure 8.8
A set is designed for viewing from only one direction.

Whereas sets usually have a lot of 3D geometry, backdrops are much less complex. A backdrop is more like a large mural that the figures stand in front of to make it look like there is something complex behind them. One advantage of a backdrop is that they are simple, requiring less geometry so they are usually faster to render. Backdrops do not require the high-polygon-count 3D models that a full 3D environment requires. High polygon counts can cause rendering to be extremely slow and in some cases slow down the editing functions in DAZ Studio while you are trying to work on your art before you render it. Even though DAZ Studio is optimized to run as efficiently as possible, if you crowd a scene with a number of high-polygon-count 3D models, it will bog down and become unresponsive.

Full 3D Environments

The most accurate and believable settings for your character in DAZ Studio are full 3D environments. A full 3D environment will give you the most accurate three-dimensional rendering because the lighting will be accurate and the distances will be consistent with your models. Full 3D environments give your characters a full range of movement capabilities. You have a lot more freedom for camera angles because you are not limited to only one direction.

The down side to full 3D environments is that they take a massive amount of polygons and texture data. They tend to create very complex scenes that often take a long time to render. Figure 8.9 shows a full 3D environment scene. As you can see, this scene is very complex even without characters. Even on a fast machine, this scene took almost two hours to render with shadows.

Figure 8.9 Full 3D environments give a more accurate feel to your art.

Another important element to remember when dealing with 3D environments is that you will have greater freedom in moving things around and customizing the setup of your scene. In the scene shown in Figure 8.9, each of the buildings, trees, chairs, lampposts, and other objects is separate. With enough elements, an entire city could be built.

DAZ has a huge variety of 3D environments that you can use for sets. Figures 8.10 and 8.11 show two more 3D environment sets.

Figure 8.10 This 3D set is a modern-day rundown city street.

Figure 8.11 This 3D set has a Mediterranean look.

Figure 8.12 shows the Mediterranean geometry from a distance. Notice that there are several locations where you can position your camera in a 3D environment set.

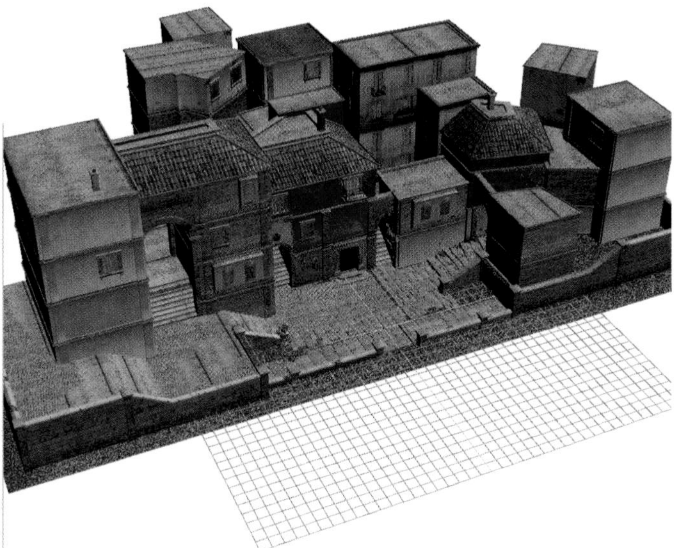

Figure 8.12
This view shows the entire environment.

Some environments from DAZ cover large areas and allow for multiple camera positions. Other environments are more limited. In the next section, we will take a look at how you can create your own environments for use in DAZ Studio using another DAZ tool called Bryce.

Before rendering a scene, you may want to look at the scene and remove or hide objects that will not be seen in the render view. This will save time during renders as the program will not have to calculate the geometry, light, and shadows of those objects.

Bryce

Bryce is a software program specifically designed for the creation of rich environments. With it, artists can quickly create realistic environments including mountains, oceans, landscapes, cityscapes, and a host of other settings. It includes a number of functions for creating trees, buildings, rocks, and other geographic features. Figure 8.13 shows a view of the Bryce interface.

The center part of the interface contains the working area, which is your window into the world you are creating. You can use the camera controls to the left of the scene view to change or adjust your view. The upper-left corner of the screen shows a small preview render window called the Nano Preview. Along the top of the screen are toolbars for creating and manipulating scene objects. Along the bottom of the screen are animation tools and selection icons. The right side of the interface contains a collection of advanced options.

Memory Dots *Nano Preview* *Tool Palette* *Working Window* *Advanced Display Palette*

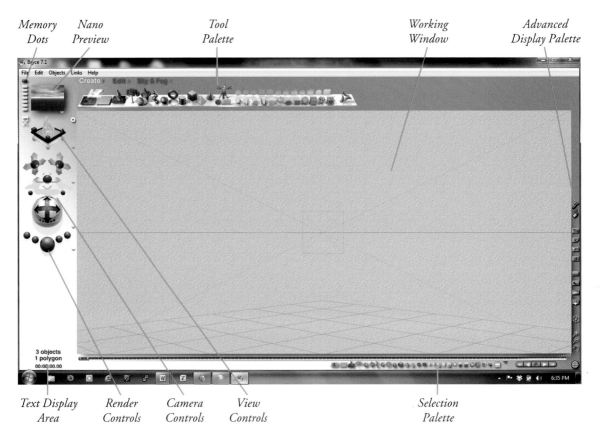

Text Display Area *Render Controls* *Camera Controls* *View Controls* *Selection Palette*

Figure 8.13 The Bryce interface contains many useful tools.

In Figure 8.13, the top toolbar contains the create tools. These tools are used for bringing new objects or lights into a scene. There are two other toolbars that occupy the same space depending on what you are creating. The three toolbars are Create, Edit, and Sky & Fog. Figure 8.14 shows the Edit toolbar with its several Edit tools.

After you create objects for your scene, the Edit tools are used to adjust or change the objects into the shapes, sizes, and placements you want.

Figure 8.15 shows the Sky & Fog toolbar. The tools in this toolbar are used for creating atmospheres for your scenes.

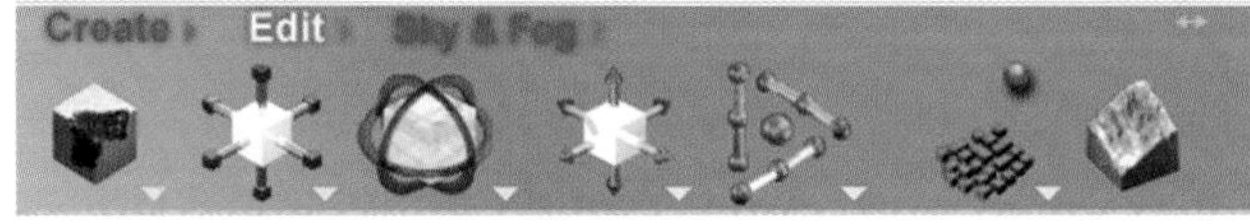

Figure 8.14 You can modify objects in Bryce using the Edit tools.

In the bottom-left corner of the Bryce interface is a small circular icon. This icon toggles between the full animation controls and the selection icons. The Animation controls are shown in Figure 8.16.

Figure 8.15 Sky & Fog tools are used for creating atmospheres.

Figure 8.16 The bottom controls toggle between selection and animation.

Building a Scene in Bryce

Bryce is a full 3D scene creation program and contains a number of tools and functions that we will not be able to cover adequately in this book. Instead, we will take a quick look at how the program is used to create a simple background. DAZ has a complete set of reference and tutorial documents that you can refer to for more information on using Bryce.

When Bryce first comes up, it will already have an infinite plane and a sky—a flat ground plane with a repeating texture that extends infinitely to the horizon. Figure 8.17 shows a rendering of the default scene.

You could just use the infinite plane and place your DAZ characters on it, but it is not very interesting. Instead, let's build some scenery elements. First, we can add a terrain. Clicking the Terrain icon, the one that looks like a small mountain, will load a terrain object into the scene, as shown in Figure 8.18.

Figure 8.17 The infinite plane extends endlessly to the horizon.

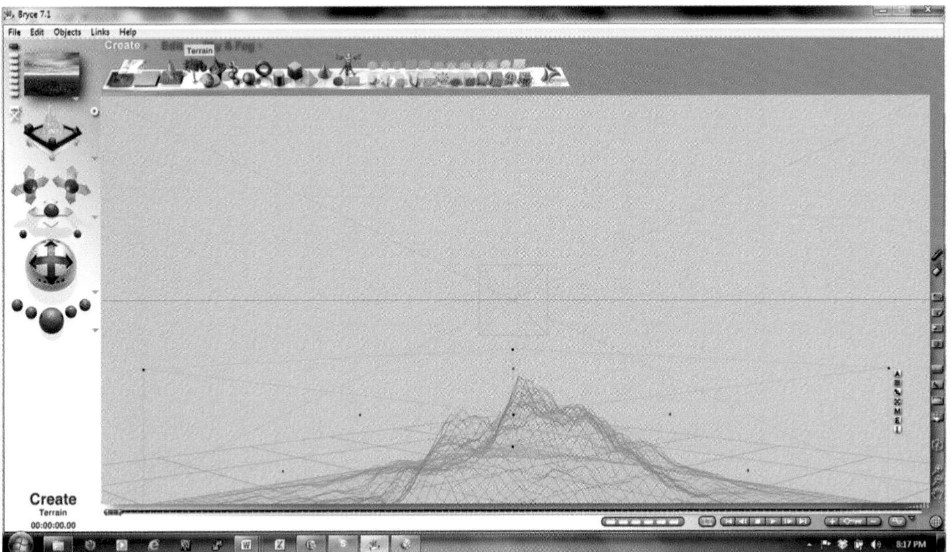

Figure 8.18
Add a terrain to the scene.

The terrain is a little small for what we want so we need to scale it up to take up more of the scene. Switch to the Edit toolbar by clicking Edit at the top of the interface. Use the Scale tool, second from the left, to enlarge the scene. Notice that the terrain scales from the center so some of it will appear to go below the infinite plane. Use the Translate tool, fourth from the left, to lift the enlarged terrain above the infinite plane. Figure 8.19 shows a rendering of the enlarged terrain in the scene.

As you can see, the new terrain looks like some rugged sandstone mountains. These mountains look cool but they are just the start. There are several possibilities for creating mountains.

Figure 8.19
The new terrain is rendered in the scene.

Editing the Terrain

Along the side of the terrain are a number of icons shown in Figure 8.20. These icons are used to bring up tools for editing your terrain.

Figure 8.20 Tools for modifying your terrain.

Select the E icon to edit your terrain. The screen will change to the Terrain Editor. Figure 8.21 shows the edit options for changing the terrain.

Figure 8.21 There are a number of options for editing your terrain object.

Terrains in Bryce are created using a height map. The height map for this terrain is located in the upper-left corner. A height map is simply a black-and-white picture in which the value dark to light represents the height of the terrain. In the upper-right corner is a view of how your terrain looks from the side. Below the side view, along the right of the screen, are modifying options for changing the look of your terrain. Clicking on a button and dragging left or right on these options will add or subtract that option from your terrain. In the above figure, the overall height of the terrain was eroded and lowered. Figure 8.22 shows the new rendered terrain.

Figure 8.22
The new terrain looks more natural.

Changing the Texture

Next, we will change the terrain's texture to give it a more tropical look. Select the M icon to bring up the Materials Lab, as shown in Figure 8.23.

The Materials Lab has a number of controls for letting the artist create an infinite variety of materials for use in Bryce objects. There is also a large number of pre-made materials that you can use in your scenes. Rather than covering how to use the Material Editor, we will just use a pre-made material.

On the left-hand side of the editor is a small window that shows a preview render of the material on the terrain. If you are using Bryce and it doesn't show a terrain view, you can change the view to terrain by clicking the triangle just below the window and selecting Current Selection from the pull-down menu.

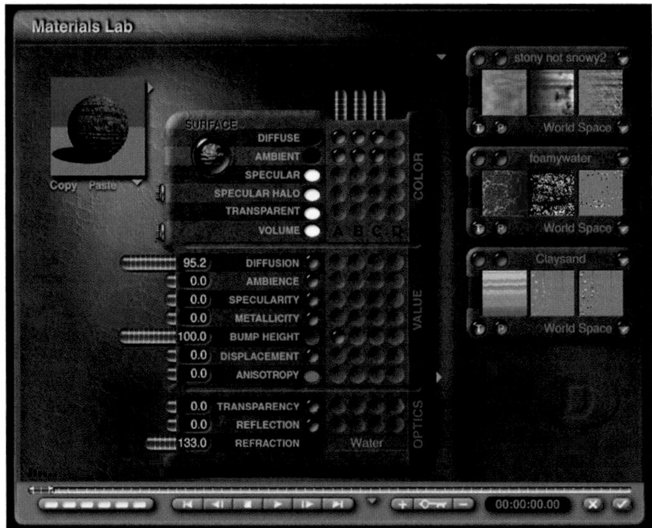

Figure 8.23
The Materials Lab is used for changing textures on terrains and other objects in Bryce.

The triangle to the right of the Preview Render window will bring up the Material Selection window shown in Figure 8.24.

The first material selection will be architectural, as shown in the figure. Select Terrain from the drop-down menu accessed by clicking the triangle in the lower-right corner of the window next to the word Architectural.

There are five categories of terrain types listed below the preview render: HeightMap, Plains, Rocky, Snowy, and Vegetation. Choose Vegetation. You should now have a selection set that looks like the one shown in Figure 8.25.

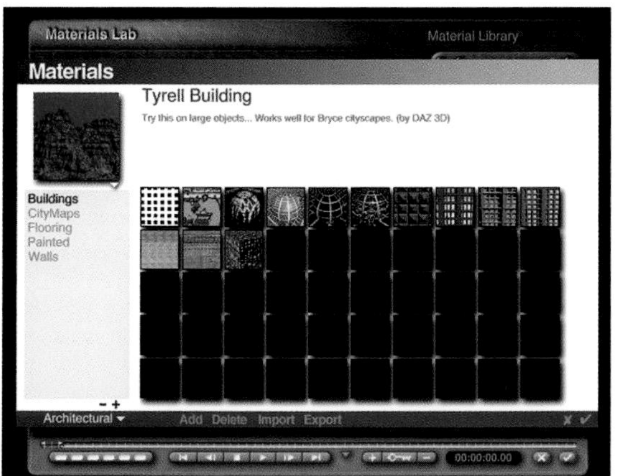

Figure 8.24 Bring up the Material Selection window.

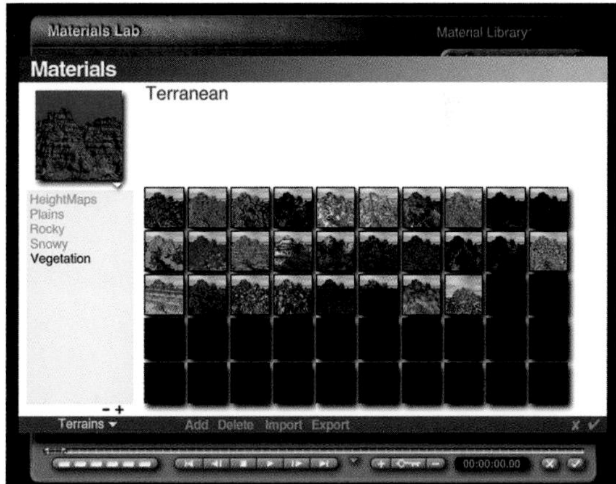

Figure 8.25 Choose the Vegetation terrain set.

You can preview each terrain in the preview window. For this scene Heavy Foliage was selected. Figure 8.26 shows the new texture rendered in the scene.

The scene is starting to look more like what we want. You can see how much difference just a few adjustments in shape and texture can make. Now add some water to the scene to make it look like a tropical island. From the Create menu, select and add a water plane. Figure 8.27 shows the render.

There are many more things you could do with this scene, like adding rocks, trees, buildings, and things but we are limited on space in this book. What we do want to go over is how to bring a DAZ Studio model into Bryce. Figure 8.28 shows a posed dragon model in DAZ Studio that we will be importing into Bryce.

In DAZ Studio, go to File>Export and change the export type to .obj format. The option screen shown in Figure 8.29 will appear. There are several options that you will need to change. Check all of the options in the left-hand column and select the bottom option in the right-hand column: Convert Maps for Bryce. In the top pull-down menu, select the Bryce option. This will export the DAZ Studio file into a format and scale needed for bringing a model into Bryce.

Figure 8.26
The new texture is added to the terrain.

Figure 8.27
The water makes a huge difference in the scene.

Figure 8.28
This model of a dragon will input into our Bryce scene.

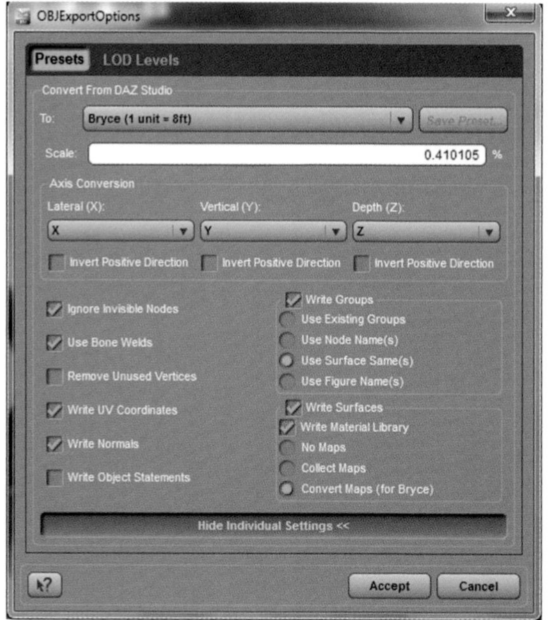

Figure 8.29
Make sure the Convert Maps (for Bryce) option is checked.

Back in Bryce, import the DAZ Studio file using the Import function in the File menu. The dragon will appear in the scene, as shown in Figure 8.30.

The dragon is now a Bryce object and you can use the Edit menu to scale, rotate, and move it around the scene.

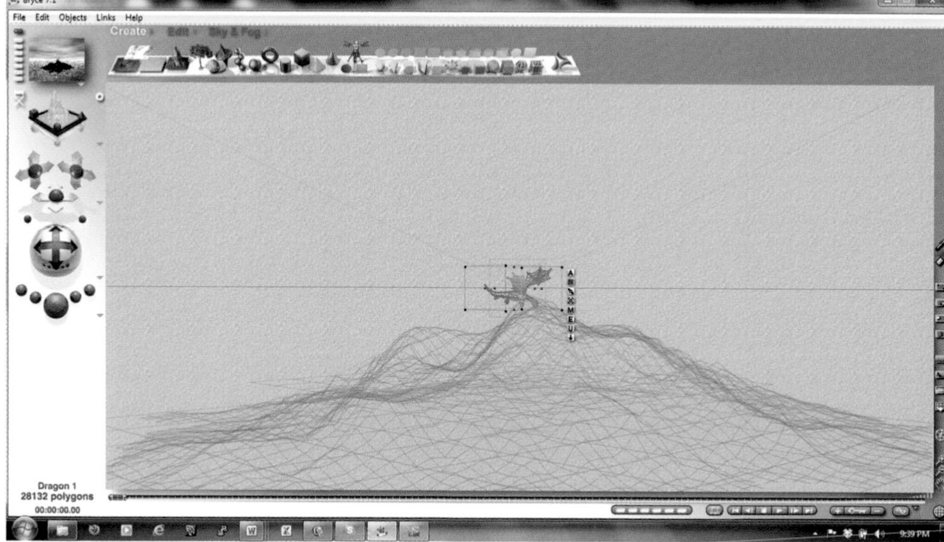

Figure 8.30
Import the dragon model into the Bryce scene.

> **Note**
>
> Objects in Bryce do not have the bone system and Morph systems that are present in DAZ Studios. The model should be posed prior to exporting. Use DAZ as your posing tool and Bryce as your stage.

In Figure 8.31, the dragon has been moved closer to the camera and rotated to face us.

Figure 8.31
The dragon is coming at us.

Now let's change the lighting in the scene. Open the Sky Lab by clicking on the cloud icon in the Sky & Fog toolbar. This brings up the Sky Lab as shown in Figure 8.32.

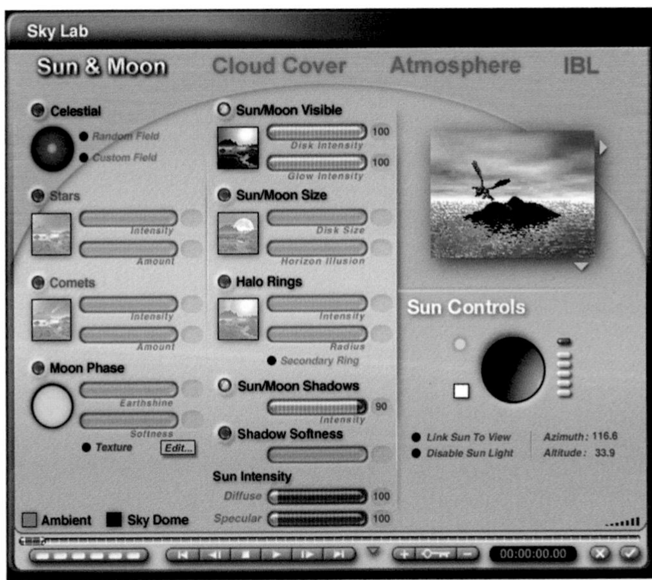

Figure 8.32
Open the Sky Lab.

The Sky Lab gives the user a number of options for lighting and atmospheric effects. Change the position of the sun and add some haze to the scene in the Atmosphere tab. Figure 8.33 shows the scene rendered with the Haze.

Figure 8.33 The scene now has some background fog.

We've only lightly touched on some of the creative possibilities available in Bryce. There are many parts of the program that we weren't able to cover. However, I am sure you can see its usefulness in creating backgrounds for your art.

Summary

To build a full scene for your characters in DAZ Studio, props and environments are essential. In this chapter, we covered different types of props and how to attach them to your characters. We also covered backdrops and environments showing how each is used in DAZ Studio. In the last section, we covered a different program called Bryce that allows the artist to create his own unique environments.

Hopefully you were able to glimpse the great variety and creative opportunities available for creating beautiful settings for your art.

In the next chapter, we will take a look at some advanced posing tools in DAZ Studio.

9

Lighting

Lighting is one of the most important things to consider when setting up a scene for a picture or animation. In life as in virtual settings, we need light to see. Without it, everything would be black. Light is what defines our visual world.

This chapter covers lighting as it relates to creating pictures in DAZ Studio. To do this, we'll start with an overview of how light works in the real world. Having a clear understanding of light in life will help you to simulate it in your art. Then we'll learn how to add lights to your scenes in DAZ Studio.

Light in Life

One of the first things that you need to understand about light is that it travels in a straight path. As light leaves an emission source, it does so in a straight course until it strikes an object. When hitting an object, light will reflect from the object in a direct angle from where it struck and continue its course until striking another object, as shown in Figure 9.1. It is important to understand this nature of light because much of what we see in life is the result of reflected light.

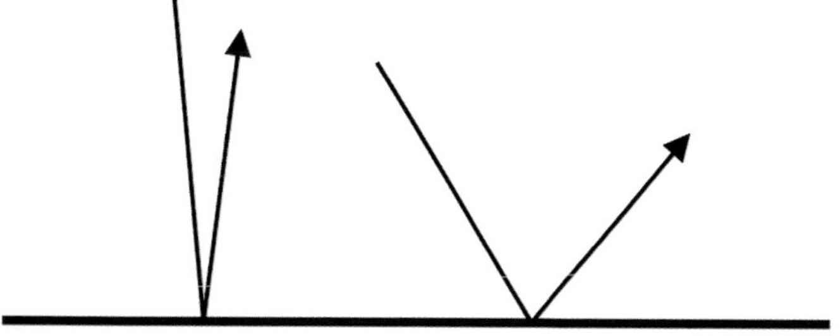

Figure 9.1
Light reflects from an object at a direct angle from where it hits an object.

Light and Shadow

When there is light, there is also shadow. A shadow is an area of diminished light caused by the object blocking some of the light from entering. The light and shadow of an object help show its shape and dimensions.

Let's take a look at how light defines a three-dimensional object. We will start with a simple shape, such as a sphere. Figure 9.2 shows a simple sphere shape.

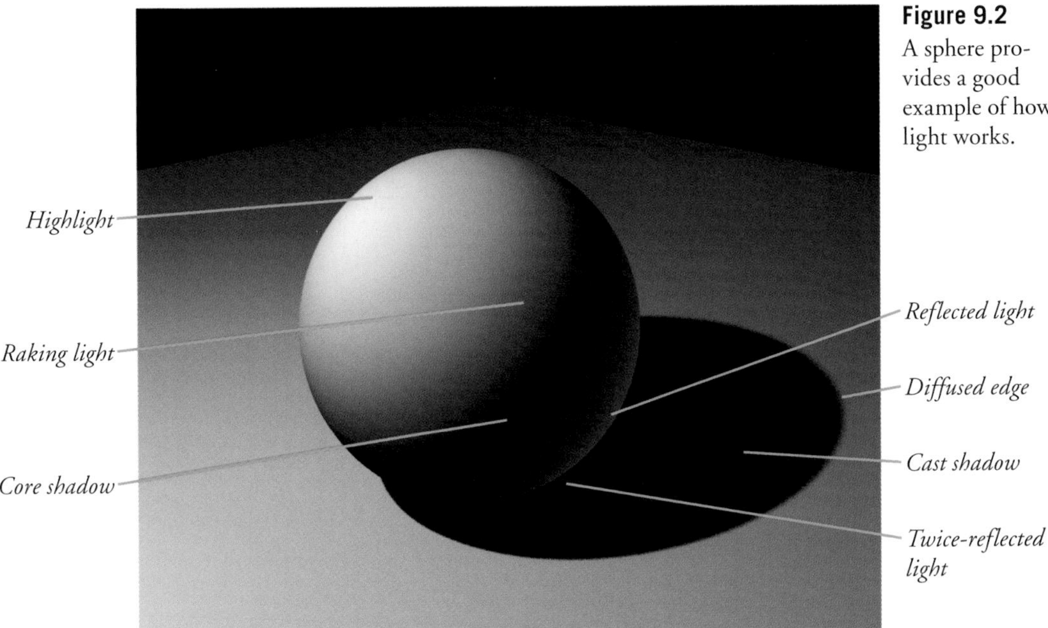

Figure 9.2
A sphere provides a good example of how light works.

Highlight

The *highlight* of an object is the area that directly reflects light from the light source to the viewer's eyes. The highlight is located on the brightest area of the ball, as shown in Figure 9.2. The highlight area is at a direct reflection angle from the light source.

Raking Light

The area that surrounds the highlight where the light is not as directly reflected is called *raking light*. The name comes from the way the light skims across the surface and hits it at an angle. This area extends outward from the highlight and gradually gets darker because the surface of the object is turning away from the light.

Light Area

The area that contains the highlight and the raking light is the *light area* of an object. Most objects can be defined as having a light area and a shadow area. Because the light area receives the most light, most of the detail in a picture is in this area.

Shadow Area

As the surface of the ball turns away from the light source, it no longer receives light directly from the light source. The area that does not receive direct light from the light source is called the *shadow area*. The shadow area generally receives the least amount of detail in a picture because there is less light to define this area.

In situations where there is only one light shining on an object, such as a ball, roughly half of the ball will be in the shadow area and half will be in the light area.

Core Shadow

There is a band of shadow that separates the raking light from the shadow area of the ball. This shadow is called the *core shadow*. The core shadow runs along the edge of the object that is directly past the influence of the light. It is a very important shadow for the artist because the core shadow, more than any other shading, defines the form. The core shadow is the darkest shadow on the ball because it receives the least amount of light.

Reflected Light

The shadow area does not receive direct light from the light source, but it does receive indirect light. Indirect light is reflected from other surfaces onto the ball. In Figure 9.2, the light that hits the table and reflects back to us also reflects back toward the ball. The reflected light gives definition to the shadow area of a picture.

Cast Shadow

Because the ball interrupts some of the light traveling from the light source to the table, there is an area of shadow on the table. This area of shadow is called the *cast shadow*.

Cast shadows are not just flat shadows. They have unique characteristics that an artist must understand to make them look correct. As the shadow becomes more distant from the object, the edge becomes less distinct. This happens because there is more chance for reflected light to reach the shadow area. The shadow has a diffused edge.

There is also a slightly lighter area just beneath the ball. This area is the twice-reflected light area. The light that is reflected to the ball bounces off the ball and into the cast shadow area, giving that area a small amount of light. This is one reason why some cast shadows seem to be lighter near the middle.

Note

When setting up lighting in DAZ Studio, you need to make sure you are accounting for both the major light sources and also for reflected light. Most pictures with a single light source in DAZ studio will look unnatural. To get a more natural look, think about how light will be reflected on your scene and add a few subdued lights to simulate reflected light.

Multiple Lights

Many times, objects we see in life have more than one light source. This is particularly true of characters or objects that are in interior settings. A single room inside a building might have many lights illuminating a character or object from multiple angles. Each light will have an effect on how the character or object looks. This can often be confusing for the artist who has to track the direction of the lights to understand the angles of the lights. Figure 9.3 shows the ball with three lights. Notice the multiple cast shadows.

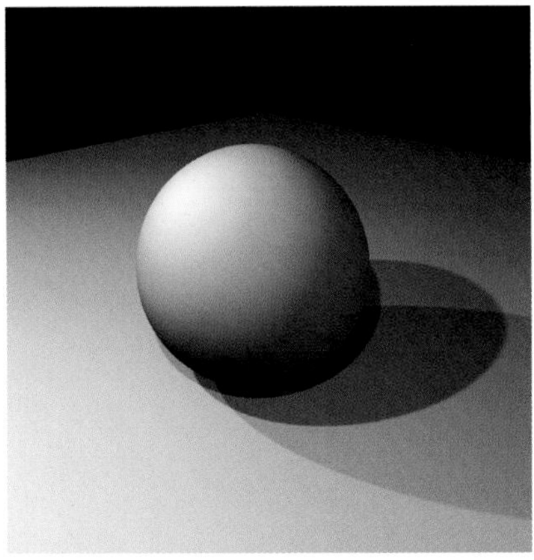

Figure 9.3
Cast shadows help to show the location of multiple light sources.

Light and Color

Each time a light strikes an object, only part of the light is reflected while some of it is absorbed into the object, thus diminishing the intensity and color of the light with each collision. The specific light reflected from an object is what determines the object's color. Let me explain how this works.

Light that is visible to our eyes varies in color based on a full range or spectrum, from red on one side to violet on the other, including all other colors in between. A good example of the full spectrum of color is a rainbow. White light is the purest form of light and contains all colors in the spectrum in equal measures. When white light strikes a red object, some of the light is absorbed into the object and is converted to energy, while the rest of the light is reflected from the object. The light that is reflected from a red object makes up the red portion of the spectrum. Thus, the red object becomes a red light source and we see the object as red.

A white object reflects white light and absorbs the least amount of energy, while a black object absorbs the most energy. That is why wearing a black shirt in the sun is so uncomfortable. The black absorbs the light from the sun, converting it into heat, while a white shirt reflects most of the sun's energy and is more comfortable.

Roughness in Textures

Every surface you see in real life has some degree of roughness. Some surfaces, such as glass or polished metal, have such a low degree of roughness that they can only be seen using a microscope. Other surfaces, such as a rock wall or gravel, have noticeable roughness. The rougher a surface is, the more it refracts light. *Refraction* is the scattering of light when it hits an uneven surface. Figure 9.4 illustrates how light is refracted from a rough surface.

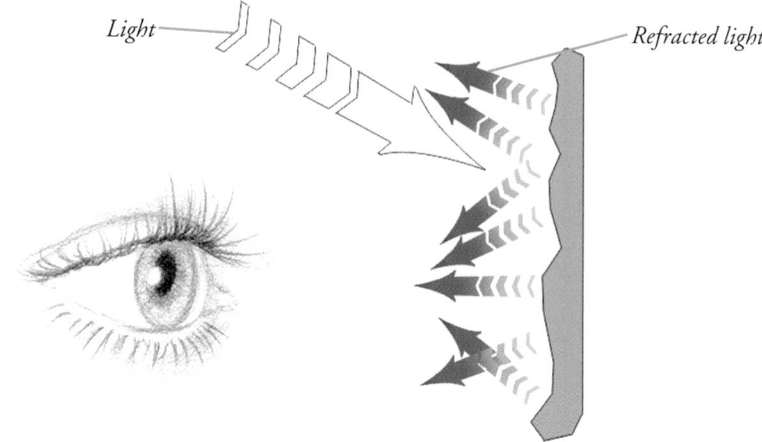

Figure 9.4 Refracted light bounces off an object in multiple directions.

Transparency in Textures

In nature, not all surfaces are opaque; some surfaces are transparent. A transparent surface allows some amount of light to pass through it, making it possible to see through the surface. For example, the glass of the car's windshield allows light to pass through it, as shown in Figure 9.5.

So what would happen to the lighting of the ball if it were transparent? Look at Figure 9.6. Notice how some of the light passes through the ball. This makes it so you can see both the front and back of the ball through the ball. It also makes it so you see the table on the other side of the ball, including the shadow of the ball. The highlight, core shadow, reflected light, and other aspects of light and shadow don't go away just because the object is transparent.

Figure 9.5 Light passes through the glass of the windshield.

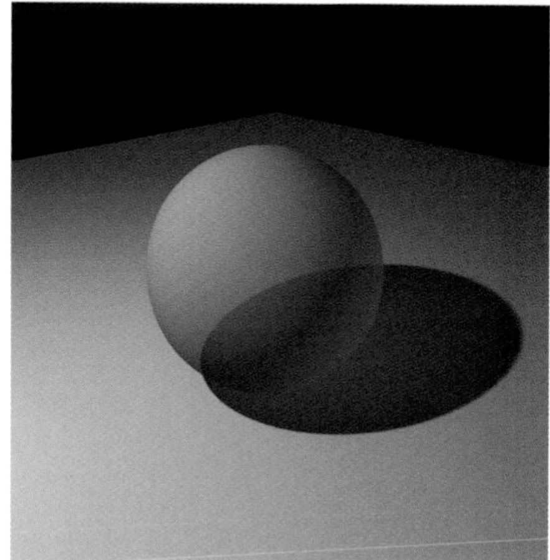

Figure 9.6 The ball is transparent, allowing us to see through the ball.

In DAZ Studio, you can control the transparency of an object in the Surfaces tab, as discussed in Chapter 5. The Surfaces tab also controls many other aspects of a surface, like reflectivity, roughness, and color.

Reflectivity in Textures

Reflectivity is related to roughness in textures. The more even and polished a surface is, the more it will tend to reflect light directly back to the viewer. A reflective surface acts like a mirror, reflecting its surroundings.

If you have reflection for higher than 0 in the Surfaces tab, your object will reflect its surroundings. The higher the strength, the more reflective your surface will be. Figure 9.7 shows the car with reflection strength set at 33%.

Figure 9.8 shows the same scene with reflection strength set at 100%. Notice how the car seems much shinier in this picture.

Figure 9.7 The car reflects its surroundings.

Figure 9.8 Higher reflections make the car seem shinier.

Setting Up Lights in DAZ Studio

When you first set up a scene in DAZ Studio, it will have the default lighting. Default lighting is designed for use in working with 3D models in a work environment and is not meant for the final lighting of a scene. For example, Figure 9.9 shows a scene rendered with the default lighting on the right and the same scene rendered with custom lighting on the left. Notice how flat everything looks with the default lighting.

Figure 9.9
Default lighting doesn't work well for rendering.

If you create and place your own lights in your scenes, you will be able to get the exact look you want for your art. Placing lights in DAZ Studio is easy and only takes a couple minutes, but it will make a big difference in your final render.

The tools for adding lights to your scene are located in the Lights tab, as shown in Figure 9.10.

DAZ Studio has three types of lights that you can add to your scene: spot lights, distance lights, and point lights.

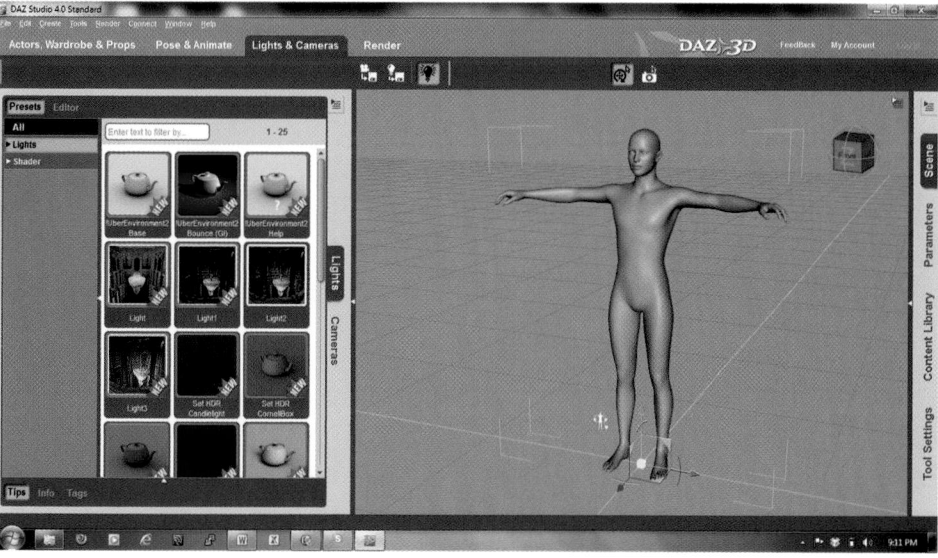

Figure 9.10
The Lights tab contains tools for adding lights to your scene.

Preset Lights

The Lights tab contains a number of preset lights. These lights give you a quick, easy way to add professional-looking lighting to your scenes in one easy step. Just find the lighting setup that you like and add it to your scene.

Custom Lights

In addition to the preset lights, you can create your own light in a scene. DAZ Studio has several types of lights that you can use. They are found in the Create menu. Simply select a light from the menu to add it to your scene.

Most scenes have multiple lights in them to get just the right lighting. This is because a single light in a scene will likely leave many areas in the dark. While lights in DAZ Studio behave much like lights in the real world, they do not have the same reflective qualities of real lights. This means that the artist has to compensate by adding lights to account for the reflective lighting found in nature.

Lighting a Scene

In this next section, you will learn how to light a scene with your own lighting setup. Let's start with the scene shown in Figure 9.9.

1. The first step to lighting a scene is to add a light. This is an outdoor street scene so use a distance light to simulate the light from the sun. Clicking on the New Distance Light from the menu will open up the Light dialog box shown in Figure 9.11.
2. Name the new light "sun" and then accept the default setting, which will place a new light source in the scene. The new light is also added to the Display Selection list, as shown in Figure 9.12.

Figure 9.11 Open the Create New Distant Light dialog box.

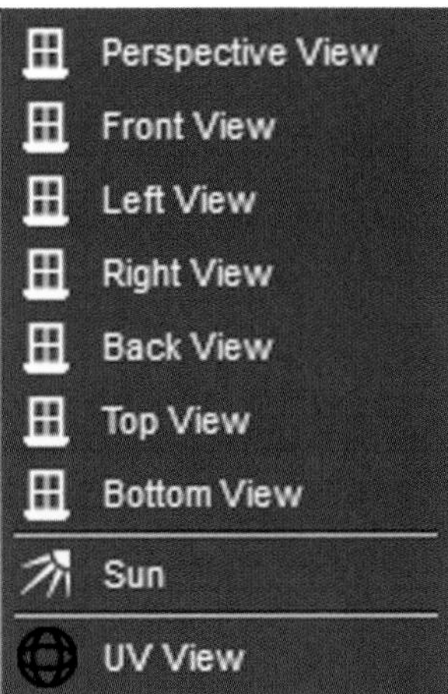

Figure 9.12 The new light is added to the Display Selection list.

This is so you can look through the light while positioning it in your scene. Select Sun from the list and now you can see the scene from the point of view of the new light, as shown in Figure 9.13.

3. Using the Camera Orbit tool, rotate the scene so the light is coming from above the scene, as shown in Figure 9.14.

Figure 9.13 The scene is viewed from the light source.

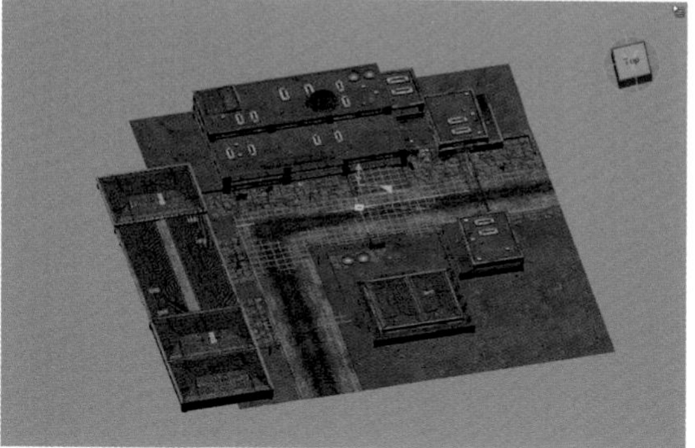

Figure 9.14 Rotate the scene to position the light in the direction you want.

4. Now, when you render the scene as shown in Figure 9.15, you'll have a strong light from above. The ground is now illuminated; however, the raking light causes the buildings to be very dark.

5. To get a more natural look, you'll need to simulate the reflected light in the scene. A good way to simulate reflected light is to add one or more lights to the scene. Add a second distant light to the scene and position it to shine from the bottom and to the side, illuminating the dark buildings as shown in Figure 9.16.

Figure 9.15 Using just one light will often cause part of a scene to be very dark.

Figure 9.16
A second light is placed in the scene.

6. In the new light's parameters, reduce the light's intensity, because reflected light is never as bright as direct light. Also, change the light color to a light blue, as shown in Figure 9.17.

Figure 9.17
Change the second light color to light blue.

7. Now, when you render the scene, the lighting on the buildings is much better, as shown in Figure 9.18. Something, however, is still missing. Notice that there are no cast shadows.

Figure 9.18
Now the buildings are more illuminated.

8. There should be cast shadows to make the scene look natural. DAZ Studio supports cast shadows using Shadow maps and Raytracing. *Raytracing* is a process where shadows are plotted based on the light's position and the shape of the object. It is a very time-consuming process; therefore, it is turned off by default in DAZ Studio. Shadow maps render faster but they are not as accurate as Raytracing. We only want the first light to cast shadows, so select it and turn Raytracing on, as shown in Figure 9.19.

Figure 9.19
Turn on Raytracing for the first light.

9. Set the Shadow Softness to 3.9% to soften the shadow edges to make them seem more natural, and increase the intensity to 150.
10. Sunlight is usually a little yellow so add some yellow to the light.
11. The finished scene is now rendered and shown in Figure 9.20.

Figure 9.20
The lighting for the scene is finished.

The above example is very simple, having just two lights, but the process works for an outdoor scene. Often, many lights will be added to a scene to get just the right feel.

Summary

Lighting is one of the most important and easiest ways to get your pictures in DAZ Studio to look great. Good lighting can make a virtual scene appear to be a real-life setting.

In this chapter, we covered a number of concepts about light, like how it reacts in nature and with objects. We also covered some ways that you can use the lights in DAZ Studio to simulate natural lighting. Setting up lights in a scene was covered, including the types of lights used in DAZ Studio and what they are generally used for.

10

Animation

Animation is the process of using a series of drawn or rendered pictures that successively show motion and displaying them to the viewer in rapid succession, giving the illusion of motion. When this happens, the slight differences between pictures give the illusion of movement. This process of showing pictures in rapid succession is the same method used in motion pictures, videos, and television. A motion picture camera does not record movement; it records a series of still images called frames. A *frame* is a single image in a series of images used in film, video, and animation.

In motion pictures and television, the frames are presented so quickly that the normal human eye does not register that they are individual frames. In motion pictures, the usual rate of pictures projected on the screen is 24 frames per second, although some will go as high as 70 frames per second. TV and video run at 30 frames per second.

3D Animation

3D animation creates individual frames from rendering a virtual scene similar to how live-action video is shot in the real world. 3D animation is kind of a blending of live action and animation techniques. The animator sets up the scene using animation-timing schedules, then shoots the animation as the 3D actors move about the stage.

DAZ Studio has a set of basic controls, called the Timeline, for the creation of animation. It has all of the basic features of a good animation tool and can create some fairly sophisticated animation once you understand how to use it.

Timeline

The Timeline tab is found on the bottom pull-up panel in the Pose & Animate tab. It is shown in Figure 10.1. There are two configurations of the Timeline. The one shown here is the advanced set of tools. You can switch between advanced and basic by using the small pull-down menu in the upper-right corner of the tool. To understand how it works, you first need to understand its basic parts.

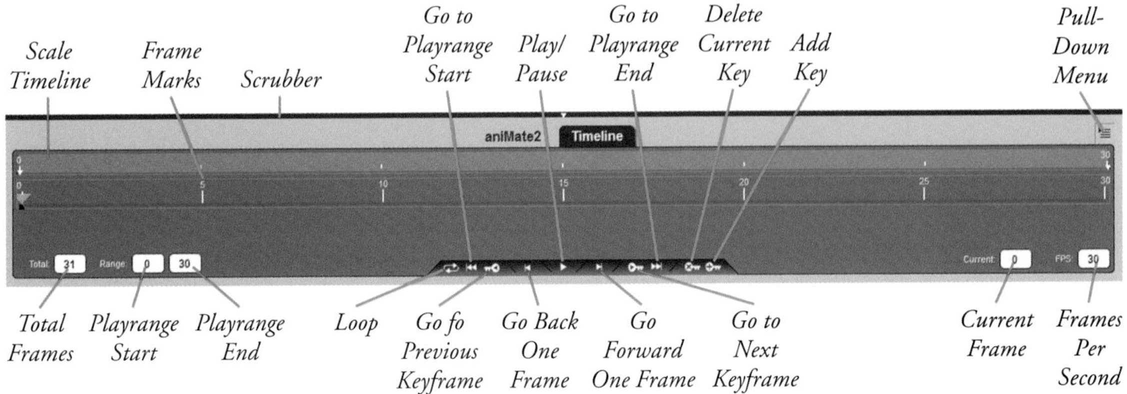

Figure 10.1 The Timeline tab contains DAZ Studio's basic animation tools.

The Timeline itself looks similar to a ruler with numbered tick marks along its length. The numbers represent frames. The frames are placed in order along the Timeline, from left to right, incrementing up as you move right along the line.

- Scale Timeline is used for zooming in and out of the Timeline.
- Scrubber is the small orange inverted triangle that moves along the Timeline. It is called a Scrubber because you can scrub it back and forth along the Timeline to find any frame you like.
- Total Frames is a counter that indicates how many total frames are in the playrange on the Timeline.
- Current Range shows the range of frames currently displayed along the Timeline. The left box shows the frame number of the first frame and the right box shows the last frame.
- Current Frame is a counter that indicates the current frame displayed in the animation. It is also the current location of the Scrubber.
- Frames Per Second or FPS shows how fast the animation will play, indicating the number of frames shown each second.

Hint

The number of frames per second is very important to the animator. Beginning animators often make the mistake of keeping the difference in movement between frames even. They do not take into account that faster movements have greater differences between frames, while slower movements have fewer differences between frames. However, movement between frames should not be sporadic, causing the animation to have a jerky appearance. Differences in movement rates should be smooth.

- Loop On/Off toggles looping on and off. If looping is on once the animation finishes running the Timeline, it starts over again. If it is off, it just goes to the end of the Timeline and stops.
- Go to Playrange Start resets the current frame to the first frame of the current range.
- Go to Previous Keyframe moves the current frame back to the last keyframe.
- Go Back One Frame moves the current frame back one frame.
- Play/Pause plays and pauses the animation. The function changes from a triangle to a square. Click the triangle to play the animation; then click the square to stop the animation.
- Go Forward One Frame moves the current frame ahead one frame.
- Go to Next Keyframe moves the current frame to the next keyframe.
- Go to Playrange End moves the current frame to the end of the current range.
- Delete Current Key removes a keyframe from the current frame.
- Add Key adds a keyframe to the current frame.

Bouncing Ball

Now that you understand the different features of the Timeline tab, let's try a simple animation. In Figure 10.2, the beach scene and the volleyball have been loaded.

In this animation, the volleyball will bounce off of the sand and up in the air.

1. Start by moving the volleyball to the top left of the screen. Note that there is a black triangle just below the Scrubber. This means that a keyframe is set for the volleyball. DAZ Studio automatically sets keyframes when you move an object.
2. Now move the Scrubber to frame 10 along the Timeline. This is where we will place the next keyframe of the animation.

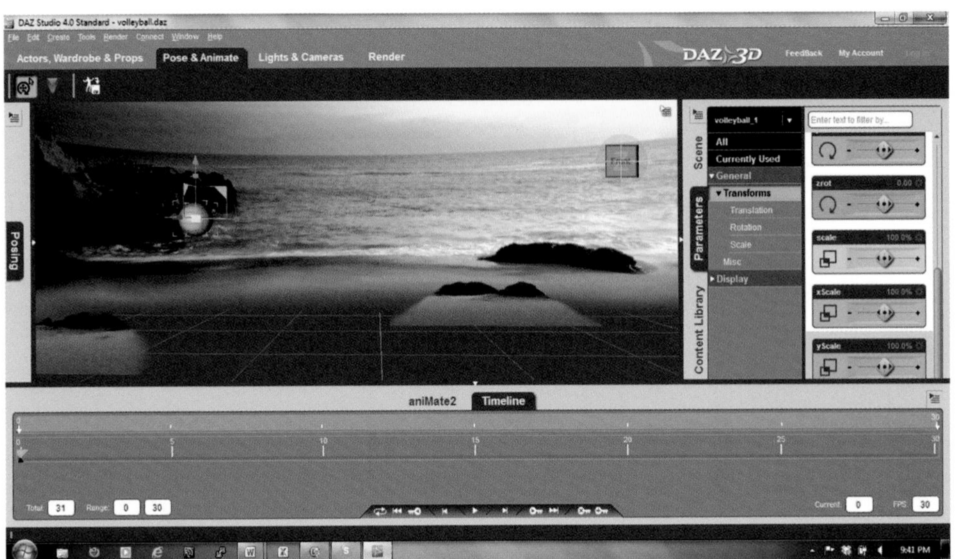

Figure 10.2
Load the beach and volleyball into the scene.

3. Move the volleyball to the center of the scene and down until it is touching the sand, as shown in Figure 10.3. A new keyframe will be created for the volleyball at frame ten.

   To get something to move, go to a different frame number and move the object to the new location. Then set a second keyframe and DAZ Studio records the scene data for the second keyframe. Now when you scrub between the two keyframes, the scene elements that are different will move frame by frame between the two

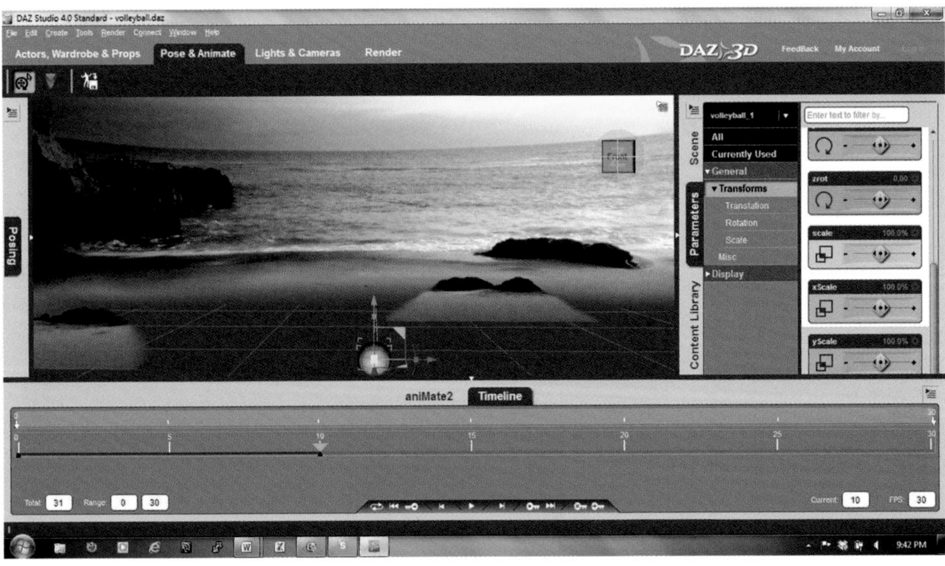

Figure 10.3
Move the volleyball to the bottom center of the scene.

positions. DAZ Studio automatically calculates the position of the moving object from one frame to the next.

4. Keyframes also apply to changes within an object, too. For example, as shown in Figure 10.4, we squashed the ball to make it look like it is hitting the sand.

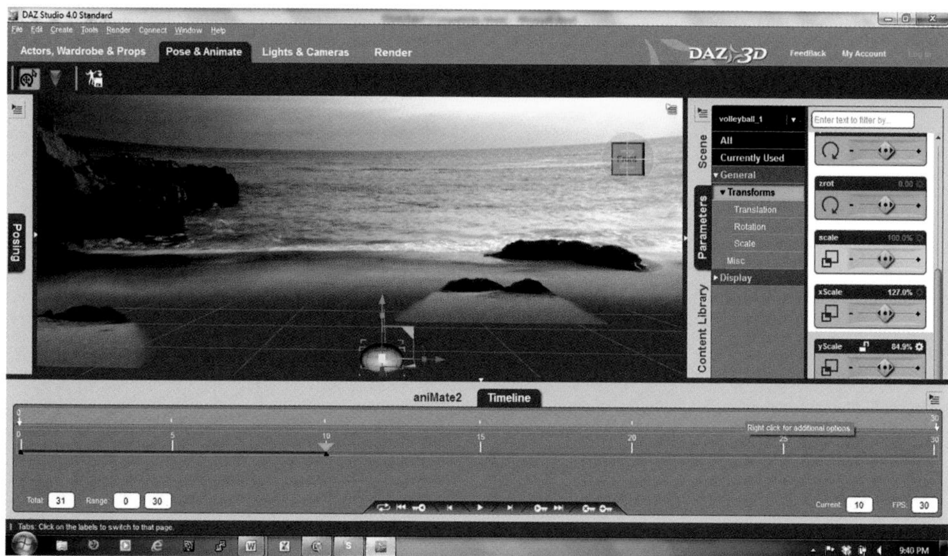

Figure 10.4
Move the volleyball to the beach.

To get the animation to look right, move the Scrubber back to the beginning frame and click the Add Key button. Clicking the Add Key button will record the ball's original round shape. Back at frame 10, give the ball a compressed look. The compression adds to the feeling of impact when the ball hits the ground. Using the Parameters tab, scale the X and Z of the ball up and the Y down to give the ball the compressed look. When the ball is exactly how you want it, add a second keyframe.

DAZ Studio automatically calculates the progression of the ball from the first keyframe to the next. If you move the Scrubber back and forth between the two keyframes, you will see the ball move and change shape.

Now the ball needs to bounce back up in the air. Move the Scrubber to frame 20 and then translate the ball up and to the right, as shown in Figure 10.5. Now, remove the compression so the ball is round again. When the ball is ready, the keyframe is set. Selecting play on the controls will now show the ball bounce.

When a keyframe is added, DAZ Studio records all of the scene information at that point. This includes not only the 3D objects in the scene but also any other objects like lights and cameras. The automatic keys set in the Timeline are only for those objects that have moved or changed. It is important to remember this aspect of keyframe animation. As a general rule, it is a good idea to set a keyframe at the start of your animation just so you lock all your scene objects in their beginning positions and shapes.

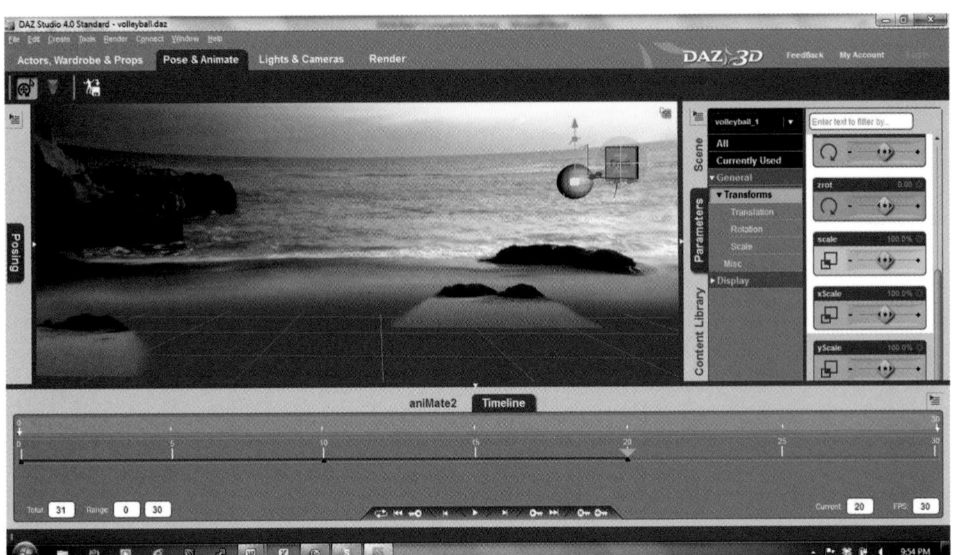

Figure 10.5
Move the ball up in the air.

Character Animation

We typically think of animation as characters moving about a scene. DAZ Studio handles character animation in the same way it does other animation. Keyframes capture character positions so all you really need to do to create a character animation is create a series of poses that you can capture as keyframes at different places along the Timeline.

Using the same systems used in posing a character, you can set up keyframes for your animation. If you think about it, keyframes are nothing more than a series of poses tied together with timing. DAZ Studio interprets the frames between each keyframe by adding in-between frames based on where you place the keyframes in the Timeline.

In Figure 10.6, Michael is loaded into the scene. Michael is standing with his hands in a fighting pose. This is a good pose for the beginning animation.

The next keyframe is an anticipation frame. To make a motion seem natural, it is usually a good idea to do a slight counter motion just before the larger motion. We want Michael to throw a hard punch with his right hand. In frame 1, have Michael twist just to his right, bring his left arm up a little, and lift his left leg as if he is just about to take a step. The movements are slight but important. Figure 10.7 shows the slight difference from Figure 10.6.

Next, plant Michael's left foot on frame 2, then create the next keyframe at frame 5 with the fully extended punch, as shown in Figure 10.8. A punch is a relatively quick action, taking just a fraction of a second, so we want to make sure it only covers a few frames.

Michael then moves from the fully extended punch to a recovery position, as shown in Figure 10.9 at frame 15.

While the total punch only took four frames, the recovery and return to the original pose takes 10 frames. The total punch animation took a total of 4 keyframes to complete. There could be more but generally fewer keyframes in an animation results in a less jerky animation. Keyframes should be set at the apex of a motion, meaning the farthest point of movement in any one direction.

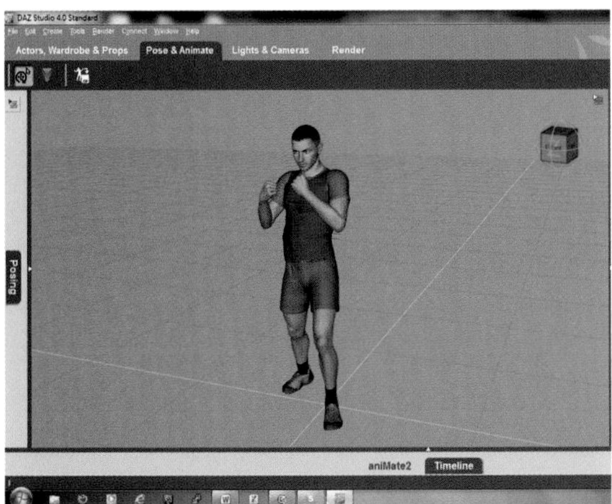

Figure 10.6 Michael stands in a fighting pose.

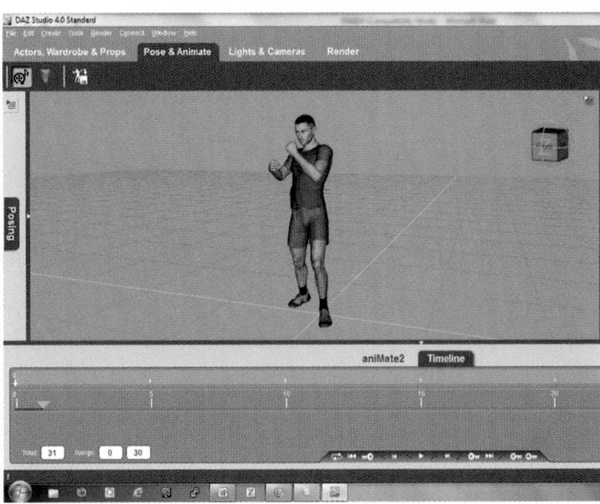

Figure 10.7 Frame one is an anticipation frame.

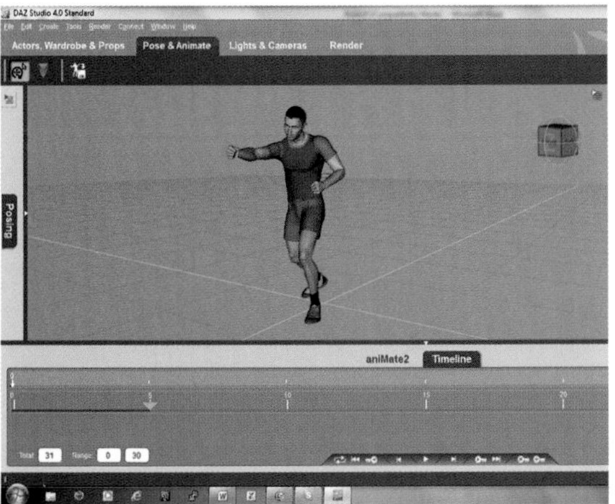

Figure 10.8 The punch is a fast movement.

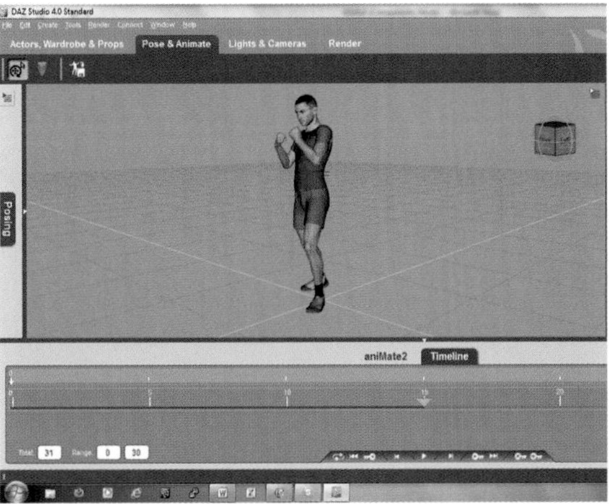

Figure 10.9 The next keyframe is the character's recovery from the punch motion.

aniMate 2

aniMate 2 is an animation plug-in that helps simplify the animation process in DAZ Studio. aniMate 2 and its aniBlock technology that stores animation sequences rather than just keyframes makes managing your animated sequences easy.

The heart of the aniMate 2 plug-in is the aniBlock. An *aniBlock* is a set of animation frames for your character that are packaged together in a single editable block. They can contain a single movement or a series of related movements. It lets the animator treat animations as a single unit as opposed to a series of keyframes.

The aniMate 2 controls are in the aniMate 2 tab shown in Figure 10.10.

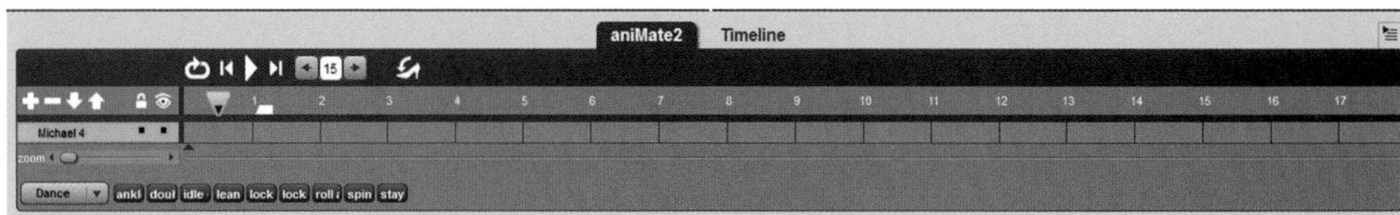

Figure 10.10 aniMate 2 can be viewed by selecting it from the tab.

- Your selected character will appear in the orange Selected Character box or you can also choose another potential character from the pull-down menu if you have multiple characters in the scene.
- The Timeline covers the central portion of aniMate 2. It is numbered in seconds not in frames. aniBlocks are placed on the Timeline to create animations.
- aniBlocks are animation sequences. They are located along the bottom of aniMate 2 in blue.
- aniBlocks are organized in the aniBlock library, which is located on the far left in a pull-down menu shown in Figure 10.11.
- aniBlocks from any library folder are placed in the Available aniBlocks area when that folder is chosen. Placing the cursor over an aniBlock will give a preview of the animation sequence. When you find an aniBlock you like, just drag it to the Timeline.

Using aniMate 2 is easy. All you need to do is select the model you want to animate, and then drag an aniBlock from the available aniBlocks area into the Timeline. aniMate automatically applies the animation to the character. Figure 10.12 shows the boxing animation loaded into the Timeline. Unfortunately, because this is a book, you can't see the animation, but take my word for it, it's cool.

aniMate will blend between aniBlocks automatically, so to add a second animation like a kick after the boxing animation, drag the kick aniBlock onto the Timeline, as shown in Figure 10.13.

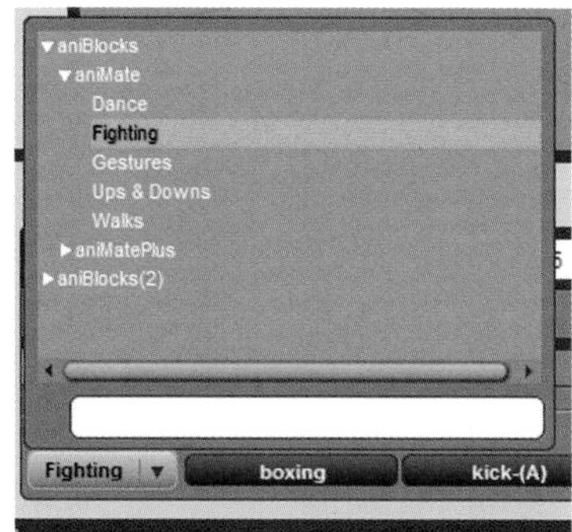

Figure 10.11 aniBlocks are stored in the aniBlock library.

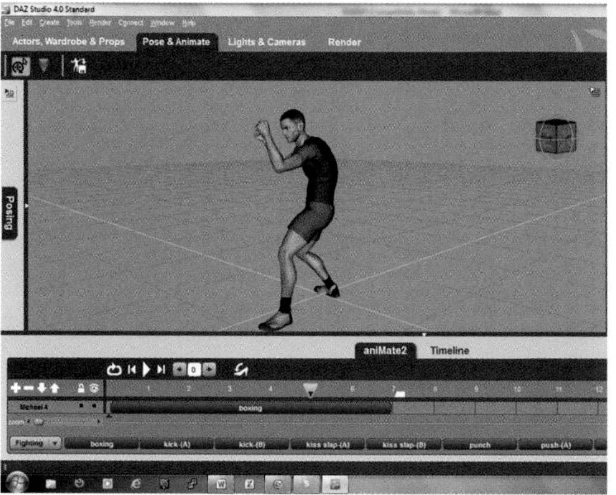

Figure 10.12 Drag aniBlocks onto the Timeline to add animation to your character.

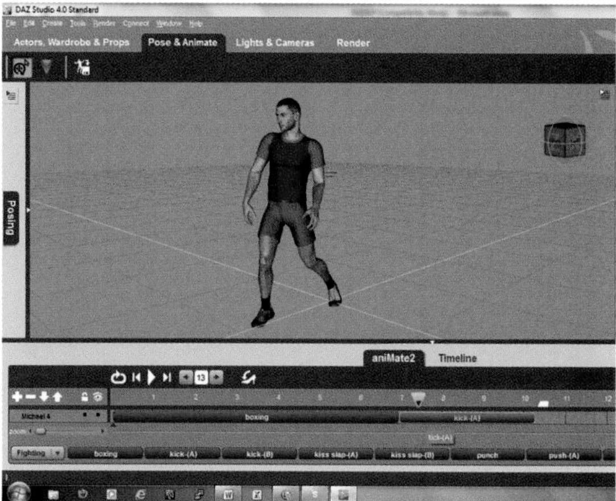

Figure 10.13 A second aniBlock is added to the animation.

If you want to adjust an aniBlock in the Timeline, simply click on the aniBlock to select it, as shown in Figure 10.14.

Once selected, you can change the length of an aniBlock by using the arrows on either side of the block. aniBlocks don't scale, so when you change the length what you are really doing is determining how long you want that animation to play. If you set the length to longer than the original animation, it will loop and start over again. If you set the length to shorter than the original animation, it will only play the animation to the point you set, then move on to the next aniBlock.

Figure 10.14 You can adjust aniBlocks in the Timeline.

The white triangle below the selected aniBlock on the Timeline is used for setting the blending length between aniBlocks. The default length will usually work well, but you can use the diamond to fine-tune your animation.

Summary

Animation in DAZ Studio is fun and easy. You can create simple object animation or complex character animation with just a few simple commands using the Timeline tool included in DAZ Studio. The Timeline lets you save poses as keyframes and then play them back as a completed animation.

For added animation fun, you can also use the aniMate plug-in. aniMate makes animation easy and fun with its aniBlock technology. aniBlocks store entire animation sequences as editable blocks.

11

Lip Sync

Animating a character often isn't complete unless you are able to make your character talk. Talking animation includes subtle movements of the head and the formation of facial mouth animations for the words the character is speaking. Usually a character will talk with a prerecorded audio track. Matching the audio track with the word animations of the character is called lip-syncing because you are synchronizing the motion of the lips with the audio. DAZ Studio comes with a plug-in, aptly titled Lip Sync, which makes the complex task of animating a talking character relatively easy. You can find the Lip Sync plug-in under Tabs in the Window menu. It is shown in Figure 11.1.

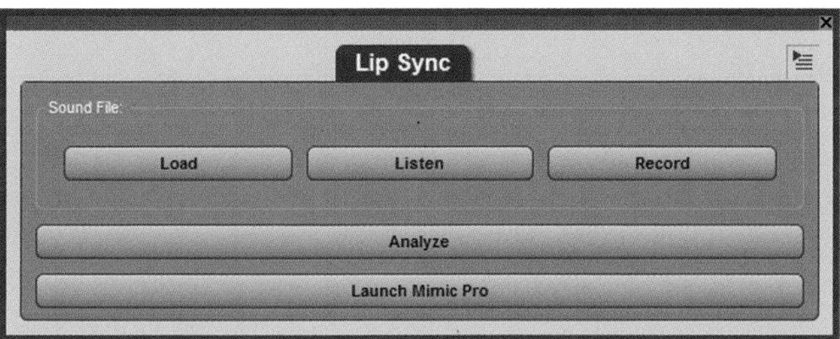

Figure 11.1 The Lip Sync plug-in.

The Lip Sync plug-in has several features. Following is a brief rundown of some of its features:

- **Load**—Click the Load button to load a new audio file. DAZ Studio supports .wav files for Windows and .aiff files for Mac.
- **Listen**—Click Listen to play the loaded audio file.

- **Record**—Click Record to record your own audio file. Click Stop when you are done recording.
- **Analyze**—Click Analyze to apply head and lip movement animation to your recorded audio file. Analyze is used for newly recorded audio.
- **Launch Mimic Pro**—Mimic Pro is a specialized lip-sync software package that automates many lip-sync functions. It will be covered later in this chapter.

We will get into how to use Lip Sync a little later. For now, let's talk about animating a talking character in general.

Animating a Phrase

In a typical lip-sync animation procedure, the animator will adjust the character's face and gestures to match the soundtrack. This is a painstaking process where facial movements and gestures have to be precisely timed to the audio. Often the animator has to move back and forth through the animation sequence to time each movement. If you have ever watched a movie where the audio is slightly ahead of or behind the video, you will understand how accurate you need to be with lip-sync animation. If it is off even just a little, it becomes almost comical.

There are two basic aspects of lip-sync animation: gestures and speech. When a person talks he rarely stands perfectly still. He will shift his stance, use hand motions, and move his head about. These small gestures can often communicate as much to the viewer as listening to what the person has to say.

Speech is the actual movement of the mouth as it makes the sounds of the dialogue. The shape of the mouth changes when we speak. Each sound has a distinct look that is recognizable. That is why people who have difficulty hearing can read lips and understand what people are saying even if they don't hear the sounds.

Gestures

Gestures are body animation, both large and small, that accompany the person's speech. They are similar to any other gesture animations, so we will not go into them in detail in this chapter. The important thing for you to remember is that once you have the facial animation matching the soundtrack, you also need to have your character perform gestures that also communicate the message. For example, if the character's speech is emotional, including gestures that convey the same emotions will help make the animation seem more natural.

> **Note**
>
> In the following example I will be using the Victoria 5 character from DAZ 3D. Victoria 5 is an add-on character that does not come with DAZ Studio 4, but is bought from the DAZ 3D store. The base Genesis model is just the beginning of what you can do with Genesis and other morph sets like Victoria can greatly expand your capabilities. Victoria 5 is the culmination of years of character development and is likely the most advanced character for Genesis at the time of this writing. Victoria has full lip-sync capabilities while other Genesis models do not.

Speech Animation

DAZ Studio provides several ways to create speech animation. Many DAZ models have built-in morphs called visemes that you can use to hand animate your characters or fine-tune animations created in the Lip Sync tool or Mimic Pro, if you have that application. Figure 11.2 shows Victoria 5 with the Lip Sync tool and Timeline up in the work area, and the Visemes morphs in the Parameters tab.

Lip Sync automates the speech animation process and gives you a way to create long animation sets without hand animating every animation change. While it is not perfect, and you will need to go through a touch-up pass over the animation, it does get pretty close to a final speech animation.

DAZ Studio makes lip-sync animation very easy. To load an audio file, just click the Load button, browse to the file you want, and load it. Alternately, you can record your own audio with the Record button. You will need a microphone with your computer

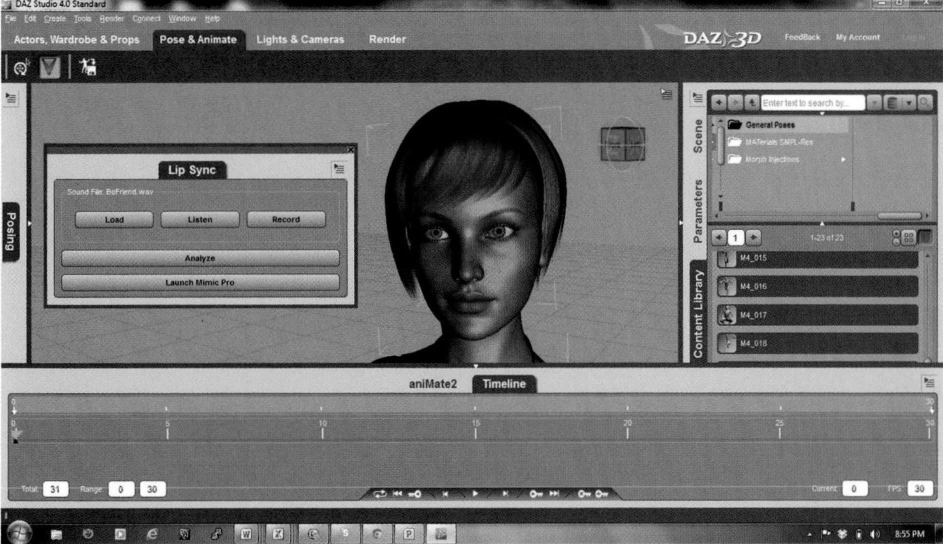

Figure 11.2 The Visemes morphs are in the Parameters tab for the character's head.

but if you have that, just click Record when you are ready to record and click it again when you are done.

When you have an audio file loaded into Lip Sync, you can analyze the file by clicking the Analyze button. Analyze will go through the audio file and apply specific facial shapes to each sound creating a lip-sync animation. Figure 11.3 shows a rendering of Victoria talking using the Lip Sync tool.

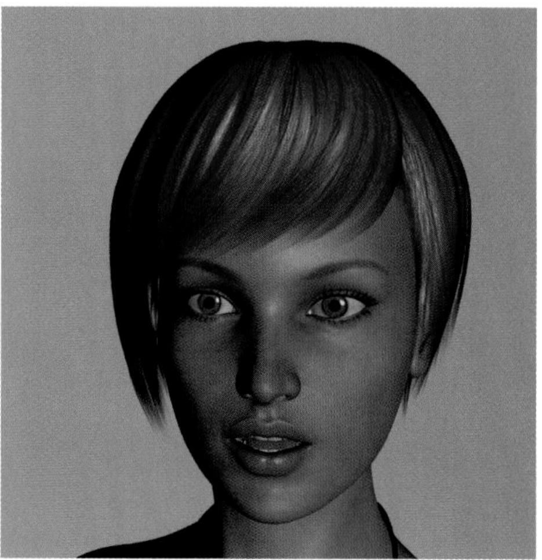

Figure 11.3 Victoria animating using Lip Sync.

If you want to animate the facial speech animation by hand, load the audio track into the Lip Sync tool and analyze it as normal. From there you can position the play head exactly where you want it and use the Viseme Morph sliders to change the facial animation and adjust the facial animation to exactly what you want. You will see the keyframes that are set in the Timeline. Just move the slider along the keyframes to the ones you want to adjust. You will notice that with every keyframe the Viseme sliders will change morph settings as shown in Figure 11.4. You can change these at each keyframe to refine the animation. Figure 11.4 shows Victoria with an AA sound.

The visemes give you very fine control over how much change in expression you want for each sound. Some people hardly move their mouths at all when they talk, whereas others are very expressive. The ranges of motion are also useful for animating a whisper or a shout.

In addition to the visemes morphs, some DAZ models will come with a pre-made set of phonemes. Phonemes are facial animations that match specific phonetic syllables. Phonemes are treated as content and are loaded into the scene the same way a preset pose is loaded. Not all characters will have phonemes and those that do usually will have them as a separate item in the store. When looking for phonemes, make sure that they are designed for the model you are working with.

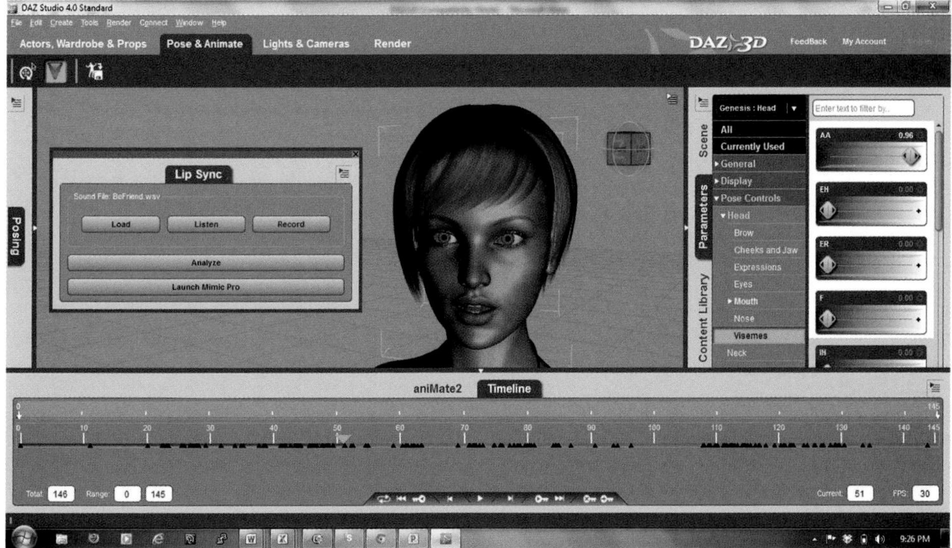

Figure 11.4 The Viseme morphs change with each keyframe.

The procedure for loading phonemes for speech animation is similar to using the Visemes morphs with the exception that instead of setting keyframes for Morph sliders, you set a keyframe where you load the phoneme. You can use the Visemes morphs to adjust the phoneme if you want, but be warned that the process is additive, meaning that you will need to zero out the visemes when you load a new phoneme.

Mimic Pro

Mimic Pro is a stand-alone program that you can use in conjunction with DAZ Studio that gives you complete control over lip-sync animation. It takes many of the features of Lip Sync and expands them. It also allows for fine editing of the phonemes, gestures, and other aspects of animating someone talking. With Mimic Pro you can have the program automatically animate the most complex voice tracks and then go in and fine-tune it with specialized tools that make animating the character's head easy and quick.

Mimic Pro works much the same as Lip Sync does using a sound file in conjunction with a text file; however, the text file is optional because Mimic Pro can work just from a sound file. Mimic Pro also has a feature where you can load a video file and then animate your character frame by frame using the video as a reference.

You can launch Mimic Pro within Lip Sync by clicking the Launch Mimic Pro button or you can open the program on its own. Let's take a quick look at how the program works. For the following example I'll be using the Victoria 4.2 character.

When you open Mimic Pro you will see the Session Manager window shown in Figure 11.5.

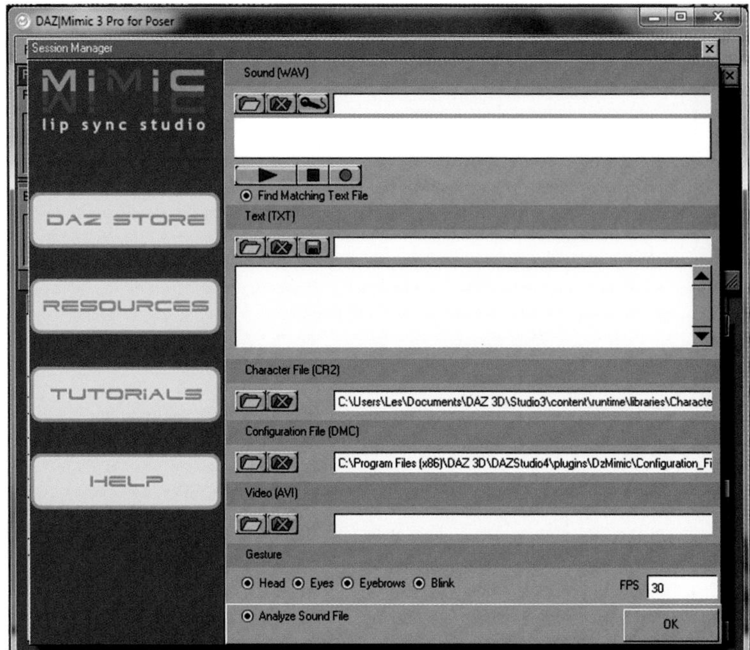

Figure 11.5
The Session Manager helps you set up your animation.

This tool allows you to set up your session by giving Mimic Pro the important information it needs to work properly. Like Lip Sync you can load a sound file, a text file, and a configuration file. The top section of the Session Manager is where you load or create your sound file. If you don't have a sound file, you can record one from the Session Manager by clicking the microphone and using your computer's mic system. The next section down is where you load or write your text file.

> **Tip**
>
> For Mimic Pro to use the text properly, it must be verbatim what is said in the audio file. For best results, write the words phonetically.

For this example, load a file from the standard library of audio and text files that comes with Mimic. See Figure 11.6.

The next section below the text file is where you tell Mimic Pro what character and configuration file you want to work with. If you've launched the program from DAZ Studio with a character selected, these two sections will already be filled in.

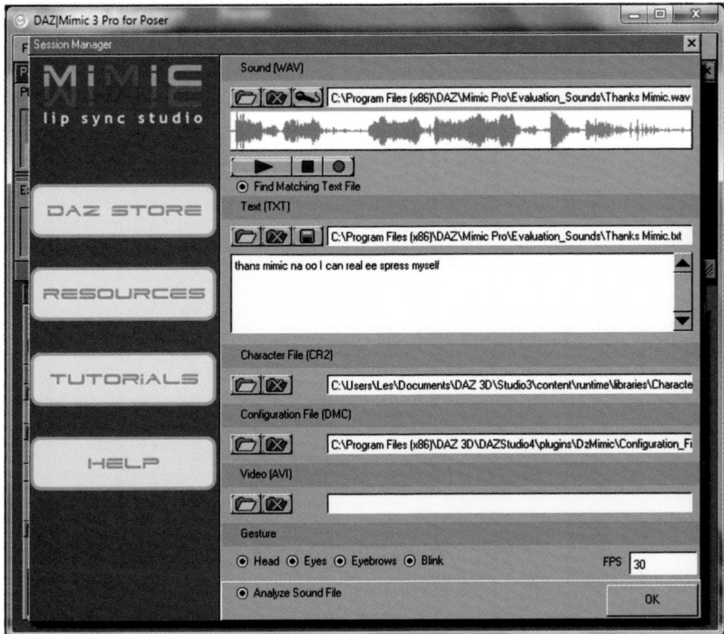

Figure 11.6 Load a file from the standard library.

> **Note**
>
> At the time of this writing the Genesis figure did not have a configuration file; therefore, I am not using that model for this demonstration.

If you have a video that you want to use as reference, you can load that under the configuration file area.

At the bottom of the Session Manager is the Gesture feature. Here you can tell Mimic Pro what gesture animations you want to include. Mimic Pro can automatically add gestures to your animation to make them look more lifelike. The items that are checked will be animated.

To the right of gestures, you can set the frame rate.

If Analyze Sound File is checked, Mimic Pro will analyze the file and automatically set up the animation.

It is a good idea to set up your animations in the Session Manager before you start, but if you forget something you can bring the Session Manager back up from the File menu. If you ever get stuck or need help, you can try going through a few of the tutorials; they can be launched by clicking the Tutorial button on the left panel.

The real power of Mimic Pro is in its editing tools. Once you are in Mimic Pro, you will be able to see your character in the Display window, as shown in Figure 11.7.

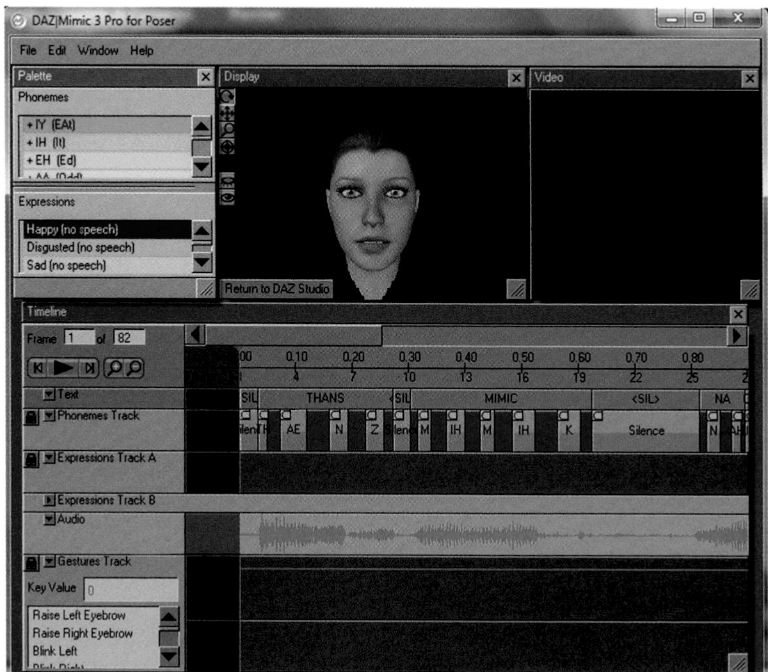

Figure 11.7
Mimic Pro has a number of great editing tools.

To the right of the Display window is the Video window. You can load video here and use it as reference for frame-by-frame comparisons. To the left of the Display window are the Phoneme and Expressions palettes. Here you can choose from a number of phonemes and expressions to add to your animation.

Below the Display window is the Timeline. You will notice that the Timeline in Mimic Pro has several sections. From top to bottom there are Frames, Text, Phonemes Track, Expressions Track A, Expressions Track B, Audio, and Gestures Track.

The Frames section measures the length of the animation in both time and frames. It also has playback, scrolling, and magnification tools to help make the process of animating easier.

The Text section contains the text of the speech in the audio file.

The Phonemes section is where you can edit the phonemes used in the animation. Here you can insert, delete, replace, and split phonemes from the Phoneme palette. You do this by selecting the area on the Phonemes Track you want to edit and then selecting the phoneme from the Phoneme palette and using the Edit menu to select the function you want to perform.

There are two Expressions Tracks. This allows you to have overlapping expressions or the blending of two expressions. You can edit the expressions in the same way as phonemes using the Expressions palette. Adding an expression is as simple as dragging one from the palette to the Expression Track and placing it were you want it.

The Audio section shows the wave file from the sound file. It is very useful in setting up precise animations.

The Gestures Track has a gesture list that you can use to add and modify the character's speaking gestures. This list is populated with the gestures you selected when you set them up in the Session Manager. Clicking any gesture on the list will bring up its Timeline. Deviation from 0 in the center of the Timeline indicates how much strength the gesture has. You can edit the strength of a gesture by moving points on the Timeline or by selecting a point and typing a value in the Key Strength window.

Click on the Play button to see how the character animates. You will notice that the animation looks a lot more natural than just using the Lip Sync tool in DAZ Studio.

As you can see, Mimic Pro has a number of great features for the serious lip-sync animator. Files from Mimic can be saved and imported into DAZ Studio. So if you have a character that you want to talk and you need the lip-sync to be accurate, Mimic Pro is the best tool for working alongside DAZ Studio.

Summary

Lip-sync animation is one of the most demanding and time-consuming animation tasks. To help artists streamline the process and automate lip-sync animation, DAZ Studio comes with a great plug-in called Lip Sync. Lip Sync can automatically add lip-sync animations and gestures to your characters based on audio and text files.

Mimic Pro is a stand-alone product from DAZ 3D that gives the animator an incredible suite of tools for creating complex and accurate lip-sync animation. With Mimic, the animator has almost unlimited control over a complex animation process.

With these two tools, DAZ 3D has taken a difficult and complex animation process and made it easy enough for anyone to use.

The next chapter deals with giving your characters greater emotion.

12

DAZ Studio 4 and Traditional Media

From this book, you can see that DAZ Studio is perfectly suited to the creation of beautiful art all on its own. However, for those of you who want a more traditional approach to art, it also works well as a source of reference for pictures. In fact, short of hiring models and setting up a scene in real life, DAZ Studio is probably one of the best sources of reference for any artist. The same features that make it such a great creative art program for characters and settings also make it the perfect source for artistic inspiration for traditional artists and illustrators.

Reference

Reference is very important to the serious artist. While drawing or painting from one's imagination may be a fun and creative experience, when it comes to depicting anything accurately in a work of art, having something to look at as a guide is a valuable aide. Most professional artists I know have extensive reference libraries. Not only do they like drawing and painting things, they also like looking at things. Artists work in a visual media. To understand how to draw something, we first have to understand what we are drawing. This understanding begins with observing.

Professional artists often spend as much time observing and collecting references as they do drawing. They do this for two main reasons: accuracy and inspiration. While artists may, with time and practice, gain mastery over a subject matter allowing for a decent depiction from their imagination, rarely will they be able to draw from imagination with the accuracy they could have if they had a reference to draw from. Often inspiration for an artist comes through closely observing something from nature.

A beginning artist will often hear the term *artistic vision*. But what exactly does artistic vision really mean? In a nutshell, artistic vision is the ability to convey in visual form something that is seen or imagined. That vision is usually an interpretation of the observed and imagined. Either way, the image is first seen in your mind before it is committed to paper or canvas. Therefore, the more you see and observe the more visual information the mind has to work with to express your vision.

DAZ Studio is a great reference tool for artists, whether beginner or master. The program is designed to let you explore creative possibilities rather than accept the limits of your own visualization or observation. With DAZ Studio's versatility in letting artists develop scenes, it also lets you experiment in ways that go well beyond what you might be able to witness in nature.

There is no substitute for observing nature in real life. Although programs like DAZ Studio go to great lengths to simulate nature with all its subtleties, no software program can include every variation found in the natural world. On the other hand, nature is limited in what it can show. Lighting, placement of objects, and even weather conditions may conflict with what you really want to portray. Artists who use DAZ Studio for reference for their work have a great advantage in that they can control every aspect of the scene allowing for a closer conformity to their own vision.

Figure Drawing

One of the greatest challenges you'll confront is drawing the human figure. Our bodies are infinitely complex yet intimately familiar, giving rise to a subject that is difficult to depict accurately yet judged incessantly.

The human figure is almost overwhelmingly complex to draw. The human figure is an organic structure that defies geometric simplification. It is composed of bones, muscles, and organs, all of which are covered by a flexible layer of skin. The body has many moving parts that make it almost impossible to define as a shape. Within its skeleton are more than 200 individual bones. Attached to the skeleton and throughout the body are more than 650 muscles. You can spend a lifetime trying to learn all the aspects of the human figure and still have more to learn. DAZ Studio can help in many ways because many of the models available for use in the program are very close to real human bodies. The artists at DAZ and many other contributing artists have gone to great lengths to create very accurate 3D models of the human form. Figure 12.1 shows a front and back view of a DAZ model. Notice how detailed the image is.

There is a big difference between drawing a stylized character on purpose and drawing a figure poorly. Because we are so familiar with our own bodies, small mistakes in construction or even in lighting will be noticed even by the casual observer. Even a stylized or cartoon figure will look bad if it isn't drawn well. Having a virtual model as reference can help to minimize mistakes.

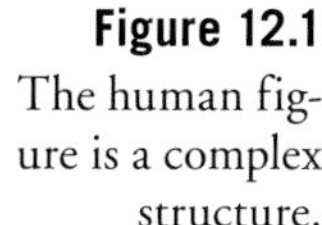

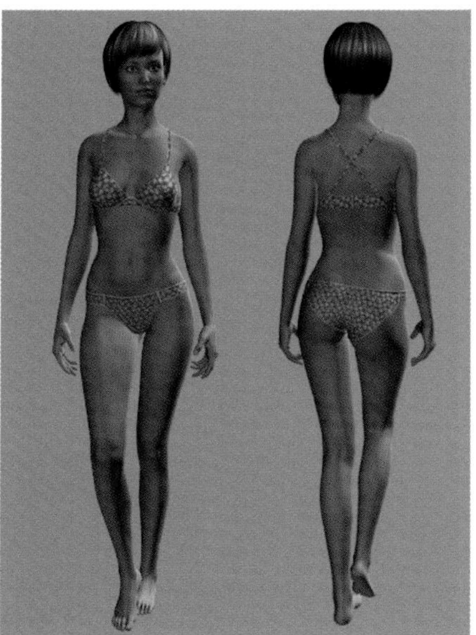

Figure 12.1
The human figure is a complex structure.

Although virtual models should not take the place of human models, they do add a valuable resource when real models are unavailable or the pose is unattainable. Often artists are faced with needing to draw a figure with no time, money, or availability of a model. Sometimes the pose needed for a drawing is something that can't be held by a model, such as requiring dynamic motion in sports or other extreme physical activity like that shown in Figure 12.2. In these situations, artists in the past had to rely on their own visualization abilities. Now, however, artists can set up models in DAZ Studio and use them as reference for their artwork.

Using DAZ Studio for Reference

DAZ Studio is a very flexible and useful tool for artistic reference; however, because of its nature as a virtual studio, care must be taken to make the reference as useful as possible. You must first determine the purpose for the reference. For example, if the only thing you need is structural information on a figure in a specific pose, a full-lighted rendering of the figure may not be needed. On the other hand, if you need lighting information, a full rendering with Raytracing will be important.

Structural Reference

Structural reference involves understanding how something is built but without an extensive amount of fine detail. Say, for example, you're working on a cartoon drawing and need to know how the arm looks in 3D space in a particular pose, like the one shown in Figure 12.3. Structural reference doesn't need a highly rendered scene with full light and shadows. In fact, shadows can often obscure important structural elements.

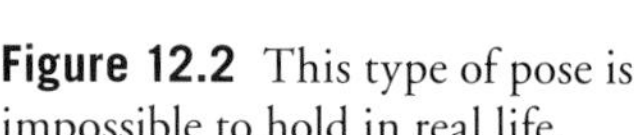

Figure 12.2 This type of pose is impossible to hold in real life.

Figure 12.3 Structural reference is more concerned with structure than lighting.

When an artist needs to understand proportions, perspective, and physical positions of the different parts of the body, structural reference is invaluable. For years artists used manikins or dolls to help them with structure. Now with highly detailed virtual models in a program like DAZ Studio, you can quickly and easily set up any pose and view it from any angle with a high degree of accuracy.

Detailed Reference

Detailed reference is having a reference as close to the finished picture as possible. With detailed reference, you use the lighting and texture information as well as the structural information to understand how to paint or draw the character or an entire setting. You'll want as much information as the reference can supply.

The creators of DAZ Studio put a significant amount of effort into creating a program that simulates the real world as closely as possible. Their rendering technology is one of the most advanced ever developed. Their characters and settings are as lifelike and detailed as possible. A lot of work went into creating scenes as true to life as if they were photographed from the real world.

For detailed reference, you will almost always need to render the scene with Raytracing turned on for at least one of the light sources in the scene. Raytracing is a complex process in which light is calculated for each pixel. It takes longer but is more accurate than other rendering methods. For example, look at the two renderings in Figure 12.4. The one on the right was rendered using no raytracing. The one on the left used raytracing from the main light.

Figure 12.4 Raytrace rendering produces a more lifelike reference image.

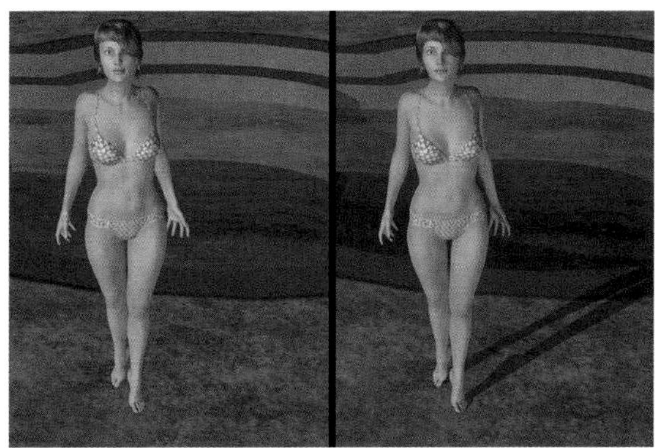

Figure 12.5 Lighting is important for any detailed reference.

Notice the difference in lighting in the renderings. The hair and nose have distinct cast shadows. The rendering on the right seems to have more depth and is more dimensional even though there is no difference between the two versions other than the rendering.

The raytraced images are more lifelike than other rendered images because they use a more advanced simulation of lighting. The problem with raytraced images is that they take a significant amount of time to render. The image on the left took less than a minute to render while the one on the right took more than 20 minutes to render.

Having good shadow information isn't just important within your character; it is also important within your scene. Notice in the two renders in Figure 12.5, the figure on the left seems to float above the ground and does not look anchored to the earth. The figure on the right looks like she is actually in the scene. The primary difference is the cast shadow created with the raytracing.

In addition to lighting, another important aspect of detailed reference is the texture information. The artists and designers at DAZ 3D have gone to great lengths to create as detailed textures as possible. To the point that even things like small skin blemishes, pores, and even single strands of hair are as close to reality as possible. Figure 12.6 shows a close-up of a character's face. Notice the incredible detail in the skin, hair, eyes, and around the mouth. This type of detail can be very useful as reference for an artist who needs realism in their work.

Much of the detail in DAZ models is in their textures. Textures for DAZ models are larger and contain more details and layers than most other 3D models. Some models have multiple high-resolution images as big as 4,000 pixels by 4,000 pixels, just for one part of the body. Textures for a character can reach as much as 70 megabytes of information. Not all models are that big, but some of the more advanced models are, and the number is going up all the time. DAZ is constantly trying to push the envelope for more and more realistic models for DAZ Studio.

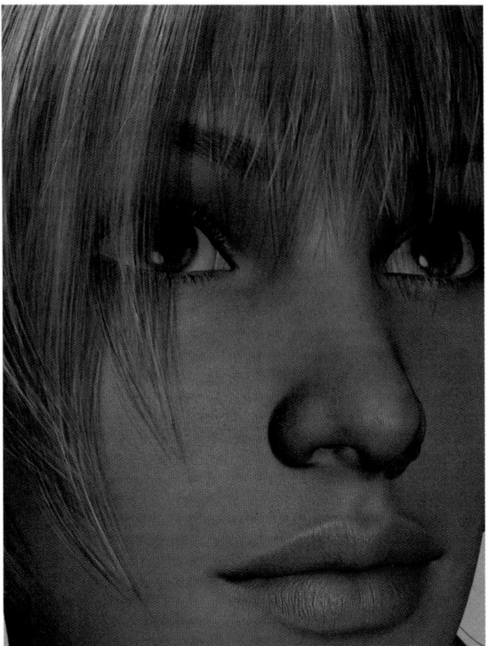

Figure 12.6
Close-up—you can see the detail in the DAZ models.

DAZ models also come with other maps that enhance detail in the models. These maps include bump maps that add surface detail like the pores on the skin and the wrinkles on the lips. Normal maps can give the same effect. Specular maps are also used for some parts of the models that are shinier than others, like the eyes. Transparency maps are used to make elements of the model transparent or see-through. In Figure 12.6 a transparency map is used on the hair.

The down side to large texture maps on models is that it creates very long rendering times. Rendering time may not be a big issue for single pictures, but it can become a real problem when developing and rendering an animation sequence where hundreds or thousands of frames need to be rendered. Basically, the greater detail and more realistic you want your picture to be, the longer it will likely take to be rendered.

Posing for Reference

One of the biggest challenges when using virtual models is to get them to look natural. This is true for both the artist whose finished product is rendered right out of DAZ Studio and for those who just use DAZ Studio for reference for their art. Whether you are using DAZ Studio for your finished art or just for reference, your work will suffer if you don't follow good practices for posing your figure.

If you have ever attended a life drawing class and worked with a live human model, you should be familiar with the term gesture drawing. A *gesture drawing* is a quick, sometimes 30-second, drawing of a model. Gesture drawings are used to reduce the model down to just a few simple lines. The reducing of a pose to just a few simple lines is an important concept for getting believable poses. The most important of these lines is the action line.

Action Lines

An *action line* is the main line of motion in a pose. It will usually follow the character's spine and one or both of the character's legs. Figure 12.7 shows the action line for a character pose.

In this pose, the action line is fairly easy to find because the legs are together and the spine is evenly arched. When the legs are separated and the curvature of the spine is more complex, the action line will work a little differently. The action line will still follow the curve of the spine, but it then follows what is known as the power leg. The power leg is the leg on the character that has the most dynamic flow of movement. Figure 12.8 shows a more complex action line.

Even in a more static pose like in Figure 12.9, there is still an action line.

The action line of the body is important because it defines the dynamic nature of your pose. The action line should flow through the limbs of the model. Sharp changes of direction should be avoided to keep your poses from looking robotic or stiff. Whenever you set up a pose for your art, draw the action line. Poses with well-defined action lines will seem more dynamic and more natural. They will have a consistent flow to the motion of the character and will have a stronger sense of cohesiveness.

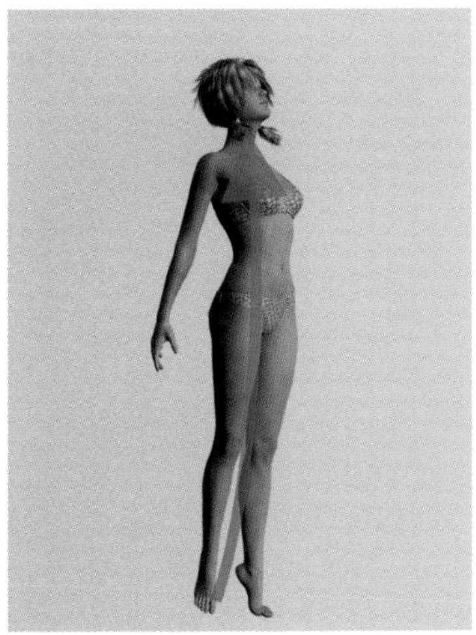

Figure 12.7 The action line follows the motion of the body.

Figure 12.8 The action line follows the power leg.

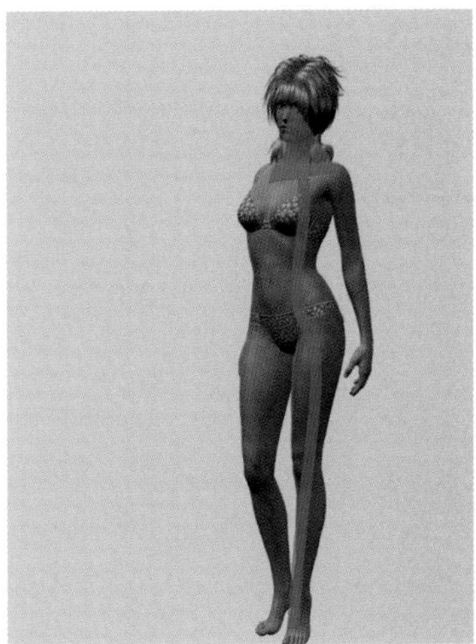

Figure 12.9 Even static poses have an action line.

Secondary Action

In addition to the main action line, there are also secondary action lines in most poses. Secondary lines are those that connect secondary dynamics with the primary motion of the body. Some of these lines are only slightly less important than the primary line. These lines are shown in red in Figure 12.10.

Like the main action line, secondary lines should have a flow to them. On a good pose, the lines will seem to fit together to give the body an overall feeling of dynamics.

Figure 12.10 Secondary action lines tie the motion of the body together.

Problem Poses

A book this size could never list every possible problem pose that you might encounter, but here are a few suggestions to help you avoid problems.

Static Torso

A common mistake of beginning artists is to move the arms and legs but leave the torso static. This creates an unnatural, almost robot look to the pose, as shown in Figure 12.11. The human torso is a dynamic system that is constantly in motion. The spine has tremendous potential for movement.

Too Much Symmetry

The pose in Figure 12.12 is an example of too much symmetry. The arms and legs are almost identical on both sides, giving the body an unnatural stiff look. In nature, we hardly ever stand in such a static position. Almost always, we will have one leg carrying most of our weight. Our arms are almost never exactly in the same pose.

90-Degree Angles

Like static torsos, arms that are at 90-degree angles give the pose a robotic look. Even with a dynamic active torso, the 90-degree angles of Figure 12.13 give the pose a stiff unnatural look.

Jerky Action Line

Action lines should flow and have a strong primary arc. Some swinging of the arc or blending between two arcs can work nicely but too many can make the pose seem unnatural, as shown in Figure 12.14.

These are just a few pointers for keeping your poses from looking unnatural. Combined with the principles about weight and balance found in Chapter 7, you should have a good foundation for creating great reference poses for your art.

Figure 12.11 Static torsos lead to robotic-like poses.

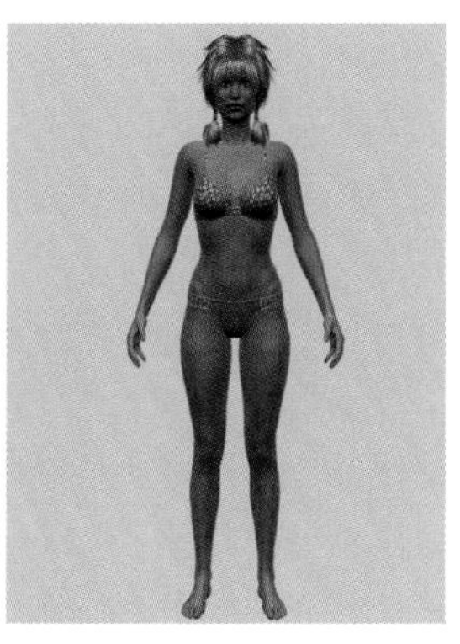

Figure 12.12 Symmetry can make a pose look unnatural.

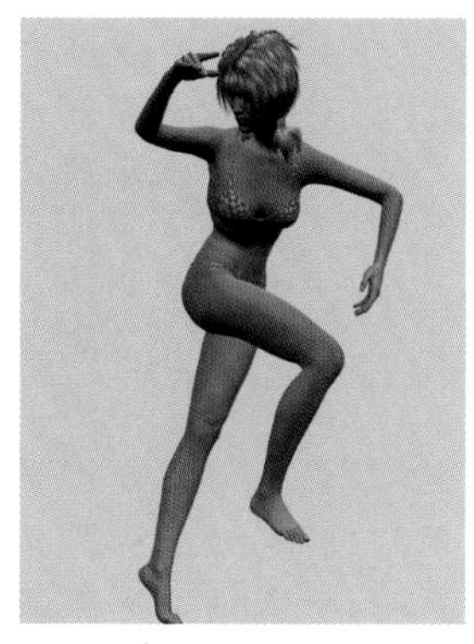

Figure 12.13 Stay away from 90-degree angles in the arms and legs.

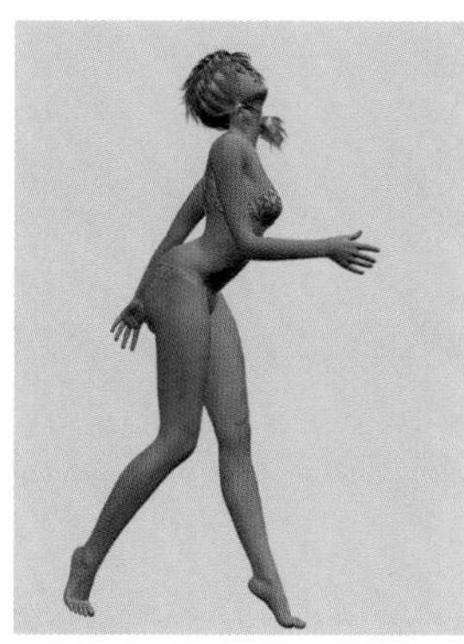

Figure 12.14 Keep the action simple.

Scene Reference

In addition to figure reference, DAZ Studio can also be a great help for setting up scenes or even landscapes without figures. A number of great sets and props can be used with DAZ Studio. Figures 12.15 through 12.18 show a few. You can find many more at www.daz3d.com.

Figure 12.15 DAZ 3D has beautiful tropical settings.

Figure 12.16 There are also winter settings.

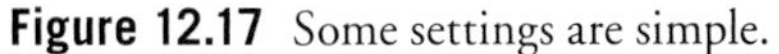
Figure 12.17 Some settings are simple.

Figure 12.18 Some settings are complex.

Summary

This chapter was primarily devoted to the artists who use DAZ Studio for reference in more traditional art media, like oil painting or figure drawing, with a little bit of help in posing to help avoid bad poses. There are also a number of settings for visualizing pictures available from DAZ 3D. DAZ Studio is a great source for reference and inspiration for the traditional artist. It creates a highly realistic scene, including lighting and characters, at the click of a mouse any time of day or night.

If you are reading the printed book, you will find two bonus chapters at www.courseptr.com/downloads. If you are reading the ebook, the bonus chapters follow.

Gallery

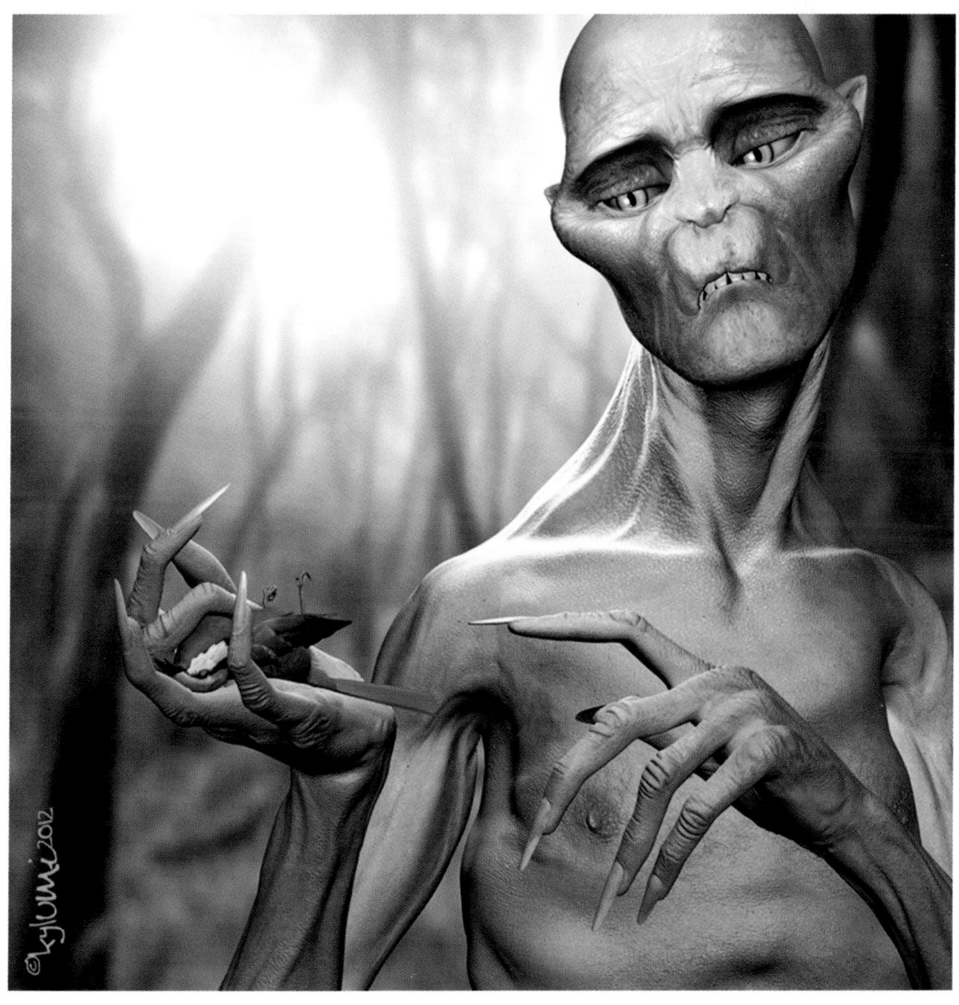

© Mike Smith

© Serhiy Maystrenko

© Paul Telesco

© Mike Smith

© Heather Douglas

© Wayne Martell

© Erik Wallace

© Lee "Maraich' Dunning

© Mike Smith

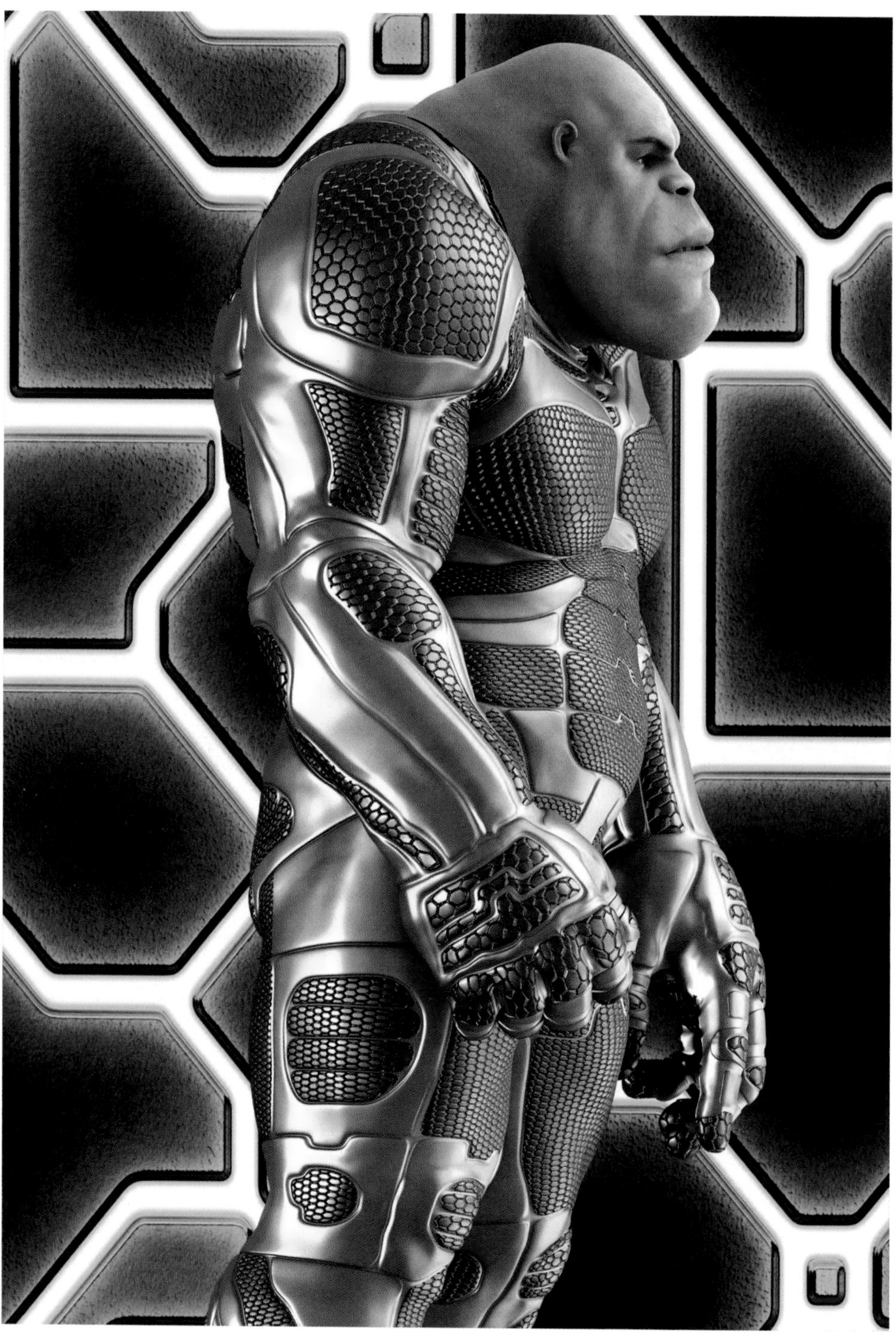

© Russ Terrell

© Ron Reisere

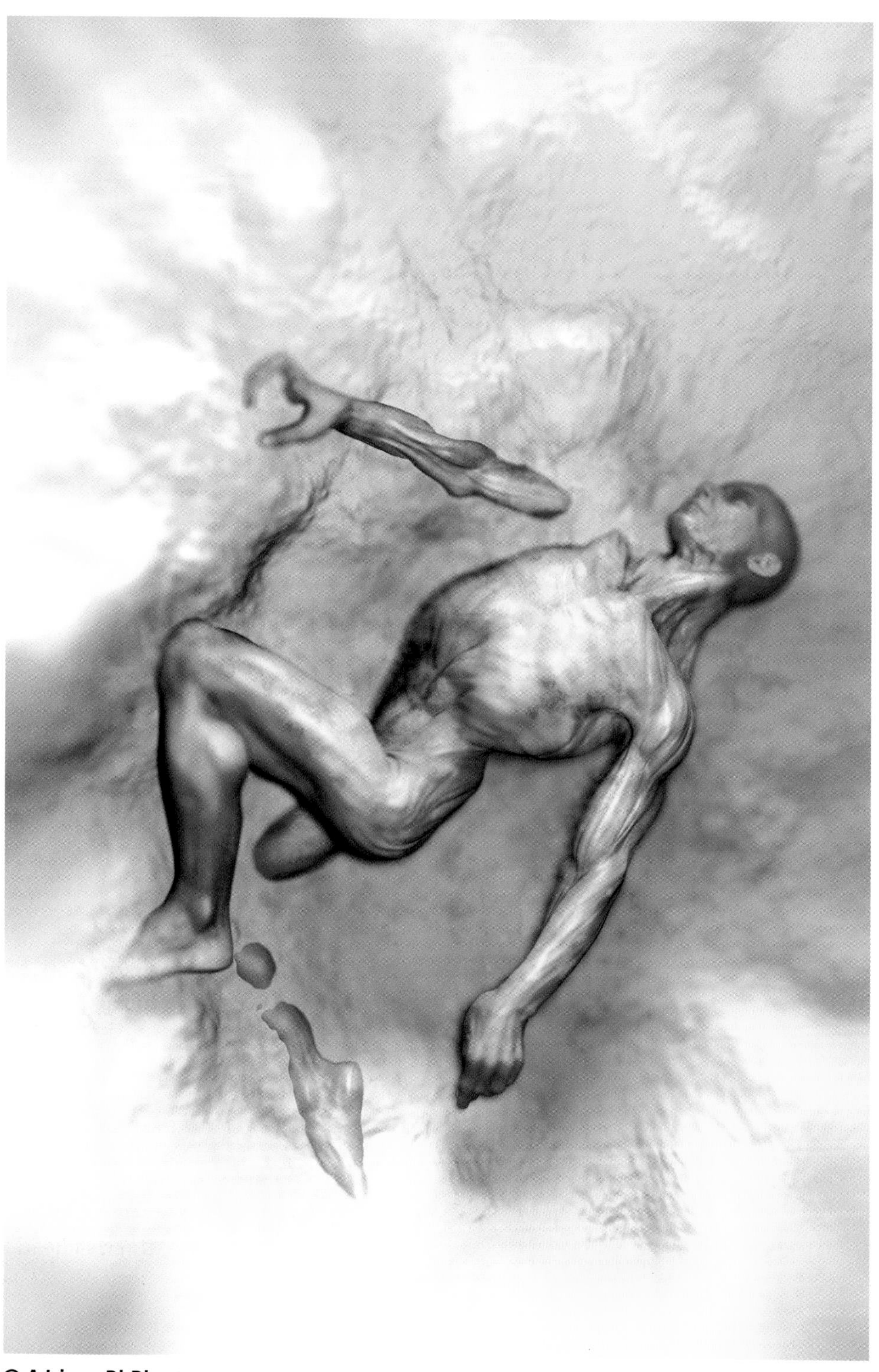

© Adriano Di Pierro

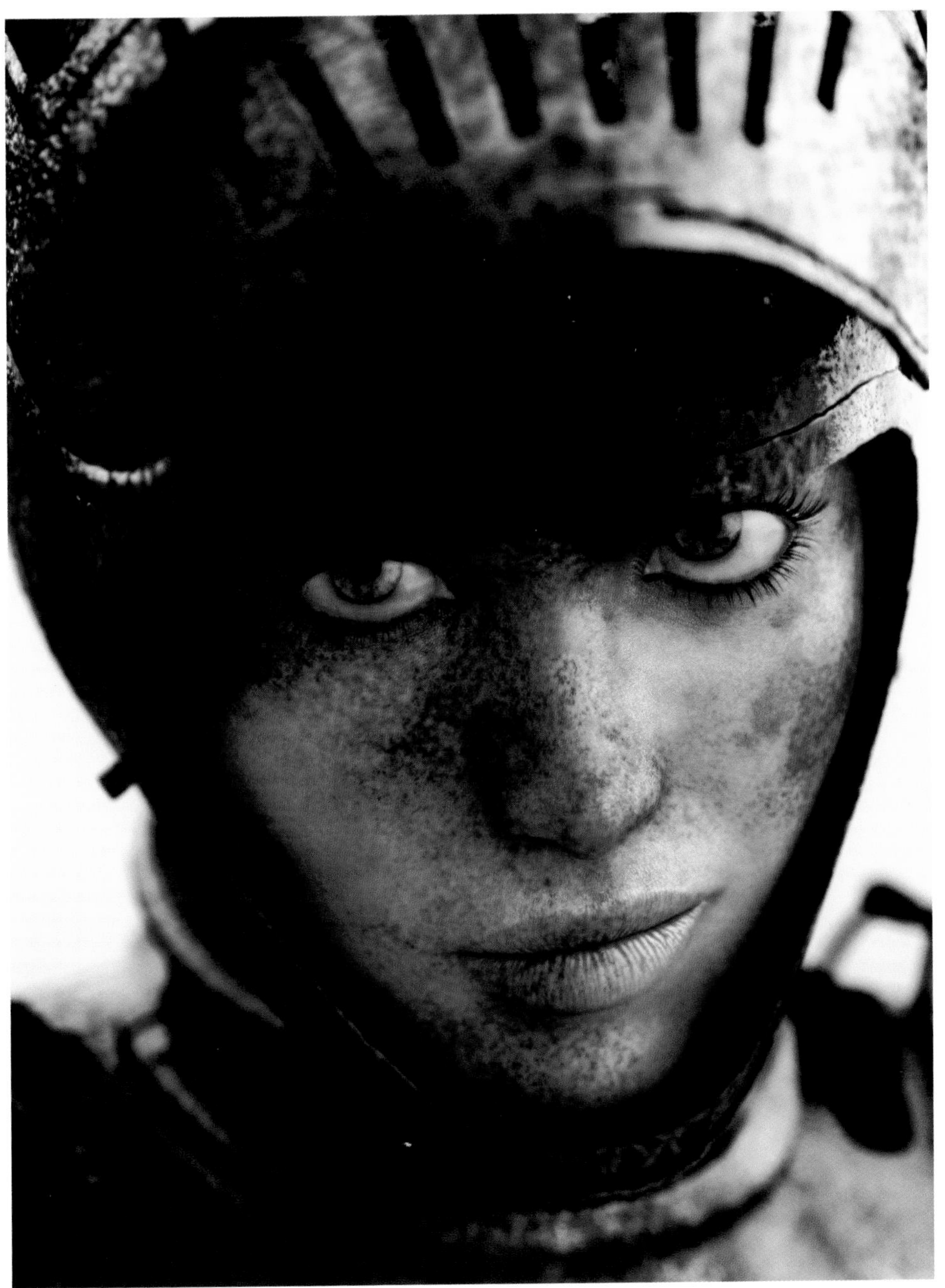

© Micah Henrie

Index

Note: Page references with a preceding E refer to page references in the bonus chapters found on the companion website (www.courseptr.com/downloads).

A

accessorizing characters, 15
action lines, 159–160
Active Pose, 85–86
activity tabs, 18–30
Actors, Wardrobe & Props tab, 19
adding
atmospheric effects, 119
clothing, 61. *See also* clothing
expressions (Mimic Pro), 151
hair, 62
keyframes, 137
lighting, 126–132
models, 42
props, 105
terrain objects, 111
vertices, 3
Add Key button, 137
Aikanaro product panels, 43
Aim function, 38
Ambient Strength, 67
Analyze button, 146
anger, poses, 99
Anger morph, 80
angles
cameras, 107
posing, 160
settings, 107
smoothing, 70
aniBlock, 140–142
aniMate2, 27, 140–142
animation, 5, 133–142
3D, 133–139
bouncing ball, 135–138
characters, 138–139
frames, 135
phrases, 144–147
Puppeteer, 92–96
speech, 145–147
talking, 143–151
Timeline tab, 134–135
applying
3D, 11–13
aniMate2, 140–142
animation, 133–139
Bryce, 109–119
clothing, 60–62
graphics, 4–9
Hexagon, E-174–E-189
lighting, 126–132
Mimic Pro, 147–151
morphs, heads, 74–79
primitives (Hexagon), E-177–E-186
Puppeteer, 92–96
areas, shadows, 123
arms, moving, 85
arranging scenes, 16, 39
art, 1. *See also* graphics
3D graphics, 9
references, 153–158
artistic vision, 154

atmospheric effects, adding, 119
audio. *See also* Lip Sync
loading, 145
Mimic Pro, 147–151
authoritarian poses, 101–102
automatic fit, clothing, 60–62
automating speech animation, 145. *See also* Lip Sync
avatars, 7–8. *See also* characters
hair, E-168–E-169
selecting, E-163–E-169
axes, 12

B

backdrops, 106–109
balance, 98
banking scenes, 34–36
Basic Child slider bar, 53
Bend slider bar box, 52
blemishes, 157
blending (Puppeteer), 92–96
bodies, 47. *See also* figures
clothing, 57–70
gestures, 144
heads, 71–79
bodybuilder shapes, 54–55
bones, 47. *See also* figures
heads, 72
rotating, 90
bouncing ball animation, 135–138
brows, 75
brushes
bump maps, E-187
models, E-187
Pinch, E-188
Smooth, E-188
Bryce, 109–119
building scenes (Bryce), 111–119
Bump, 68
bump maps, E-187
buying software, 14

C

calculating progression, 137
Camera Orbit tool, 129
cameras, 12
angles, 107
controls, 109
moving, 36–38
positioning, 16
views, 12
Camera tab, 27–29
cast shadows, 123
centering scenes, 39
chairs, posing in, 88–92
characters, 4, 45. *See also* figures
accessorizing, 15
animation, 138–139
clothing, 57–70
faces, 71
figures. *See* figures
heads, 71
Lip Sync, 143–151
loading, 15
posing, 16, 83–92
props, 103–106
selecting, E-163–E-169
cheeks, morphs, 77
cities, 108. *See also* environments
close-ups, 158
clothing, 57–70
applying, 60–62
morphs, 62–64
options, E-166–E-168
surfaces, 65–70
V4 Morph Magnet Fit, 63–64
Collada Export Options dialog box, E-170–E-171
colors, 3
Diffuse Color, 66
lighting, 124, 130
compatibility, E-165–E-166
compression, 137
Concentrate morph, 80
concepts, 3D, 11–13

configuring
3D models, E-173–E-190
aniMate2, 140–142
animation, 133–139
Bryce, 109–119
exporting, E-171
lighting, 16, 123, 126–132
Mimic Pro, 147–151
posing, 88–92
Puppeteer, 92–96
ready-made poses, 96
scenes, 111–119
Connect menu, 18
Content Library tab, 24–25
controls
aniMate2, 140
animation, 133–139
cameras, 109
Convert Maps (Bryce), 117
core shadows, 122–123
costumes, E-163. ***See also*** **clothing**
Create menu, 18
Create New Distant Light dialog box, 128
Create toolbar (Bryce), 110
Current Frame, 134
Current Range, 134
customizing
3D models, E-173–E-190
aniMate2, 140–142
animation, 133–139
Bryce, 111–119
lighting, 123, 126–132
Mimic Pro, 147–151
scenes, 108

D

DAZ Studio. ***See*** **software**
defining shapes, 154
dejected (sad), posing, 101
design, 3D graphics, 8–9
details, references, 156–158
dialog boxes
Collada Export Options, E-170–E-171
Create New Distant Light, 128
Export File, E-170
Diffuse Color, 66
diffused edges, 122
Displacement, 68
Display Selection list, 128
distance lights, 127
Dolly Zoom/Focal Zoom toolbar, 33, 36–38
dragging objects, 44. ***See also*** **moving**
dragons, 117–118
drawing
figures, 154–155
gestures, 158
references, 153–158
Draw Style toolbar, 33
drop shadows, 122

E

edges, 4
diffused, 122
settings, 106
vertices, 3
editing
Mimic Pro, 150
terrain, 113–114
Edit menu, 18
Edit mode, 93–94
Edit toolbar (Bryce), 110
effects
atmospheric, 119
special, 5
emotions, 79–81
Lip Sync, 144
poses, 99
environments
Bryce, 109–119
props, 105–106
settings, 106–109
examples, Hexagon, E-189
Export File dialog box, E-170
exporting models, E-170–E-172

expressions, 72
adding (Mimic Pro), 151
brows, 75
faces, 79–81
Lip Sync, 144
Expressions palette (Mimic Pro), 151
Extrude Surface tool (Hexagon), E-180
eyes, 73, 157
morphs, 76
moving, 74

F

faces, 3–4, 71
animation, 144
expressions, 79–81
parts, 71–79
features
faces, 71–79
Hexagon, E-187–E-189
Lip Sync, 144
software, 15–16
figures, 47–56
clothing, 57–70
costumes, E-163
drawing, 154–155
models, E-164
parts
moving, 51–56
selecting, 47–51
posing, 83–102
Puppeteer, 92–96
selecting, 96–102
File menu, 17
files, audio, 148. *See also* audio
fine art , 3D graphics, 9
fitting
clothing, 60–62
V4 Morph Magnet Fit, 63–64
fog, 119. *See also* Sky & Fog toolbar
formatting. *See also* configuring
3D models, E-173–E-190
Hexagon, E-174–E-189
FPS (Frames Per Second), 134
Frame/Aim toolbar, 34, 38–40
Frame function, 38
frames
animation, 135
keyframes, 137
views, 39
Frames Per Second. *See* FPS
functions
Aim, 38
Frame, 38
Import, 117
Smoothing, 69

G

games, video, 7
Genesis models
clothing, 57–70
props, 103–106
selecting, 48
shaping, 53–56, 59
geometry, 3D, 107
gestures, 144
drawing, 158
Mimic Pro, 151
Glossiness, 67
graphics
3D, 1–10
applying, 4–9
gravel, 124
groups, morphs, 75–79

H

hair, 61–62, 157
avatars, E-168–E-169
hands, moving, 91
happy (joy), posing, 100–101
heads, 71
morphs, 74–79
parts, 71–79
posing, 72
visemes morphs, 145
Help menu, 18

Hexagon, E-174–E-189
hierarchies of body movement, 84
highlights, 122
hips, 49
rotating, 52
horizons, 111
human figures, 154. *See also* figures

I

icons (Hexagon), E-176
illustrations, 5–6. *See also* images
images, 1–10. *See also* graphics
Import function, 117
importing models, 117, E-186
infinite planes, 111
Inflate tool (Hexagon), E-188
installing software, 13–14
interfaces
Bryce, 109–119
Hexagon, E-174–E-189
navigating, 16–30

J

jaws, 72
morphs, 77
jerky action lines, 160
jewelry, 103. *See also* props
joy (happy), posing, 100–101

K

keyframes, 137
kicking, 51

L

layouts, 16–30
posing, 88–92
legs, 52
libraries, references, 153. *See also* references
lighting, 121–132
colors, 124, 130
configuring, 16, 123
positioning, 129
presets, 128
references, 155
reflection, 121–123
rendering, 156–157
setups, 126–132
shadows, 122–123
Lighting model, 69
Lights & Camera tab, 19
Lights tab, 27
Light tab, 127
limitations of 3D models, E-166
lines, 2
action, 159–160
Hexagon, E-188
lips, morphs, 79
Lip Sync, 143–151
lists
Display Selection, 128
scenes, 33
loading
audio, 145
objects, 44
scenes, 15, 42–46
Victoria model, 60
wardrobes, 58

M

maps
bump, E-187
Convert Maps (Bryce), 117
shadows, 131
specular, 158
Materials Lab (Bryce), 114
media, references, 153–158
menus, 17–18
Mimic Pro, 147–151

models
3D, 1–4, 107
creating, E-173–E-190
limitations, E-166
adding, 42
brushes, E-187
exporting, E-170–E-172
figures, 47–56, E-164
Genesis
clothing, 57–70
props, 103–106
selecting, 48
shaping, 53–56, 59
heads, 71–79
Hexagon, E-174–E-189
importing, 117, E-186
Lighting, 69
modifying, 54, E-175
references, 156–158. *See also* references
shaping, 53–56
surfaces, E-188
vertices, E-188
Victoria
loading, 60
morphs, 62
viewing, E-176
modifying
keyframes, 137
models, 54, E-175
morphs, 63
objects, 91, 110
perspective, 37
scenes, 32
textures, 114–119
morphs
Anger, 80
clothing, 62–64
Concentrate, 80
expressions, 79–81
groups, 75–79
heads, 74–79
V4 Morph Magnet Fit, 63–64
visemes, 145
motion
range of, 72
synchronizing, 143
motion pictures, 3D graphics, 4–5
mountains, adding, 111
mouths, morphs, 77
moving
arms, 85
body movement, 47, 83–92. *See also* figures
bouncing balls, 135–138
cameras, 36–38
eyes, 74
hands, 91
legs, 52
objects, 45
parent-to-child rotations, 86
parts, figures, 51–56
scenes, 34–36
shoulders, 85
multiple lights, 123
muscles, 47. *See also* figures
My Stuff tab, 21, 42

N

Nano Preview, 109
natural poses, 97–99
nature, observing, 154
navigating
3D models, 1–4
animation, 133–139
Hexagon, E-174–E-189
interfaces, 16–30
Puppeteer, 92–96
scenes, 31–33
software, 15–16
toolbars, 33–46
wheel mouse buttons, 42
necks, pivot points, 72–73
Normal tool, 68
noses, morphs, 77

O

objects, 1
dragging, 44
keyframes, 137
loading, 44
modifying, 91, 110
selecting, 45
terrain, adding, 111
observation, 153
Opacity, 67
opening. ***See also*** **loading**
Create New Distant Light dialog box, 128
Sky Lab (Bryce), 118
wardrobes, 58
options, clothing, E-166–E-168
orbiting scenes, 34–36
Orbit/Rotate/Bank toolbar, 33–36
origins, 12

P

Pan/Dolly toolbar, 33, 36
panels
Aikanaro product, 43
Scene, 32
Panels tab, 20–21
panning scenes, 36
pants, 58. ***See also*** **clothing**
Parameter Settings window, 56
Parameters tab, 24, 56, 145
parent-to-child rotations, 86
parts
of bodies, 156
figures
moving, 51–56
selecting, 47–51
heads, 71–79
modifying, 91
perspective, 12, 156
zooming, 37
phonemes, 146, 151
phrases, animation, 144–147
pictures. ***See*** **images**
Pinch brush, E-188
pivot points, 40
necks, 72–73
skulls, 73
placement of lights, 127
planes, infinite, 111
plug-ins
aniMate2, 140–142
Lip Sync, 143–151
point lights, 127
polygons, 2–4, 107
Pose & Animate tab, 19, 134
posing
Active Pose, 85–86
characters, 16, 83–92
creating, 88–92
figures, 49, 83–102
Puppeteer, 92–96
selecting, 96–102
heads, 72
references, 158–161
troubleshooting, 160–161
types of, 156
in work areas, 85–88
Posing tab, 26
positioning
cameras, 16
lighting, 129
scenes, 39
in work areas, 85–88
PowerPose tool, 50–51
eyes, 73
presets, lighting, 128
previewing
Bryce, 109
rendering, 114
Preview mode, Puppeteer, 94–95
primitives (Hexagon), E-177–E-186, E-188
products, viewing, 42
programs. ***See*** **plug-ins; software**
progression, calculating, 137
proportions, 156
props, 5, 103–106, E-163
characters, 103–106
environments, 105–106
loading, 15

purchasing software, 14
purpose of poses, 97
putting on clothing, 60–62

R

raking light, 122
range of motion, 72
raytracing, 131, 155–156
ready-made poses, 96
recording audio, 145
Record mode, Puppeteer, 96
references, 153–158
details, 156–158
posing, 158–161
scenes, 161–162
structures, 155–156
Reflection, 68
reflections
lighting, 121–123
textures, 126
refraction, 68, 124
registering software, 14–15
rendering, 12
lighting, 156–157
previewing, 114
scenes, 16
terrain, 112
Render Library tab, 29–30
Render menu, 18
Render tab, 20, 29
Reset toolbar, 34, 40
right-handed props, 104. *See also* props
Right Panel tab, 24
rocks, 124
Rotate tool, 86–87
rotating
bones, 90
hips, 52
parent-to-child rotations, 86
scenes, 34–36
roughness in textures, 124

S

sad (dejected), posing, 101
Scale Timeline, 134
Scale tool, 88
scattering of light, 124
Scene panel, 32
scenes, 4, 12
animation, 133–139
arranging, 16
centering, 39
configuring, 111–119
customizing, 108
environments, 107
lighting, 127. *See also* lighting
lists, 33
loading, 15, 42–46
modifying, 32
navigating, 31–33
panning, 36
references, 161–162
rendering, 16
tools, 17
zooming, 36–38
Scene tab, 24, 48
scoreboards, 5
screens, navigating, 16–30
Scrubber, 134, 136
secondary action lines, 160
selecting
bodies, 49
characters, E-163–E-169
Genesis model, 48
hair, E-168–E-169
objects, 45
parts, 47–51
poses, 96–102
terrain, 115
sequences, animation, 140. *See also* animation
Session Manager (Mimic Pro), 148
settings, 4, 103, 106–109, 161–162. *See also* scenes

setups. ***See also*** **configuring**
lighting, 16, 126–132
Mimic Pro, 148
posing, 88–92
Puppeteer, 92–96
ready-made poses, 96
shadows, 107, 155
areas, 123
lighting, 122–123
maps, 131
shaping. ***See also*** **morphs**
characters, 16
defining, 154
Genesis models, 59
models, 53–56
Shaping tab, 21–23
shoes, 61. ***See also*** **clothing**
shoulders, moving, 85
skeletal systems, 47. ***See also*** **figures**
skin, 157
skulls, 72. ***See also*** **heads**
pivot points, 73
Sky & Fog toolbar, 110, 118
Sky Lab (Bryce), 118
Smooth brush, E-188
smoothing, 3
angles, 70
Smoothing function, 69
software
Bryce, 109–119
installing, 13–14
Mimic Pro, 147–151
navigating, 15–16
registering, 14–15
updating, E-165–E-166
sound. ***See*** **audio**
special effects, 5
specular maps, 158
speech animation, 145–147
spot lights, 127
static torso poses, 160
storage, animation sequences (aniMate2), 140–142
structures, references, 155–156
surfaces, 124
clothing, 65–70
models, E-188
Surfaces tab, 23
surprise, posing, 100
symmetrical poses, 160
synchronizing motion, 143

T

tabs, activity, 18–30
talking animation, 143–151
terrain
editing, 113–114
objects, adding, 111
rendering, 112
selecting, 115
textures, modifying, 114–119
textures, 3, 107, 157
modifying, 114–119
reflections, 126
roughness in, 124
transparency in, 125
thighs, 50
3D (three-dimensional)
animation, 133–139
concepts, 11–13
environments, 107–109
geometry, 107
graphics, 1–10
models, 1–4
creating, E-173–E-190
limitations, E-166
primitives (Hexagon), E-178, E-188
Tiles, 69
Timeline tab, 27, 134–135
aniBlocks, 141
toolbars, 33
Bryce, 110
navigating, 33–46
tools
Active Pose, 85–86
Ambient Strength, 67
animation, 134
Bryce, 110
Bump, 68

Camera Orbit, 129
Diffuse Color, 66
Displacement, 68
Extrude Surface (Hexagon), E-180
Glossiness, 67
Hexagon, E-174–E-189
Inflate (Hexagon), E-188
Normal, 68
Opacity, 67
PowerPose, 50–51, 73
Reflection, 68
Refraction, 68
Rotate, 86–87
Scale, 88
scenes, 17
Tiles, 69
Translate, 87
Universal Manipulator, 44, 48, 52, 86

Tools menu, 18
Tools Settings tab, 25–26
Total Frames, 134
traditional media references, 153–158
Translate tool, 87
transparency in textures, 125
troubleshooting posing, 160–161
TV, 3D graphics, 4–5
twice reflected light, 122
types
of environment props, 106
of lights, 127
of poses, 86, 96–102, 156
of shadows, 122–123

U

Universal Manipulator tool, 44, 48, 52
parent-to-child rotations, 86
updating software, E-165–E-166
Utilities tab (Hexagon), E-188. *See also* tools
UV sets, 69

V

V4 Morph Magnet Fit, 63–64
Vantage/Orbit Cube toolbar, 33, 41–42
vertices, 2–4
models, E-188
Victoria model
loading, 60
morphs, 62
video
3D graphics, 4–5
games, 7
viewing
models, E-176
products, 42
Viewport Options toolbar, 33
views, 12
cameras, 12
framing, 39
View Selection toolbar, 33
virtual models, 155. *See also* models
visemes morphs, 145
vision, artistic, 154

W

wardrobes, 57–70
weapons, 103. *See also* props
weight, 99
wheel mouse buttons, 42
Window menu, 18, 50
wireframe meshes, 3
work areas, posing, 85–88

X

X axis, 12

Y

Y axis, 12

Z

Z axis, 12
zooming, 36–38